EX LIBRIS

Where to Watch Birds in Devon and Cornwall

David Norman and Vic Tucker

HARRISON 83

CROOM HELM
London & Sydney

Croom Helm Australia Pty Ltd, First Floor,
139 King Street, Sydney, NSW 2001, Australia

British Library Cataloguing in Publication Data
Norman, Dave
   Where to watch birds in Devon and Cornwall.
   1. Bird watching—England—Devon
   2. Bird watching—England—Cornwall
   I. Title II. Tucker, Vic
   598.2'07'2344235   QL690.G7
ISBN 0-7099-1428-8

Dedication

This book is dedicated to our wives, Karen and Sylvia, in
gratitude for their patience and support as we toiled over the
book, and their tolerance of freezing dawn outings, muddy
wellies, bird notes strewn around the house and all the other
symptoms of ornithology.

Designed and Typeset by Columns of Reading
Printed and bound in Great Britain

Contents

Foreword

Acknowledgeme

This is my first foreword. I've written several actual books – but never a foreword – so this really is my very first. Come to think of it, my books didn't have a foreword at all, so I suppose forewords can't really be necessary. As I recall they are, however, usually written by jolly important famous people, like royalty or newsreaders. That's probably why my books didn't have one – I don't know any royal persons, or newsreaders, at least none that would waste their name writing forewords for my silly books. So, does the fact that I've been asked to write this one mean that I am now considered a famous important person? I'm definitely not royal, and I've never read the news – except in my morning paper, if you see what I mean – and I don't feel important. Nevertheless, I am most certainly honoured and surprised that they have asked me, rather than Prince Charles. After all, he owns most of the places mentioned in this book. Mind you, I reckon I've been birding in Devon and Cornwall more than he has. I once saw him on Scilly and he didn't even have his 'bins' with him. He never even gave a passing Red-Rumped Swallow a second glance!

Well now . . . I expect you're wondering if people who write forewords actually read the books. Probably not: but I have read this one. It is very good. It tells you all the places you can go whilst you're waiting to get over to Scilly; and when you're on your way back. In fact it may convince you to avoid Scilly altogether. (But if you can't resist it, Scilly is in here too.) There are lots and lots of splendid birdy areas in Cornwall and Devon, and this book not only tells you precisely how to find them, but when to go there and indeed when to avoid them. It should provide a historic service to West Country birding by scattering the twitchers all over the two counties so they don't all try and pack into one bush at Porthgwarra. (Oh . . . if you don't know where Porthgwarra is, turn to page 211.) I was going to write pages and pages about why this is such a good book, but I suggest you read it now, and then you'll find out for yourself. OK?

That is the end of the foreword. God bless you all.

BILL ODDIE

Acknowledgements

We wish to express our gratitude to Peter Harrison for finding the time, despite a very heavy workload, for his line drawings, drawn specially to enhance our book. Grateful thanks to Roger Penhallurick for much practical, and academic, advice and wisdom so freely given. Stan Gay eagerly helped with the text of Gerrans Bay and Fal Estuary areas. Many people helped in various ways, offering helpful comments and advice, and all are warmly thanked. Among them we would particularly mention Roger Smaldon for his help and encouragement. Local observers in less ornithologically known districts such as north and northwest Devon also provided valuable advice. Peter Welch drew all our site maps.

During the book's development over the past two years we have been most reliant on the guidance and support given by Croom Helm staff, without whom this book would have been impossible, and on David Christie's expertise in editing the drafts.

The authors would be pleased to receive any additional information or ideas which might be incorporated in future editions of this guide and hence benefit future users. Correspondence (s.a.e. if reply needed) should be addressed c/o Croom Helm Publishers, marked for the attention of David Norman and Vic Tucker.

Authors' Note

Bird Name Plurals: There is no uniform practice among birdwatchers over use of plurals. Some watchers, particularly referring to wildfowl and waders, prefer to avoid plural *s*, e.g. '100 Teal' rather than '100 Teals'. For the sake of uniformity, we have agreed with the publisher to use plural *s* throughout our text.

Introduction

The object of this book is to guide the reader to areas of ornithological interest in the two counties of the extreme southwest of Britain, Devon and Cornwall, and their offshore islands. The information contained in the text is the distillation of thousands of hours' birdwatching experience in the region by the two authors. Our aim has been to make this book really useful by including local knowledge, the tricks of the trade, developed over the years with a 'feel' of when and in what conditions an area is most worth visiting. Information on occurrences is based on events over the past two decades, during which birdwatching has developed as a mass hobby, although we have also tried to indicate the latest trends and discoveries.

We have selected areas which have proved consistently worth visiting. Many species occur just about anywhere, but our chosen locations are based on the following rules:

1. Those which hold a high *density* of birds, whether breeding, migrating or wintering.
2. Those which form a *specialised* habitat where bird species occur which might not be found elsewhere.
3. Areas which are *representative* of their type, e.g. a wood with a good range of birds which might also occur in less accessible areas nearby.

There remains, however, ample scope for discovery, by visiting little-studied districts, or by visiting well-known bird sites during different conditions or times of the year from other watchers. Knowledge of the distribution and movements of birds can progress only if someone is prepared to try out ideas.

It is not enough to know that a locality is good for seeing birds. At most birdwatching sites, factors such as tides and winds, as well as season, are of paramount importance in

7

planning your visit. Much valuable information is obtained from county bird reports, but these assume quite a high degree of knowledge. It is not their function to explain in detail the background behind records, or to cover ancillary factors such as timing a wader-watch for high tide (vital if time and effort are not to be wasted). Birdwatching visitors with limited time to spare will find our treatment of these topics particularly useful in planning their stay.

County bird reports, which list what is known to have occurred within each county during any one year, are produced by the Devon and Cornwall Bird Watching and Preservation Societies, two parallel organisations through which regular birdwatching excursions take place in both counties, with local experts in charge. The national Royal Society for the Protection of Birds also has branches throughout the country which are particularly helpful to children, and to beginners of all ages. Membership of any of these organisations has another advantage, in the long run the most important of all: the conservation of birds, by protecting the birds themselves and the habitats in which they live.

'How do I identify the birds I see?' is a question to which the answers are outside the scope of this book. There are good field guides, illustrating several 'action' poses of the same species, in positions most usually seen and in varying plumage stages. Beware of some bird books which confuse the beginner by omitting common British birds and substituting species which would probably not be found in this country.

Features of the Region's Birdlife

As the mildest part of Britain, the region plays host to many wintering birds which normally move further south, including waders (e.g. Avocet) and regular Blackcaps and Chiffchaffs; in severe winters, large numbers of birds move across from the east coast to shelter. Frost-sensitive species such as Cirl Bunting, resident here, are rare elsewhere. Areas of non-intensive farming with overgrown hedges remain, holding a good variety of small birds. Extensive valley woodlands, particularly on moorland fringes, hold many breeding residents and summer migrant songbirds, plus a healthy population of larger birds such as Buzzard, Sparrowhawk and Raven. The higher moors form a southern outpost of several breeding species usually found in Scotland and the Pennines, e.g. Ring Ouzel and Golden Plover. The hundreds of miles of rocky coast with offshore islands still hold a number of seabird colonies, while protruding headlands near seabird feeding and migration routes enable a wide range of these birds to be seen passing in spring and autumn. Our southerly position means that spring often arrives early (from late February) and that autumn birds linger well into November; it also makes the region an arrival point for southern migrants such as Hoopoes in small numbers each spring. As we stand at the side of Britain which faces the New World, American wanderers are noted most autumns after westerly winds.

On the debit side, oil pollution at sea is regular, and mass tourism has driven breeding terns and waders off mainland beaches. In terms of habitat, we have much running water, but few lowland lakes and reservoirs. Although seabirds are well represented, some species such as Tree Sparrow, common farther east, are almost absent. Birdwatchers are still thinly spread over most of the region and we still have gaps to fill in our knowledge of a number of species. Thanks largely to the Isles of Scilly and Lundy, plus a few outstanding coastal headlands on the mainland, the list of passage migrants and rare vagrant species is extremely long; we have not attempted to compile a total list, since it would be out of place in a practical guide where information about typical occurrences is more relevant than that on isolated sightings.

Geographers separate Devon and Cornwall from the rest of southern England by the 'Tees-Exe line' drawn on a map from Teesmouth in northeast England to the Exe estuary in South Devon. To the west and north of the line lie upland regions with hills, rocks and deep offshore seas; to the east and south lie mainly lowlands and shallow muddy coasts. The peninsula is therefore classed with Wales, northern England and Scotland as a hill area. The hills and the position facing the Atlantic ensure a mild, damp and windy climate; severe gales are frequent in winter on exposed coasts and high hills, preventing tree growth and leading to boggy ground conditions through the high rainfall. Snow and ice can occur on the mainland, particularly on the moors where snowfalls are sometimes very large, but thaws usually arrive swiftly in the coastal lowlands. Prolonged hard frosts are uncommon in the far west of Cornwall and almost unknown on the Isles of Scilly. Most of the regions's rivers are short and fast-flowing; the weathered granite masses of Bodmin Moor in Cornwall and Dartmoor in Devon are the origin of most of the larger rivers. High Willhays on Dartmoor (about 627 m) is the region's highest point. Exmoor, which lies across the North Devon-

Climate and Geography: some general points

Somerset boundary, falls partly within our scope; we have also included, for completeness of county coverage, the sandy heathland ridges and valleys of east Devon, which are geographically distinct from the rest of the region.

Birdwatching in Devon and Cornwall has given the authors a great many memorable and exciting days. There have been dawn watches at St Ives when the sea was strewn with tens of thousands of migrating seabirds during hurricane-force winds; days when some tiny rare Asiatic warbler was found feeding in a remote cove; days when the moorland woods were full of singing Pied Flycatchers and Redstarts in all directions; winter days when swerving wader flocks shimmered silver over the mudflats as a Peregrine hunted overhead. Birdwatchers surely cannot be immune to the interest of seeing other wildlife, and we can well remember occasions when a seawatch was interrupted by a 30-ft (9-m) Basking Shark rolling lazily up to the surface just offshore, or when a magnificent Red Deer stag ran past during a winter moorland visit. We hope that, by giving you the benefit of our experience, we may give you the chance to see and appreciate these sights for yourself.

Observe the 'Country Code'

This book tells you how and where to find birds. What you do when you find them should also be considered; don't forget that the birds' welfare always comes first, and you should try to minimise disturbance of the bird itself or its habitat. Act with due regard and respect for the countryside, farmland, crops, livestock and private property. Observe the 'Country Code' at all times. Don't forget that it is illegal to disturb most breeding birds at the nest, particularly less common species. Wherever you are watching birds, the best technique is invariably to stop, wait silently and look carefully; not only will you avoid disturbing birds, but you will see far more.

How To Use This Book

We often meet inexperienced but keen birdwatchers who rely heavily on field guides and books listing areas of ornithological interest. Many are frustrated and disappointed by inadequate information: for instance, if a book says 'Dartmoor: Ring Ouzels', where do you start looking in 400 square miles (1036 km^2) of heather, rocks and bog? They are also given the impression that there will always be birds at a particular area in all conditions — yet very few spring migrants, for example, will be seen arriving at southerly coastal watchpoints in an opposing northerly gale. Birds undertake complex movements influenced by many factors such as weather, tides and seasons; human disturbance may also cause them to change quarters (for example, a group of ducks flying from one lake to another when disturbed by sailing). We have set out to highlight these factors to give you the best chance of success at each area you visit.

Throughout the text we have given measurements in those units most readily understood by the majority of English readers. Distances are normally stated in miles, followed by the metric equivalent in kilometres (occasionally metres). Altitudes are given in metres, as on all modern Ordnance Survey maps. For surface areas, we have given the imperial measurement, followed by the metric one.

Habitat

This section aims to paint a 'word picture' of each area and its scenery. The extent of the area covered and main bird-habitat zones are indicated. Where the birdwatcher is likely to see other easily visible wildlife, such as deer, seals or butterflies, a brief note is included.

Measurements

The Information Sections for Each Site

11

Species

This section does not list every species found in an area; for reasons of space, common birds are usually excluded. We have aimed to give a sample of the main species of interest, and what they are doing (breeding, moving through, or turning up in cold weather). Frequency of occurrence and scale of numbers involved will guide the visitor on what to expect —whether single birds, small parties, or flocks of hundreds of a particular species. A few ornithological 'goodies' which might be encountered are also mentioned.

The text is arranged in broadly chronological order to help the reader to follow the pattern of bird events through the year. At the start of the section, some reference is made to the general ornithological importance of the area. No attempt is made to give specific dates, as the 'Calendar' section gives further details on when each species usually occurs.

Timing

How to avoid a wasted visit! How to judge appropriate weather conditions for what you hope to see: bird migration is heavily dependent on weather, and a mass of birds along the coastline one day may all have departed by next morning if conditions change. How to judge when particular groups of species will be most active: a dawn watch, for instance, often yields rich results. How to plan your visit to avoid human disturbance which may frighten birds off or make them difficult to see (don't forget that one form of disturbance is thoughtless birdwatchers!). How to pick tides to see roosting or feeding waders on different estuaries. Accurate use of this section is *essential* if you want best results from the book.

Access

How to get there from main towns and A-class roads, down minor roads, and what paths to take when you arrive. Often a maze of country roads leads to a birdwatching site; we have described one practical route. How far you need to walk around the area. Use this section in conjunction with the map provided.

Note Special access restrictions, such as a military firing range or a wardened nature reserve, may mean that you need to plan your visit in advance, so check this section for possible problems beforehand. If an area includes private farmland, you should in all cases seek permission from the farmer before deviating from public footpaths. To follow detailed directions, a 1:50,000 Ordnance Survey map will be a great help; the number of the appropriate map is given beside the heading for each locality.

Calendar

This is a quick-reference summary section, so all information has been condensed and abbreviated as far as possible. The calendar year has been split into seasons which relate to the majority of ornithological events, although obviously some species will not fit this pattern exactly. *Winter* is December-February as far as the larger numbers of winter bird visitors to our region are concerned; *Spring* is March-May as far as most arriving migrants are concerned; *Summer*, in terms of maximum breeding activity and little migration movement, can be extended only over June and July, with some species starting to move even in the late part of this period; *Autumn* is protracted, with migration from August to November. These are not, it should be noted, the same as normal human definitions of seasons. Many people, for example, might take a 'summer holiday' in late August, but if they visited a Guillemot colony then they would find that the birds had finished breeding and departed far out to sea. To avoid confusion we have repeated these groupings of months by name in each Calendar section.

Within the section we have included the most likely peak periods for each species or group of species; if no further qualifying comment is made, the bird concerned may be looked for with equal chance of success at any time during the season, or peak numbers may occur randomly whenever conditions are most suitable during these months. Where several species or groups are listed in the same period, we have mentioned them in the order most usual in field guides, to facilitate quick reference to identification points in a suitable book.

Glossary of Terms Used and Useful Addresses

For ease of use of the text, and to enable the reader to understand what other birdwatchers are discussing, we have used a number of words and expressions which may need explanation. We have avoided 'jargon' for its own sake, but the terms listed below serve the double function of making a clear ornithological point and being in familiar use by experienced watchers in the region. They fall into four categories: terms used to describe birds, or groups of birds, and their actions; weather phenomena; geography; and initials of relevant organisations.

Bird Terms

Activity Times:
>*Crepuscular* – Active in dim light at dawn and especially dusk, e.g. Nightjar.
>*Diurnal* – Active in full daylight.
>*Nocturnal* – Active at night, e.g. most owls; many small insect-eating passerines are nocturnal fliers (navigating by stars) when migrating.

Auk – A seabird of the Guillemot-Razorbill family.

Brownhead – A female or immature of certain northern ducks, usually Goldeneye, Smew, Red-breasted Merganser, Goosander.

Coasting – Diurnal movement against a headwind by groups of migrants, e.g. Swallows and pipits, following major landmarks and coastlines. Most noticed on autumn days with a light-moderate wind from southwest or west.

Commic Tern – A sea tern, Common or Arctic, not specifically identified.

Common Woodland Passerines – Those small birds resident in most English woods, e.g. Dunnock, thrushes, tits, Nuthatch, Treecreeper, Wren.

Ducks, Dabbling – Surface-feeders such as Mallard and Teal.

Ducks, Diving – Species which seek food entirely by swim-

14

ming underwater, e.g. Tufted Duck, Pochard.

Fall – Mass arrival of night-flying migrants, e.g. warblers, flycatchers, along the coastline when conditions prevent them from continuing their journey. Winds from fine high-pressure weather areas on the Continent, combined with cloud, mist or drizzle at our end, are most likely to cause this, as large numbers of birds set off in the fine conditions and are then forced down.

Feral – Introduced here by man and now living in the wild state, e.g. Canada Goose, Ruddy Duck.

Hirundine – A bird of the swallow-martin family.

Irruption – An arrival of certain specialised feeders from the Continent, e.g. Waxwing and Crossbill, when their population is high and food runs short in their native areas. Irruptions vary greatly in size from year to year and are more marked in eastern Britain; only larger arrivals extend to us.

Movement – A long-distance purposeful journey, e.g. migration or search for food, rather than a routine local activity.

Movement, Weather – Mass movement of wintering species, e.g. wildfowl, open-ground species such as Lapwing, winter thrushes, into our region when ice and snow prevent feeding in other parts of Britain and the adjacent Continent.

Off-passage – Used to describe a migrant which makes an extended stop-over to rest and feed, maybe for weeks, before resuming its journey.

Open-ground Species – Species which tend to use treeless expanses, open fields, moors and downs, e.g. plovers, larks.

Overshoot – In spring and early summer, 'exotic' species such as Little Egret, Hoopoe and Golden Oriole migrating into southern Europe from Africa may overshoot their normal range and be carried to Britain by high pressure with following winds.

Passage Migrant – A bird which occurs only when passing through on migration between summer and winter quarters.

Passerine – 'Sparrow-like', small perching birds; used to describe all small landbirds.

Pelagic – Feeding over areas of deep sea and not normally seen near the coast except when visiting nest sites, e.g. small petrels, or when displaced by gales.

Raptor – A diurnal bird of prey, e.g. Kestrel, buzzards; excludes owls.

Ringtail – Female or immature Hen or Montagu's Harrier.

Sawbill – A duck of the Red-breasted Merganser-Goosander-Smew group, with a serrated bill edge to grasp fish.

Seabird – One of the mainly pelagic or coastal species or groups of birds, not normally seen inland, e.g. shearwaters, Gannet, skuas, most gulls.

Seaducks – Marine diving ducks not normally seen on fresh water, e.g. Eider, scoters.

Seawatch – A prolonged watch over an area of sea through binoculars or telescope from a coastal headland, scanning to pick out passing seabirds. Views can be distant and considerable skill is needed to make accurate identifications. Most likely to be productive in poor visibility or onshore winds. In wrong conditions can be unrewarding, but on good days thousands of birds may pass.

Shank – A medium-sized wader of the *Tringa* genus, e.g. Redshank, Spotted Redshank, Greenshank.

Vagrant – A rare, accidental visitor from other countries, mainly at migration times.

Wader – A bird which feeds in mud, water or marsh, e.g. Dunlin, Curlew, but including some plovers and Woodcock which have adapted to drier ground.

Warbler, Phylloscopus – A 'leaf warbler', e.g. Willow, Wood, Chiffchaff and scarcer related species. For quickness, often shortened by birdwatchers in the field to 'Phyllosc'.

Warbler, Sylvia – One of the larger scrub-haunting warblers, e.g. Blackcap, Whitethroat. (Note: The other main warbler groups have fewer species and we have named these individually in the text.)

Wild Swans – Whooper or Bewick's Swans, uncommon winter visitors to our region, rather than the introduced Mute Swan.

Winter Thrushes – Those which come across from northern Europe in winter, chiefly Fieldfare and Redwing flocks, but Blackbirds and Song Thrushes also arrive to join local birds.

Wreck – An arrival of exhausted and hungry seabirds, e.g. petrels, Little Auks, after prolonged severe gales at sea, occasionally driven far inland.

Weather Phenomena

Anticyclone (or High) – An area of high barometric pressure, where fine clear conditions predominate, from which winds flow out to neighbouring regions. High pressure is defined as over 1000 millibars, sometimes reaching 1040 in strong anticyclones. Such conditions encourage migrants to start off.

Depression (or Low) – A system of low pressure, generally originated over the Atlantic and drifting eastward towards

Britain unless pushed back by high pressure over the Continent. As it drifts, with winds revolving in a clockwise direction and strong at times, water is drawn in to create an unstable weather zone with rain and cloud. Low pressure is defined as under 1000 millibars and may drop to 950 (rarely lower) in deep depressions, with strong gales.

Front – A sharp division between two air masses of different temperature and humidity, drawn together in a depression. Fronts passing overhead are often accompanied by rainfall and poor visibility. They usually herald a change in temperature, wind direction and humidity as the new air mass arrives. Passerine migrants tend to land and seabirds may fly close inshore to avoid the front. A *cold front* precedes the arrival of cold, clear polar air, often with intermittent heavy showers, and characteristically with west or northwest winds. A *warm front* brings milder, cloudy and damp conditions, often with southwest winds. In a normal depression, warm fronts arrive first, and the wind swings clockwise towards northwest when cold fronts arrive later.

Thermal – A rising current of warm air over land, often used by soaring raptors to gain height without exertion.

Geographical Features

Brake – A dense area of trees and bushes, often on sloping ground.

Carn (Cornwall) – An open hilltop vantage point.

Dyke – An embanked marsh-drainage ditch.

Escarpment – A prominent edge of a hill or ridge from which the land drops away steeply.

Leat – Artificial freshwater channel fed off a stream to supply water to a village.

Tor (chiefly Devon) – A protruding mass of granite boulders standing on a moorland hilltop.

Organisations

CBWPS – Cornwall Bird Watching and Preservation Society. Current Secretary: Mr FHC Kendall, 33 Victoria Road, Bude, North Cornwall.

DBWPS – Devon Bird Watching and Preservation Society. Current Secretary: Mr FD Holmes, Wichinor, Princetown Road, Dousland, Yelverton PL20 6NJ.

NT – National Trust. Regional Office: Killerton House, Broadclyst, Exeter.

RSPB – Royal Society for the Protection of Birds. Regional

Office: 10 Richmond Road, Exeter.

RSPCA – Royal Society for the Prevention of Cruelty to Animals. See telephone directory.

SWWA – South West Water Authority (issues reservoir permits). Contact: Fisheries and Recreation Officer, 3-5 Barnfield Road, Exeter, tel. Exeter 31666, for details.

Other Useful Addresses

Forestry Commission. District Office: Bridge House, Okehampton, Devon.

Nature Conservancy Council (NCC) (controls National Nature Reserves). Regional Office: Roughmoor, Bishops Hull, Taunton, Somerset.

Dartmoor National Park. Office: Parke House, Bovey Tracey, South Devon.

Cornwall Trust for Nature Conservation Ltd. Mrs D Johnson, Relubbus Lane, Goldsithney, Penzance.

Devon Trust for Nature Conservation Ltd, 75 Queen Street, Exeter.

A Comparison of the Birdwatching Areas

To assist the reader in selecting areas to visit, we have drawn up an analysis of the main habitats visited by birdwatchers in Devon and Cornwall. Under each habitat heading we have listed those examples included in this book, and given our assessment of their comparative quality derived from our personal knowledge and experience and from other reports which we know to be reliable. Three stars (***) are awarded to areas which have consistently provided good results, the scale descending to one star (*) for areas of more limited local interest or which less often provide interesting birds. The assessment is relative to other sites in *our* region; we have not attempted to make comparison with national standards. The ratings should be used in conjunction with the relevant instructions on how to watch each area.

Reed-beds

The Habitat Types

Otter Estuary *
Exe: Dawlish Warren * and Exminster Marsh-Topsham **
Slapton ***
Beesands *
Hallsands **
South Milton Ley (Thurlestone area) ***
Marazion Marsh ***
Lower Moors, St Mary's, Isles of Scilly ***

Seawatch Points

Exe: Langstone Rock, Dawlish Warren **
Hope's Nose ***
Start Point *
Prawle Point ***
Rame Head *
Bass Point, The Lizard **
Porthgwarra ***

Porth Hellick Point, St Mary's, Isles of Scilly **
Peninnis Head, St Mary's, Isles of Scilly **
Horse Point, St Agnes, Isles of Scilly *
North Cliffs, Tresco, Isles of Scilly *
St Ives Island ***
Hartland Point *
Morte Point (North Devon coastline) *
Capstone, Ilfracombe (North Devon coastline) *

Seabird Breeding Stations

Budleigh Salterton-Ladram Bay *
Hope's Nose **
Berry Head **
Start Point *
Isles of Scilly ***
Tintagel-Boscastle ***
Lundy ***
Heddons Mouth area (North Devon coastline) **

Lowland Heaths

East Devon Commons ***
Haldon ***
Chudleigh Knighton Heath **
Lizard peninsula at Goonhilly Downs * and Predannack **

Open Moorland

Soussons area **
Cranmere Pool, North Dartmoor ***
Dozmary Pool area, Bodmin Moor **
Land's End Moors ***

Coniferous Forest

Hennock *
Haldon Woods ***
Soussons *
Bellever (Soussons-Postbridge area) *
Burrator *
Bodmin Moor plantations (Upper Fowey Valley) **

Open Turf: airfields/golf courses

Dawlish Warren Golf Links *
Little Haldon Golf Course *
Thurlestone *
Predannack, Lizard peninsula **
St Mary's Airfield, Isles of Scilly ***

Davidstow Airfield ***

Sheltered Coastal Bays

Exe Estuary off Dawlish Warren *** and Exmouth **
Torbay **
Start Bay ***
Plymouth Sound **
Whitesands Bay **
Gerrans Bay ***
Carrick Roads, Falmouth ***
Falmouth Bay ***
Helford Passage (Falmouth area) **
Mounts Bay ***
St Ives Bay ***

Shingle Beaches

Slapton **
Beesands *
Northam Burrows (Taw-Torridge) *

Sand Dunes

Dawlish Warren **
Hayle Towans *
Braunton Burrows (Taw-Torridge) **

Passerine Migration Watchpoints

Start Point **
Prawle Point ***
Rame Head **
Lizard area ***
Porthgwarra ***
Isles of Scilly ***
Hartland Point *

Woodlands (deciduous and mixed)

Stoke Woods **
Yarner Wood ***
Dartington **
Okement Woods *
Plymbridge **
Chapel Wood, Spreacombe (North Devon coastline) *
Tarr Steps, Exmoor **

Estuary Mudflats

Otter Estuary *

Exe Estuary ***
Kingsbridge Estuary **
Plym Estuary (Plymouth area) *
Tamar-Tavy, including St John's Lake and the Lynher **
Fal Estuary **
Hayle Estuary ***
Camel Estuary **
Taw-Torridge Estuary *

Water Meadows

Exe at Exminster Marsh ***
South Huish (Thurlestone) **
Amble Marshes, Camel Estuary **

Reservoirs, Lakes and Pools

Burrator Reservoir **
Slapton Ley ***
Beesands Ley **
Siblyback Reservoir **
Crowdy Reservoir ***
Dozmary Pool *
Swanpool, Falmouth *
Stithians Reservoir ***
Porth Hellick Pool, St Mary's, Isles of Scilly **
Abbey and Great Pools, Tresco, Isles of Scilly ***
Tamar Lake ***
Arlington Lake (North Devon coastline) *
Wistlandpound Reservoir (North Devon coastline) *

Birdwatching Sites

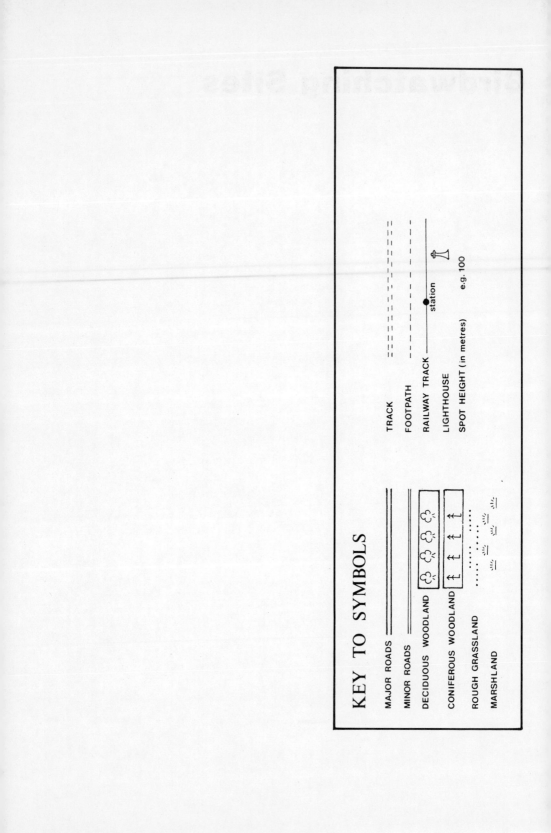

KEY TO SYMBOLS

MAJOR ROADS

MINOR ROADS

DECIDUOUS WOODLAND

CONIFEROUS WOODLAND

ROUGH GRASSLAND

MARSHLAND

TRACK

FOOTPATH

RAILWAY TRACK ●——— station

LIGHTHOUSE

SPOT HEIGHT (in metres)   e.g. 100

General Map of Main Birdwatching Sites

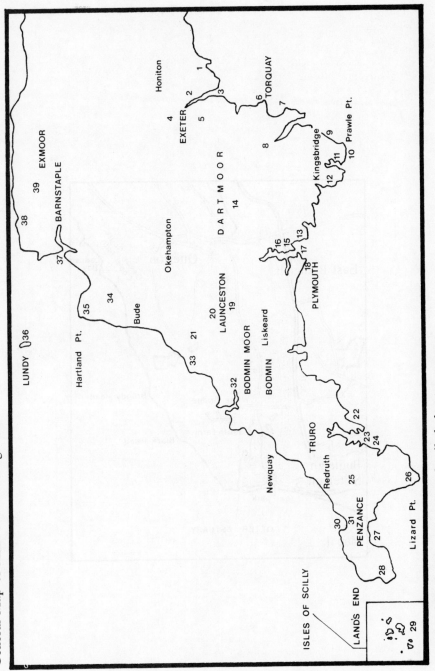

Note: Numbers correspond to detailed chapter maps.

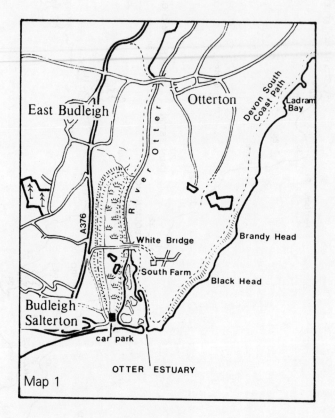

East Budleigh

Otterton

Devon South Coast Path

Ladram Bay

River Otter

A376

White Bridge

Brandy Head

South Farm

Black Head

Budleigh Salterton

car park

OTTER ESTUARY

Map 1

1 Otter Estuary and Budleigh Salterton

(Map 1 and
OS Map 192)

The east Devon coast between the Axe and Exe valleys is composed chiefly of sandstone cliffs up to 170 m high, with numerous small coves and coastal stream valleys. The only lowland is the Otter, a ½-mile (0.8-km) estuary of mud and saltmarsh adjacent to the town of Budleigh Salterton. The pebble beach forms a bar across most of the estuary mouth. A narrow strip of meadow, backed by trees and thickets, borders the west side of the river, together with a tiny reed-bed. Immediately above the open estuary, moving north towards Otterton village, the river is far narrower, with shallow clear stretches and gravel bars. Budleigh Salterton itself is well wooded, with large mature gardens and ornamental conifers.

Habitat

This is a well-known area locally for general birdwatching, with a good cross-section of the region's waterside and farmland birds, although none is restricted to this area alone. Interesting residents include Barn Owls (sometimes seen over the meadows at dusk) and Little Owls (occasionally encountered perched on a hedge or stump in daytime). Kingfishers are seen frequently, either moving upriver to breed, or (more usually) hunting the saltmarsh channels at other seasons; Grey Wagtails are also widespread here, and Dippers are resident on faster-flowing stretches around Otterton and above. All three species of woodpecker occur regularly in the valley, although the Lesser Spotted is more elusive, possibly seen in the topmost branches of riverside trees.

In winter this estuary usually shelters half a dozen Little Grebes, while Cormorants and Grey Herons stand sentinel along the banks. Ducks are not numerous, but a few Wigeons and Teals fly over from the Exe to feed; the most frequent diving ducks are one or two Goldeneyes, but scarcer species such as Long-tailed Duck have occurred, and parties of up to a dozen Red-breasted Mergansers turn up irregularly. Canada

Species

Geese frequently graze on saltmarsh islands, and flocks of up to 40-50 may visit for short periods. Water Rails, rarely seen, are often heard screaming in the reed-bed. On the narrow mudflats waders are limited: Dunlins are the only small ones regularly present, except for a single Common Sandpiper which often remains to winter, flying off low with stiff, flickering wingbeats when disturbed. Larger common waders such as Oystercatcher, Lapwing, Redshank and Curlew are generally seen, as are Snipe in neighbouring boggy fields. A watch off the beach can be worthwhile: single divers and Slavonian Grebes are reported in most winters. Shags are present, and parties of seaducks may be found. Up to 200 Common Scoters in a tight black raft, together with a dozen Velvet Scoters (uncommon in Devon) and a few immature Eiders, have been seen in some winters; they move eastward and sit off rocky coves towards Sidmouth at times. Nearer, look across to Otterton Ledge rocks which project seaward on the east side of the river mouth; a few Purple Sandpipers regularly feed here.

Passerine species by the estuary include Meadow and Rock Pipits in winter, together with several Stonechats perched on posts and fences. Bearded Tits have been found in the small reed-bed, where Reed Buntings are often seen, and town parks or roadside gardens are shelter for Blackcaps, Chiffchaffs or Firecrests in most winters. Another possible is Crossbill: small groups have occurred in the strip of pines overlooking the east bank of the estuary mouth.

In spring, as few other gaps occur in the coastal cliffs, the estuary and surrounding fields and bushes attract passerine migrants. Yellow Wagtails and Wheatears turn up on the cricket field just behind the beach car park, while Blackcaps, Whitethroats, Willow Warblers and Chiffchaffs follow riverbank path bushes and nearby hedges. The district is not known for rarer migrants, but Hoopoes have occasionally been seen on the cricket pitch. In several recent springs the sibilant, jingling song of Serins has been heard from ornamental fir trees in Budleigh; this tiny yellowish finch may occur anywhere in the district. Cliffs east of the Otter as far as Ladram Bay hold breeding seabirds: up to 15 pairs of Fulmar and 30-40 each of Shag and Cormorant, plus hundreds of Herring Gulls. Inland, small riverbank Sand Martin colonies, together with resident Kingfishers, Dippers and Grey Wagtails at nest sites, make an interesting upriver walk. Autumn brings less noticeable passerine migration, but waders are more varied, often with two or three Greenshanks, their 'tew-tew' flight calls ringing over the estuary, and irregular flocks of smaller species such as Ringed Plover and Turnstone. Offshore, migrant Sandwich Terns move west and other seabirds such as skuas may be driven in by rough weather.

Wader-watching is easiest away from high tide, as high-water **Timing** roosts on saltmarsh islands may be invisible. Early mornings following southeast winds are best for spring arrivals, especially on weekdays as many walkers use the riverbanks on fine weekends. The area is less easy to watch in high winds, except for perhaps an autumn seawatch in strong southerlies. Flattish sea conditions are needed to spot divers etc. from the beach.

Budleigh Salterton, on A376 southeast of Exeter, can be **Access** reached via Exmouth along the coast, or inland over Woodbury ridge on minor roads. The estuary mouth car park is at the far east end of the seafront, and birds can often be seen from the car. From here, walk along the pebble ridge for views out to sea and up the estuary between the raised saltings. Then take the raised estuary bank path northward: easy walking for $\frac{1}{2}$ mile (0.8 km) up to the minor road at White Bridge at the head of the estuary. On the left, after the cricket pitch, are boggy meadows and a small reed-bed. From White Bridge either continue upriver towards Otterton (about $1\frac{1}{2}$ miles/$2\frac{1}{2}$ km) for riverside birds, or cross the bridge and turn right down the partly wooded east bank towards the sea. From here you can continue eastward on the coast footpath towards Ladram Bay (3 miles/5 km) for winter seaducks or summer seabirds.

From White Bridge, turn back left along the minor road to the edge of the meadows, then left again on a public footpath where the trees start; this leads back south towards the car park. For small birds in the town, look for well-timbered parks and avenues: there are many suitable localities. Do not trespass onto private property.

Resident: Shag, Cormorant, Grey Heron, Buzzard, Sparrow- **Calendar** hawk, Kestrel, Lapwing, Stock Dove, Barn, Tawny and Little Owls, woodpeckers, Kingfisher, Rock Pipit, Grey Wagtail, Dipper, Reed Bunting, Raven.

Dec-Feb: Maybe Red-throated or Great Northern Diver, Little Grebe, chance of Slavonian Grebe, Canada Goose, Shelduck, Wigeon and Teal (irregular), Eider, Common and possibly Velvet Scoters, Goldeneye or Long-tailed Duck (irregular), Red-breasted Merganser, Water Rail, Oyster-catcher, Dunlin, probably Purple Sandpiper, Redshank, Common Sandpiper (most years), Curlew, Snipe; one or two Blackcaps, Chiffchaffs or Firecrests in town; Stonechat, possibly Bearded Tit or Crossbill (irregular).

Mar-May: Little Grebe (Mar), Fulmar, Canada Goose, Wheatear and Sand Martin (mid Mar on), Sandwich Tern (late Mar on); a few migrant waders, e.g. Greenshank, Whimbrel, mostly mid Apr-May; breeding gulls and other seabirds on cliffs, chance of Hoopoe; commoner small migrants peak late Apr, chance of Serin from mid Apr.

Jun-Jul: Breeding residents and seabirds, Shelduck, Reed and Sedge Warblers, chance of Serin; scattering of waders and Sandwich Terns in Jul.

Aug-Nov: Fulmars mostly Aug; waders in small numbers mainly Aug-Sep, inc. Turnstone, occasional Spotted Redshank and often Greenshank; terns and maybe Arctic Skua to early Oct; common passerine migrants to end Sep; winter visitors return by Nov.

2 East Devon Commons

This collective title is given to the sandy lowland heaths on the ridge between the lower Exe and Otter valleys, often known as 'Woodbury area' from Woodbury village and common near the centre. The 7-mile (11-km) stretch of commons reaches a height of around 180 m on the west-facing side, sloping more gently eastward. Width of heath varies from a few hundred metres to nearly 2 miles (3 km), broader in the central and southern parts. Vegetation consists of open heather, gorse and Bracken, boggy hollows with birch and willows, stands of pine and larger woods, predominantly coniferous with some Beech. The area contains sand quarries, a few small pools, and a reservoir at the south end. This is a good district for lizards, snakes and butterflies.

For convenience we have included the geographically related area of Muttersmoor, across the Otter just west of Sidmouth.

Several specialised birds, virtually absent from the remainder of our region, occur regularly in small numbers. Red-legged Partridge is a recent introduction into the northern commons, which also hold a good number of Common (Grey) Partridge. A few Barn Owls are still believed to live on neighbouring farmland, and there is a fair chance of finding Lesser Spotted Woodpeckers in the tops of deciduous trees. Woodlarks are thinly spread over the whole area: seen flying up from shelter in Bracken, their extremely short tail is conspicuous, but they are more easily detected by the musical spring songflight over woodland edges and clearings. Small numbers of Dartford Warblers have traditionally been present here where deep heather and gorse exists; they are currently almost extinct after a series of bad years, but will probably re-establish themselves. Hawfinch and Crossbill are also specialised, scarce breeders, probably present regularly but overlooked. The

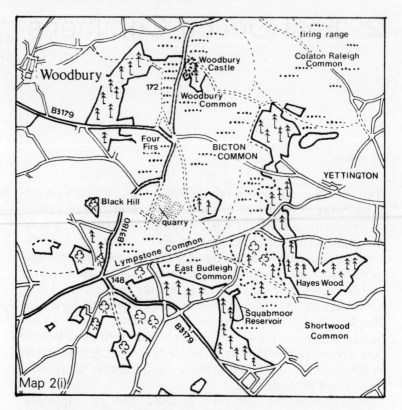

Map 2(i)

stout but secretive Hawfinch, often given away by 'tick' calls as it moves through treetops, turns up all over the area intermittently, in singles or occasionally family parties; the true population is unknown but probably several pairs breed in wooded districts (recent reports have come from Higher Metcombe and Hayes Wood, at opposite ends of the ridge). Crossbill numbers vary annually: after an invasion year, when Continental birds arrive, dozens forage through the pine clumps; in quieter years few are seen, but Hayes Wood is again a possible area.

In winter the commons hold several other species of interest; some luck is needed to find them. Hen Harriers, usually single brown ringtails, have become regular over larger open stretches, where Merlins also hunt intermittently. Woodcocks occur in greater numbers than elsewhere in the region, particularly in cold spells when dozens may arrive. Among a few Snipe in boggy hollows and streamside areas, the scarcer Jack Snipe may be encountered; it is probably regular throughout the area in suitable habitat, but most recent detailed observations are of single figures in the north

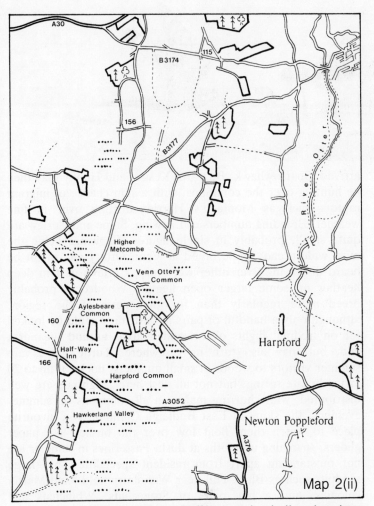

Map 2(ii)

around Venn Ottery. Water Rails occur in similar situations. At least one Great Grey Shrike usually winters on the heaths, pale front prominent as it perches on some vantage point; in early or late winter/early spring it may be seen anywhere, but midwinter sightings are most likely in the southern half, particularly on bushy slopes of East Budleigh Common towards Squabmoor Reservoir. In damp willow and birches, flocks of up to 40 Siskins and a few Redpolls probe for seeds.

Siskins are also prominent in early spring, moving up in flocks (sometimes totalling hundreds) into pinewoods as the weather warms. Although a few Hen Harriers and an occasional Great Grey Shrike turn up in new areas early on, most activity is in late spring, when breeding waders, passerines and other specialised heathland visitors have

Nightjar

arrived. Sparrowhawk, Buzzard, Kestrel and Hobby may then be hunting over the commons, with a slim chance of migrant raptors such as Montagu's Harrier drifting over in fine weather. Breeding numbers of Lapwing, Snipe and Curlew are quite small, probably in single figures, Lapwings being the most widespread; Snipe breed at Venn Ottery and might be heard displaying over other wet areas; Curlews nest in deep heather on some larger open heaths. Woodcocks probably breed more regularly than in other parts of the region, although only a handful of pairs at best; they could be looked for on 'roding' flights over wooded areas around the north end, but may also turn up elsewhere. Turtle Doves are summer visitors to woods in small numbers; flocks of up to 20 arrive in late spring, but not all nest here. Nightjars are well distributed, with churring males on all commons on summer evenings; the slope of East Budleigh Common is a favourite place to watch them float low over the bushes like paper gliders, snatching up moths at dusk. Passerines in summer are not outstanding apart from resident specialities, but large sandpits such as Black Hill near Woodbury hold Sand Martin colonies, and a few pairs of Stonechats, Whinchats and Wheatears nest on larger open heaths. Wood Warblers may be heard trilling in Beech woods and Grasshopper Warblers reel from low scrub and bramble patches on the edge of several heaths.

After the breeding season, the area appears relatively quiet. There are occasional sightings of migrant harriers or other raptors, although in this large area the chances of seeing a 'good' species are not very great.

Timing

Not particularly vital for winter, but avoid wet weather or very high winds. Freezing conditions may bring influxes of Woodcocks or other winter visitors. In summer, mornings and evenings are best, most specialised heathland visitors being crepuscular; a dusk visit is best for Woodcock, Nightjar or Grasshopper Warbler, but in midsummer Nightjars are unlikely to be active before 21.30 hours. Anticyclonic days with fine southeasterlies are most likely for arrivals of migrant raptors or Turtle Dove flocks. The most accessible commons are heavily walked over on fine weekends, so arrive early unless you are prepared to walk well away from the roads.

Access

From the north end, A30 Exeter-Honiton trunk road passes the area; B3180 runs south down the ridge towards Exmouth. A3052 between Exeter and Sidmouth cuts across the centre at Half Way Inn. From Exeter direction, B3179 through Woodbury village gives access to the ridge at Four Firs. A maze of minor roads crosses the commons from east to west, the remotest areas from road access being the centre of Woodbury/Colaton Raleigh heaths and Aylesbeare Common.

Note Parts of the Colaton Raleigh common in particular are used as a military training area at times; details may be obtained from the Commando Training Centre at Lympstone (tel. Topsham 3781) or local police stations.

Those with limited time will probably go for one of the following:

Venn Ottery From A3052/B3180 junction at Half Way Inn, turn north up the B road then right after a mile (1.6 km) onto a minor road. After ¹2 mile (0.8 km) the common is on the left; breeding waders and Grasshopper Warblers are likely in summer, probably Jack Snipe in winter.

Aylesbeare Common From Half Way Inn, this is within the first mile (1.6 km) on the right as you go north up B3180; likely to have breeding Curlews and perhaps Dartford Warblers. RSPB sanctuary Apr-Sep: contact Society for details.

Woodbury Common Half a mile (0.8 km) north of B3180/3178 junction at Four Firs, Woodbury Castle tumulus and pinewood is one of the highest points, with views over the surrounding commons and Exe valley; Woodlarks and Curlews may be found nearby, while Nightjars are often heard.

East Budleigh From Four Firs turn south on B3180, passing Black Hill quarries on the left after ¹2 mile (0.8 km), and drive towards Budleigh Salterton for 2 miles (3 km); the third minor road left leads up past woods and small lakes onto the common. Park in the dirt car park on the right at the hill crest. The bushy slope below overlooks Squabmoor Reservoir, a good summer Nightjar and winter Great Grey Shrike area. Explore left into Hayes Wood and along tracks on the far side of the road.

Muttersmoor From A3052 into Sidmouth, reach the seafront and turn right; continue along the minor road west from the front up Peak Hill, stop in the car park at the crest and walk inland. Nightjars and Grasshopper Warblers, together with common passerines (Stonechat, Linnet and Yellowhammer), may be found; also a vantage point for a passing migrant raptor if you are lucky.

Access on foot is unrestricted on most heathland, which is crossed by numerous paths, but be careful not to disturb ground-nesting birds.

Calendar

Resident: Sparrowhawk, Buzzard, Red-legged and Common Partridges, Barn and Little Owls, woodpeckers inc. Lesser Spotted, Woodlark, maybe Dartford Warbler, Hawfinch, Redpoll, Crossbill, Reed Bunting.

Dec-Feb: Possible Hen Harrier or Merlin, Water Rail, Woodcock, Jack Snipe and Snipe, Great Grey Shrike, winter thrushes, Brambling, Siskin, Redpoll.

Mar-May: Most winter visitors leave by late Mar, but Siskin may stay later. Breeding wader species arrive on sites: Lapwing, Curlew, Woodcock, Snipe from Apr. Stonechats move up from valleys. Summer visitors arriving: Sand Martin and Wheatear from late Mar, most others from late Apr inc. Hobby, Cuckoo, Tree Pipit, warblers inc. a few Wood and Grasshopper, maybe Redstart in woods, Whinchat; Turtle Dove and Nightjar mostly from late May. Occasional migrant raptors, mostly May.

Jun-Jul: Breeding residents and summer visitors most active singing in Jun, but Nightjar and Grasshopper Warbler heard all summer.

Aug-Nov: Resident species have parties of juveniles moving about in Aug. Otherwise relatively quiet, but single raptors may be noted; Hobby or Montagu's Harrier in Sep, Hen Harrier, Peregrine or Merlin in Oct. Winter visitors from late Oct.

3 Exe Estuary: General Introduction

(Maps 3(i) and 3(ii) and OS Map 192)

Habitat

At the west side of Lyme Bay, the Exe has 6 miles (9$\frac{1}{2}$ km) of tidal mudflats, over a mile (1.6 km) wide in places, between Exeter and the sea. Dawlish Warren sandspit extends eastwards across the mouth. Tidal mud tends to be more sandy in the lower estuary. Extensive *Zostera* (eelgrass) beds grow in sheltered areas. The river is tidal up to Countess Wear, on the edge of Exeter. Water meadows up to a mile (1.6 km) wide flank the upper west bank, separated from the tidal channel by Exeter Canal. A tidal reed-bed lies opposite Topsham at the head of the estuary. Shooting is banned on the west bank, and Dawlish Warren is a nature reserve. The estuary mouth is heavily used by holidaymakers in summer, and water sports are increasing.

Species

The estuary flats form southwest England's most important wader and wildfowl feeding area, with up to 20,000 waders of 20 species and several thousand ducks. Numbers of some species, including Brent Goose and Black-tailed Godwit, are recognised as internationally important. The shallow sea is attractive to passing gulls and terns, and to grebes and seaducks in winter. Together with surrounding farmland, the area holds an extremely wide variety of birds.

Main Birdwatching Zones

Because of the size and complexity of the area, we have split the text into zones with local specialities, concentrating on those with easiest access and most birds, although anywhere around the banks may repay investigation.

West bank: *Dawlish Warren; Powderham and the Park; Exminster Marshes and the Canal.*
East bank: *Exmouth.*

37

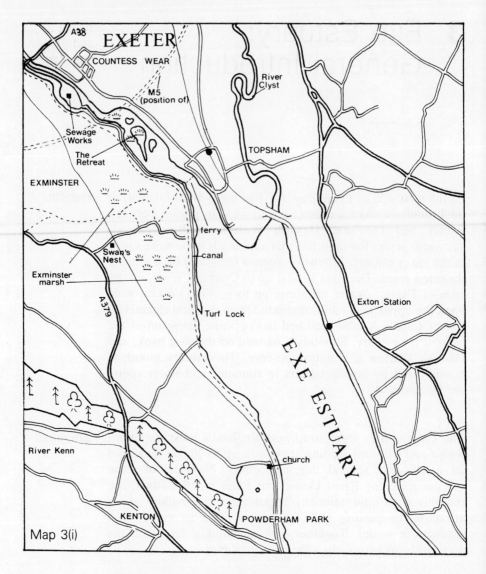

Map 3(i)

Dawlish Warren

Habitat

A mile-long (1.6 km) sand dune spit projecting eastward across the estuary mouth, the seaward side heavily used by the public. Offshore lie shallow waters, with extensive sand bars at low tide. The centre of the Warren is a dune slack with bushes and a small reed-bed. The inner (facing upriver) side of the spit is a golf course, with *Spartina* saltings in the bay behind. The tip of the peninsula curves upriver, leaving a sheltered

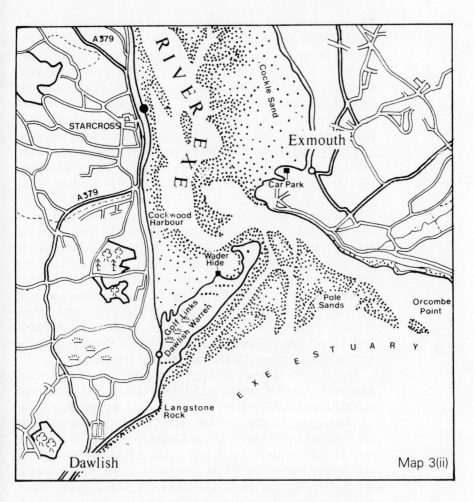

Map 3(ii)

tidal bay behind the dunes, overlooked by a birdwatching hide
near the golf course. The area is well known botanically, with
rare Sand Crocuses and orchids. To the west, along the seawall,
grass-topped Langstone Rock projects seaward.

Species

This excellent area for waders and waterbirds is much visited
by birdwatchers. Winter brings large high-tide roosts of waders
and hundreds of Brent Geese often close in front of the hide.
Oystercatchers (usually over 1,000 and sometimes over 3,000),
Dunlins (hard to count, often 2,000-3,000) and several
hundred Bar-tailed Godwits are the principal species, with a
couple of hundred Ringed Plovers, Grey Plovers and Curlews;
a few dozen Knots, Sanderlings and Turnstones are also likely.

Larger species roost in packs along the tideline, while smaller waders mass on mud and gravel near the hide. Generally, waders using the lower estuary are those adapted to coarse, sandy mud. Shelducks and larger gulls also feed in the bay. Goldeneyes and Red-breasted Mergansers in flocks of up to six fish on the estuary behind the Warren, occasionally accompanied by the smaller Long-tailed Duck. Farther in behind the spit, hundreds of Wigeons graze among saltings, and Grey Herons or Kingfishers may be found along muddy Shutterton Creek entering the main channel. Peregrines often take advantage of the concentration of birds by hunting in this section of the estuary.

On shore, a Short-eared Owl often sits in the Marram Grass among dunes near the point, and a Snow Bunting might be found on the beach in hard weather. A few Reed Buntings are still present in the central bushes, and Water Rails in the reeds. Bearded Tits have occurred several times in the flooded depression, and Chiffchaffs or Firecrests often winter around the edges in small numbers. Among the deserted seafront arcades, a party of Cirl Buntings may be found in low bramble and Tree Lupins; Stonechats and a Black Redstart may be with them, or along the seawall towards Langstone.

The sea off Dawlish Warren is one of the region's main wintering areas for marine waterfowl, with divers, grebes and seaducks regularly present. A typical watch will produce up to 15 Slavonian Grebes, which dive in shallow water just offshore, and probably a Great Crested Grebe or two farther out. In most winters, up to half a dozen Red-throated Divers are dotted across the whole Langstone Rock-estuary mouth area, joined by the occasional larger Black-throated or Great Northern; the relatively shallow sheltered sea here suits Red-throated best, indeed this is their most regular West Country haunt. Small packs of Eiders, mostly brown or patchy immatures, are often present, sometimes coming close in off Langstone, where Shags perch on the projecting jetty. Common Scoters are seen in tight packs of 200 or more off Langstone, the occasional white bar on an outstretched wing revealing a few Velvet Scoters in their midst. A dozen or so Red-breasted Mergansers often feed across the bay, while less common visitors such as a Scaup or Red-necked Grebe may join them in hard weather. Check in winter for Turnstones and Purple Sandpipers among the weedy rocks below Langstone at low tide. Watching off Langstone may be long-distance and a telescope is helpful; estuary ducks will also roost offshore, and Wigeons often sit in thousands well out to sea.

Large numbers of gulls use the estuary mouth. After onshore gales thousands, mostly Black-headed, gather along the shore and seawall to scavenge cast-up marine life; they may be joined by a Mediterranean Gull, or more frequently a Little Gull fluttering over the breakers. Occasionally after high winds, when dunes and beach suffer severe erosion, a Great Skua comes into the bay to harry Herring Gulls over the sand bars.

Wheatears arriving along the front are soon followed by the spring's first 'kirrick' calls of Sandwich Terns. Spring tern movement attracts many birdwatchers; later in the season, mixed flocks plunge for fish close off the beach or drop in to roost in the tidal bay among waders. Although Sandwich are always most noticeable, migrant Little Terns, up to 40 hovering over the sea on peak days, are far more numerous here than elsewhere in the region. Common Terns, sometimes joined by darker Arctics, may be briefly numerous according to weather conditions, but soon continue eastward. In the second half of spring there is a good chance of a Roseate Tern, often coming to roost among the Sandwich flock; up to ten of these scarce terns have been seen. Other sea migrants may include single Arctic or Pomarine Skuas, while Eiders and sometimes a flock of Great Crested Grebes remain offshore. Meanwhile, Willow Warblers and other spring migrants sing from Sallows in the centre of the Warren; Sedge and Reed Warblers turn up in the reeds, one or two staying to breed. When breezes blow from the Continent, a Hoopoe may be probing among the dunes, or sometimes an Osprey or harrier circling in overhead. On such days the wader roost is a colourful sight, with resting northbound birds in breeding plumage including hundreds of chestnut-fronted godwits, Grey Plovers, and scurrying groups of Sanderlings. Many Whimbrels fly in off the sea, and it is worth a search among smaller waders for an oddity such as a Kentish Plover.

Summer is quieter for birds, although Whitethroats and Reed Buntings will be seen, while a few terns remain offshore and parties of Eiders still occur. Cirl Buntings breed behind the coast near Langstone, and the red sandstone embankment west of the rock has several pairs of Sand Martins nesting. Even while the beach is still thronged with holidaymakers, the first terns and Arctic-nesting waders return. Several hundred Oystercatchers will probably have summered on the estuary flats.

Autumn is protracted, with large parties of waders and terns staying to feed around the estuary mouth for weeks at a time.

Screaming juvenile Sandwich Terns fly in across the dunes, pursuing parents which have caught sand-eels offshore; up to 200 of this species are regularly present. Among several dozen Commic terns there may be an Arctic or Roseate, more difficult to identify at this season, and four or five Littles. Often a Black Tern joins them for a few days. This source of food attracts Arctic Skuas, which may dive in across the roost to rob arriving birds. Waders number several thousand, with an early passage of Ringed Plovers and Sanderlings, the former sometimes reaching 500 birds although Sanderlings seldom top 100. Through mid autumn patient watchers may pick out several Curlew Sandpipers or pale, short-beaked Little Stints among teeming Dunlins. Wheatears are a familiar sight in the dunes, and small numbers of migrant warblers feed in the central bushes.

Most terns move out from mid autumn, although skuas, Gannets and other seabirds may still gather offshore during gales later in the season. Large numbers have sometimes been seen (100 Arctic Skuas, several Great Skuas and hundreds of Gannets in a day), and maybe even a Sabine's Gull. After a really rough autumn spell, check in the lee of Langstone Rock for a sheltering ocean-wanderer—a phalarope, perhaps, or rotund Little Auk. In late autumn the first Brent Geese drop in; recently they have arrived earlier and in bigger groups. Large wintering packs of plovers, Dunlins and godwits may be chased by both Peregrines and Merlins, although the smaller falcon may find Meadow Pipits on the golf links easier prey. As the last summer migrants pass through, Wigeons reappear in whistling thousands, and birdwatchers search the sea again for divers and grebes.

Powderham and the Park

Habitat

The 1-mile (1.6-km) wide central estuary tidal flats are bordered on the west by the wooded parkland and fresh water of Powderham Park, the Earl of Devon's estate. A herd of several dozen Fallow Deer, easily seen, grazes in the grounds near the castle. The small River Kenn runs through the estate into the estuary in two branches, the northern one widened into a shallow mere, often overflowing into neighbouring fields. North of the park, low-lying meadows behind the estuary seawall slowly widen northward towards Exminster

Marsh. The main deepwater channel of the estuary flows close in off the embankment bend.

The park boundary and seawall northward are one of the region's most popular areas for autumn and winter wader-watching. The meadows behind the seawall area are a high-tide roost for waders from nearby mudflats. The balance of species is different from that at Dawlish Warren, with more species adapted to probing soft mud. Curlews and Black-tailed Godwits predominate; the flock of 600 Black-tailed, smart birds in flight with black and white wing-stripes, is one of Britain's largest gatherings. Recently Brent Geese, as they have increased, have spilled over from the estuary to graze in meadows when other food is short. Rich mud off the embankment attracts many waders, including a few Green-shanks and one or two Spotted Redshanks, the latter often noticed by their 'chew-it' call. Avocets, based farther upriver, sometimes feed down this far and at high tide may float buoyantly in a group among Shelducks, easily overlooked because of their similar colours. Views may be long-distance and telescopes are recommended.

Species

Flocks of up to 1,000 dabbling ducks rest on mudbanks. Among hundreds of Mallards and Teals, the elegant shapes of 40-50 Pintails may be picked out; smaller numbers of Gadwalls and Shovelers join them, mainly in severe weather. On deeper stretches there are generally several Goldeneyes or Red-breasted Mergansers fishing, along with plentiful Cormorants. Grey Herons stand poised along the waterside. Sometimes the whole mass of ducks and waders erupts as a Peregrine dives to make a kill.

The park serves as a roost for Redshanks, Spotted Redshanks and Greenshanks, which usually fly in to the River Kenn or pools at high tide. Greenshanks particularly favour the park, although the main flock of 200 or more Redshanks may move elsewhere if disturbed. These freshwater habitats hold dozens of wintering Teals and often Canada Geese, up to 100 strong, probably breeding birds from farther up the Exe valley and Crediton; the goose flock is worth checking for an occasional (escaped?) Barnacle Goose. Kingfishers may speed along the waterside, and sometimes a Green Sandpiper stays to winter on a sheltered channel.

Spring brings large flocks of Whimbrels and 'red' breeding-plumaged godwits dropping in on the mud; Sandwich and Common Terns, or sometimes Little, fly up the estuary following the rising tide, and Greenshanks, usually in twos and threes through winter, become more numerous. The park's large trees hold a heronry of up to 40 pairs, and provide nesting territory for many Stock Doves. Kestrels, Buzzards and Sparrowhawks are often seen circling overhead, while Great Spotted and Green Woodpeckers fly across the clearings. Open spaces are frequently dotted with pairs of Shelducks prospecting Rabbit burrows to breed in.

In autumn the park is again worth a look for shanks with up to 40 pale-fronted Greenshanks and several Spotted Redshanks among scores of Redshanks. Two or three Green Sandpipers, and perhaps a Wood Sandpiper, may be present by freshwater pools in early autumn. Most watchers visit the seawall in hopes of an Osprey fishing off the bend, as this impressive raptor is recorded annually, in some years staying on the estuary for weeks. Sometimes a Hobby comes down from the marshes to try a small wader meal. In the Dunlin flocks you may find other migrant waders, if close views are possible. American vagrants, e.g. dowitcher, have been seen in park pools.

Most winter ducks do not return until late autumn, but Teals have often been noted in the park from the end of summer; in colder weather flocks of Tufted Ducks, found in few places locally, may join them on the pools.

Exminster Marshes and the Canal

Habitat

On the west side of the upper estuary, water meadows intersected by drainage dykes are up to a mile (1.6 km) wide. Beyond lies low rolling farmland. The old Exeter Canal, now used mostly for angling and rowing, runs down the outer marsh edge, entering the estuary at Turf Lock. Beyond here the estuary seawall embanks a smaller area towards Powderham. This top section of tidal flats is particularly soft, and rich in food. No shooting is permitted on the canal banks, but a private shoot operates on the water meadows. Opposite the marsh, between the canal bank and Topsham village across the river, lies an extensive tidal reed-bed through which the river flows before reaching open mudflats.

In winter the grazing marshes' attractiveness to birds often depends on water levels. Floods lying in the fields may attract large flocks of ducks and waders: hundreds of Wigeons, and smaller numbers of Teals, Pintails and Shovelers; Snipe may be present in scores and cold spells often bring thousands of Lapwings from farther afield. Two or three hundred Golden Plovers and a variable number of Ruffs, usually single figures, stay all winter; in snow they may be joined by parties of White-fronted Geese, which soon leave because of shooting, or by a wild swan, usually Bewick's, grazing among Mute Swans. Fieldfares and Redwings can be seen in hundreds. The canal sometimes holds a surprise such as a Red-throated Diver or Long-tailed Duck, watchable at close range from reed-fringed banks; often Kingfishers sit by lock gates. Rough fields at the south end of the marsh towards Turf are likely to harbour a few Short-eared Owls, which rise and beat slowly across dykes on winter afternoons; in years when vole 'plagues' occur, they are very prominent, half a dozen or more patrolling the marsh. The declining Barn Owl might still be seen; sometimes they roost in ivy adjacent to Topsham reed-bed, where an occasional Smew or Goosander appears in bad weather and the 'ping' calls of Bearded Tits have been heard. Green or Common Sandpipers often winter here.

The upper estuary flats are notable for 30 or more wintering Avocets (increasing annually) off Turf. Those wintering on the Tamar are believed to pass through at the start and end of the season, when extra groups appear briefly. The main Exe flock may move between Turf, Topsham across the river, and Powderham, but by careful timing (see that section) close views can be obtained of these elegant waders sweeping the shallows off the lower marsh. Apart from other interesting regulars such as Spotted Redshank, the mudflats are the site of a massive roost of Black-headed (over 5,000) and Common Gulls from the Exe valley farmland. Peregrines are often seen overhead. Goldeneyes are frequent on the main channel, reaching 30-40 at times, and small groups of Scaups sometimes winter off Turf.

Spring's earliest arrival is often Garganey, with one or two of these scarce ducks on freshwater channels and pools in the marshes. Sadly they do not stay to breed, but Shovelers which often arrive may breed in small numbers if trampling cattle allow. Wheatears and Sand Martins usually pass up the marsh edge soon after the Garganeys. From mid spring a variety of warblers, including Sedge, Reed and sometimes Grasshopper, arrives to sing along the canal banks. Large flocks of

Species

Drake Garganey

HARRISON 83

Whimbrels, reaching 100 or more, rest on the meadows before continuing overland. Oddities can include a Spoonbill on Turf mudflats for a few days, or a passing Marsh or Montagu's Harrier quartering the fields. Perhaps unexpected is the passage of tern flocks moving north inland along the outer marsh edge on fine evenings; generally they spiral high over the canal banks before flying high towards Exeter. Groups of Sandwich, Common and even dark-chested Arctic Terns have been seen passing, and this is also a good time for waders such as Whimbrel and Common Sandpiper flying over.

Breeding species in the meadows include a scattering of Lapwings, with one or two pairs of Shelducks in nearby farmland. Over recent seasons the tiny colony of Yellow Wagtails, on the western edge of their breeding range, has become less regular, although a few still turn up each spring. The aggressive Canada Goose, however, is now often present in summer and likely to breed. Common breeding raptors and Grey Herons are frequent hunters in the fields. A more localised speciality is Cirl Bunting, which occurs in farm hedgerows and sheltered valleys behind Exminster village. Swallows and House Martins nest plentifully around local barns and farmhouses; in late summer many feed over the marsh dykes, where they may be chased by a Hobby, and frequently caught by the slim falcon's unerring accuracy. At the end of the breeding season, thousands of Swallows and Starlings roost overnight in Topsham reed-bed, milling around before dropping in at last light. This concentration of birds is an attraction to predators; sometimes two or three Hobbies hunt here, and the endless babble of Starlings is silenced when Sparrowhawks glide over.

Passage waders on the marshes often include two or three Green Sandpipers, while flocks of shanks and godwits return early to the mudflats. Look also for the odd Little Stint or Curlew Sandpiper feeding off Turf canal exit with Dunlins. Early autumn can be productive around Turf, with a good chance of an Osprey fishing, causing gulls and waders to fly up in great alarm. Black Terns or Little Gulls may dip over the canal's wider stretches, and there are various small migrants in reeds and bushes. Late season has produced unexpected 'wrecked' seabirds during gales, such as an exhausted Pomarine Skua by the lock and a tiny Little Auk resting on the canal. It will be the end of autumn before Avocets return, and ideally a visit to see them should be left until winter.

Exmouth

At the east side of the estuary mouth, Exmouth waterfront gives views out to sea, across the fast-flowing channel to Dawlish Warren, and up the estuary mudflats. High cliffs rise from the east end of the seafront. Behind the town lies a wide, sheltered estuary bay with beds of *Zostera* (eelgrass), an important wildfowl food.

Habitat

In winter the bay at the rear of the town is the estuary's main feeding zone for Brent Goose, Wigeon and Pintail: whistling rafts of up to 5,000 Wigeons are often at close range; Brent Geese, increasing recently, now top 2,000 at times but partially disperse as food runs short; the graceful Pintail can exceed 100 in number. This bay forms the largest wildfowl concentration in our region, and the winter watcher is almost certain to see large flocks. The deeper water of the main tideway is favoured by fishing Red-breasted Mergansers; sometimes a Long-tailed Duck stays a week or two, and auks are often present in small numbers. At the seaward end of town, where Orcombe cliffs starts, seaweed-covered boulders attract a regular flock of around a dozen Purple Sandpipers, accompanied by Oystercatchers and Turnstones. Groups of Eiders in assorted immature plumages often swim near the rocks; farther out there may be Slavonian Grebes, divers and

Species

scoters, but these move about between Exmouth and the Warren according to wind and tide.

Spring brings large numbers of terns feeding offshore, often picking up sand-eels churned up by the rising tide breaking over sand bars, or moving up past the seafront into the estuary at high tide. They roost on the Warren but dozens may be seen off this side; all commoner sea terns occur here, but Roseates are identified more often from the other side. Terns are also Exmouth's main attraction in autumn, often chased by one or two Arctic Skuas; in stormy conditions larger movements of seabirds might be seen off Orcombe cliffs. There have been scattered reports of Little Auk or Grey Phalarope off Orcombe in the autumn.

Timing
(all sites)

Most waders and ducks are at great distances from the observer at low tide. Best watching is generally within the two or three hours before high tide, as birds move closer to the banks, and at main roosts such as Dawlish Warren for an hour or so across high tide. Avocets at Turf are best seen when feeding nearest the bank about two hours before high water. All times should be weighed against the height of the tide; spring tides may force birds to abandon feeding sooner, and even to abandon normal roosts (at the Warren they may have to roost on the beach and are frequently disturbed). Terns tend to join the Warren roost when there is some mud left in the tidal bay, two or three hours before or after high tide, or on neap tides; rising tides encourage them to fly upriver as far as Turf. High-pressure weather, with winds from a southerly quarter, is best for all spring arrivals; eastern migrants such as Black Tern arrive mostly in autumn easterlies. Strong south-west winds with rain battering the coast in autumn produce concentrations of seabirds off the coast and occasional 'wrecked' birds as far up as Turf. Freezing weather elsewhere brings influxes of wildfowl and open-ground species on the marshes; periods of heavy rain, flooding meadows, may also encourage birds to come from the estuary to feed. Short-eared Owls on the marshes or Warren point fly mostly in late afternoons. For raptors such as Peregrine or Osprey, a wait of at least two or three hours at vantage points along the estuary banks is needed. For views of divers and grebes on the sea, choose a calmish sea; in a swell watch from Langstone top. Avoid watching the mudflats from the west bank in early mornings when light glare is against you, and choose days when wind in these exposed spots will not prevent keeping

Peregrine

HARRISON 83

focus on distant birds. Do not try for Avocets in late afternoons, when their white shapes blend with roosting gulls. For ducks or divers on the canal, try weekdays or early mornings (less disturbance).

The reed-bed roost at Exminster Marsh-Topsham end should be watched from about two hours before dusk, in fine weather, for spring tern and wader movements, or at similar times in early autumn for roosting birds.

Coastal districts are heavily used by walkers at weekends, and by holidaymakers in summer; in July or August especially, early morning visits are best. Windsurfers may disturb wildfowl off Exmouth on fine weekends, especially Sundays, so try other days or early morning if possible (if tides are suited).

Dawlish Warren is reached from A379 Exeter-Dawlish road, turning south around Cockwood Harbour bridge, or east at the start of Dawlish town. Go under the railway bridge onto the Warren, then left towards the main estuary, or right for the seawall and Langstone. For sea views walk right along the seawall to the rock; climb the steps with care and scan from

Access (all sites)

the top. A walk west towards Dawlish may produce winter grebes or summer Sand Martins.

For the wader roost and estuary mouth, turn into the left car park. Walk along the dune crest overlooking the beach, or past the central marsh and bushes. Walk to the narrowest part of the dunes, then left beside the golf course end to reach the green corrugated bird hide facing the roost bay. A logbook of observations is kept inside. If you continue to the far tip of the Warren afterwards, avoid flushing roosting birds when passing the bay. Short-eared Owls are most likely in the far dunes.

The Warren is managed as a nature reserve by Teignbridge Council, who employ a full-time warden. Access for individuals is unrestricted (but please keep off fenced study areas); large parties should contact the Warden, Peter Nicholson, to avoid clashes over use of the hide. Guided walks are available in summer. Contact Peter via Teignbridge Council Planning Department, Courtenay St, Newton Abbot, Devon.

Powderham From A379, travelling north from Dawlish Warren, fork right at north end of Starcross village on a minor road between park and estuary. Stop and look across the park and pools from roadside pull-ins. For the estuary bank, continue to the sharp bend beside the church, and park. Walk north along a track leading to the estuary bank. A footpath leads to Turf Lock (see below), 1$\frac{1}{2}$ miles (2$\frac{1}{2}$ km) along the bank.

Exminster Marshes From A379, turn down the lane towards Swan's Nest Inn at the south end of Exminster village. Bypass the inn entrance and continue over a humpbacked bridge across the railway; stop to check fields on either side if flooded. Cross the first major dyke and stop at gravel parking to look around the central marsh. A small path starting at left leads across fields to the marsh edge and views of the tidal reed-bed. From here you can walk down the canal towpath to Turf. Alternatively, continue to the end of the central track, bumpy but driveable. Walk up onto the canal bank and south towards Turf, watching adjacent fields for Short-eared Owls in winter. Avocets and other waders are on the estuary opposite you. For better views, cross the lock gates and watch upriver along the outer marsh bank; also look down the estuary channel for diving ducks.

If access to the east bank is needed, a passenger ferry operates between the outer marsh bank and Topsham across the narrow tidal Exe channel. Stand on the slipway and signal: the boatman will come across. The ferry operates from 09.00 to 17.00 hours in winter, extending to 20.00 hours in summer, daily except on extreme low tides.

A rough (often overgrown) path leads up the outer canal bank north past the reed-bed towards Exeter.

Exmouth From Exeter, take A377 south; or, after visiting the previous points, turn right at Countess Wear roundabout on the edge of Exeter and south via Topsham. Follow signs through Exmouth centre to the seafront and try various points. For Eider and Purple Sandpiper try the far end: a path leads up onto Orcombe cliffs. For the estuary, drive back past the docks and turn left to Imperial Road car park (past station), which gives open views over the mudflats. Winter birdwatching boat trips upriver start from the docks.

Calendar

Resident: Grey Heron, Eider (some years), Sparrowhawk, Buzzard, Pheasant, Coot, Lapwing, Oystercatcher (non-breeders summer), Stock Dove, Barn Owl, woodpeckers, Stonechat, Cirl Bunting, Reed Bunting.

Dec-Feb: Divers, especially Red-throated, Slavonian and Great Crested Grebes offshore, Little Grebe, Cormorant, Shag, occasional Bewick's Swan and White-fronted Goose, Brent Goose, Shelduck, possibly Gadwall, Wigeon, Teal, Pintail, Shoveler, probably Tufted Duck, maybe Scaup, Common and perhaps Velvet Scoters, Goldeneye, probably Long-tailed Duck, Red-breasted Merganser, occasional Goosander or Smew, Peregrine, Water Rail, Avocet, Ringed Plover, Golden Plover, Grey Plover, Turnstone, Dunlin, Knot, Sanderling, Purple Sandpiper, Redshank, Spotted Redshank, Greenshank, Common and Green Sandpipers, probably Ruff, Curlew, Black-tailed Godwit, Bar-tailed Godwit, Snipe, Jack Snipe, rarely Great Skua, gulls, Short-eared Owl, Kingfisher, Chiffchaff, Black Redstart, winter thrushes, maybe Bearded tit, occasional Snow Bunting.

Mar-May: By mid Mar, Wheatears first seen on coast, probably Garganey on marshes; first Sandwich Terns offshore by end of third week. Avocets and most wildfowl leave by mid Mar. Slavonian Grebes flock in Mar before leaving, a few stay to mid Apr. Passage divers (most Red-throated) through May. Whimbrel and Common and Green Sandpipers move up through marshes; migrant shanks pass from mid Apr, peak end Apr. Reed and Sedge Warblers and Yellow Wagtail arrive mid-late Apr. Short-eared Owl occasional to early May. Main tern passage mid Apr-May, mostly end Apr and first half May, when Roseate usually seen. Occasional Arctic or Pomarine Skua early May. Occasional scarcer migrants, e.g. Osprey, Marsh or Montagu's Harrier, Kentish Plover, Hoopoe, end Apr through May. Shovelers and Shelducks breed. A few Great Crested Grebes, Common Scoters and auks on sea, passing Fulmars, Gannets and Kittiwakes.

Jun-Jul: A few Sandwich Terns summer, maybe Common Scoter. From end Jun-early Jul, first waders returning, a few terns arrive, staying off-passage until autumn. Adult Shelducks fly north to moult from end Jun.

Aug-Nov: Common, Green, maybe Wood Sandpipers Aug-early Sep on marshes, migrant warblers, Wheatears and wagtails; hirundines and Starlings roost in reed-bed, with Hobby and other raptors in pursuit, from Aug, hirundines leaving through Sep. Terns feeding Aug-early Sep, a few Black Terns through Sep. Arctic Skuas frequent, chasing terns from mid Aug. Small numbers of Little Stints and Curlew Sandpipers through Sep, often Osprey staying. Peregrine, Merlin and Short-eared Owl mostly Oct-Nov. Arctic, Great and maybe other skuas, or Sabine's Gull, offshore in gales Sep-Oct. Maybe Little Auk or Grey Phalaropes Oct-Nov. Divers and grebes arrive from mid Oct, mostly late Nov. Snow Bunting occasional on beach and Black Redstarts arrive, late Oct-Nov. Wildfowl return from late Sep, but mostly Nov. Few Avocets until late Nov.

4 Stoke Canon Meadows and Wood

(Map 4 and OS Map 192)

Habitat

Approximately 2 miles (3 km) of low-lying river valley north of Exeter, bordered along the east flank by Stoke Woods, a mixed wood on a steep hillside, designated as a Country Park. The River Exe meanders through meadows liable to flood. Above Stoke Canon, towards Brampford Speke village, the river is faster and shallower, with shingle bars. Below Stoke Canon village, the Exe and Culm rivers converge; willow and Alder trees line the banks, and at low river levels mudbars are exposed.

Species

This is a convenient area close to Exeter to see woodland and waterside birds. The attractiveness of the valley meadows to different species depends on water levels. Flocks of up to 100 Canada Geese drop in to graze outside the breeding season. Winter floods bring varying numbers of dabbling duck, mostly Wigeons with 200 most years and over 500 at times. The slender Pintail is less common but there are often ten or more in midwinter, usually in larger flood patches. Teals occur in scattered parties generally totalling under 100, but are less affected than other ducks in dry winters. Shovelers are seen sporadically in twos and threes. On the river, up to five brownhead Goldeneyes are sometimes joined by Tufted Ducks. Freeze-ups may bring a Goosander or other unusual displaced duck. Hundreds of Lapwings and dozens of Snipe feed in damp fields, while Common and Green Sandpipers winter in ones and twos on sheltered riverbanks and pools, the Green Sandpipers looking like large House Martins as they fly up. The riverside is always worth watching, with Dippers bobbing in shallows near Brampford Speke, while Kingfishers and Grey Wagtails feed all along. Parties of up to 40 Siskins forage in overhanging trees, and mixed flocks of other finches feed on stubble fields near Stoke Canon village. Woodcocks are sometimes flushed from quieter parts of the wood.

53

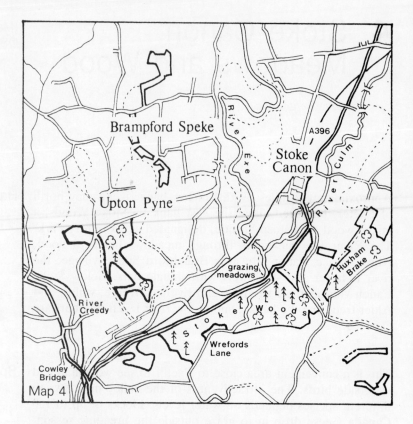

Woodland species such as woodpeckers (with a regular pair of Lesser Spotted), thrushes, tits, Nuthatch and Treecreeper are encountered; visit a cross-section of habitats, including mature Beeches for woodpeckers and undergrowth for small passerines.

Spring arrival can be noticeable as birds funnel up from the Exe estuary. Garganeys sometimes drop in on remaining flood pools, Greenshanks stop off on shingle bars beside teetering parties of Common Sandpipers, and large groups of Swifts and hirundines follow the waterway. A pair of Canada Geese often tries to breed, while Lapwings are regulars with two or three usually tumbling over meadows in display flight. Kingfishers often nest in one of the bigger riverbanks and Sand Martins can be watched entering nest holes just below Brampford, where 20 or more pairs breed, although they sometimes lose their nests if the river rises unexpectedly. One or two Sedge Warblers sing in damp thickets. Little Owls and Cirl Buntings occur in small numbers on neighbouring farmland, but are easily missed. The wood is worth a visit when summer visitors have arrived, with commoner warblers such as Blackcap, Garden Warbler, Willow Warbler and Chiffchaff in good numbers. Several trilling Wood Warblers can be heard, particularly in Beeches. Less common for Devon are one or two Turtle Doves, and, in some years, Nightingales skulking in dense undergrowth in the lower wood, near the bottom of Wrefords Lane.

Early autumn, with low river levels leaving exposed mud, is good for waders. Greenshanks and Common and Green Sandpipers are most frequent; twos and threes are usual but sometimes up to ten Green Sandpipers rise from the mud with loud 'tluee' calls. A Wood Sandpiper might also occur. Lapwings and Common Gulls flock in the fields, where various small migrants such as Yellow Wagtail and Whinchat are often found. Apart from frequent Sparrowhawks, predators hunting over the riverside may include Hobby or Barn Owl.

Timing

Duck numbers increase greatly when meadows flood after heavy rain; partial floods are present most winters. Flood pools at migration periods may also attract waders, or rarely Garganey. Frozen conditions can bring scarcer wildfowl in winter. Evening visits in late summer/early autumn can be good for waders moving, and perhaps Barn Owl. Disturbance by public use can be a problem in the wood on fine summer weekends; try mornings for songbirds in spring.

Access

A396 Exeter-Tiverton road runs north from Cowley Bridge on the edge of Exeter. For the water meadows continue 1 mile (1.6 km) and park beside the wood, in a small lay-by on the right after passing two signposted woodland entry points. Cross the main road and take the gated footpath left across fields to Staffords Bridge; scan around from here. Alternatively, several roadside pull-ins on the left up the main road give views over likely flood areas. Park near the foot of Wrefords Lane, which joins from the right halfway along the wood (do not park on main road), and look left across the Culm-Exe meeting point. In summer check the wood near the lane: the small valley behind is good for most woodland birds. Try also turning right up the lane and stopping at car parks on the right for more mature stands of trees.

The north end of the valley can be viewed by continuing up the A396, crossing the river Culm at the start of Stoke Canon village. Turn immediately left down the lane past a bungalow estate; look across nearby fields. Follow the lane around to a rail signal box and gated crossing point, then take the public footpath for ¼ mile (400 m) to Brampford Speke riverside.

Calendar

Resident: Sparrowhawk, Buzzard, Lapwing, Stock Dove, Barn and Little Owls, Kingfisher, woodpeckers inc. Lesser Spotted, Grey Wagtail, common woodland passerines, Dipper, maybe Cirl Bunting, Raven.

Dec-Feb: Cormorant, Grey Heron, Canada Goose, Wigeon, Teal, Pintail, Shoveler (irregular), maybe Tufted Duck, possible Goosander or Smew (hard weather), Goldeneye, Common and Green Sandpipers, Woodcock (Stoke Wood), Snipe, Stonechat, winter thrushes, Brambling, Siskin, Redpoll, other finches.

Mar-May: Most ducks leave by early Mar. Chiffchaff and Sand Martin arrive by late Mar. Canada Geese start nesting. Migrant Greenshank, Common and Green Sandpipers, other passing migrants and summer visitors peak late Apr-May.

Jun-Jul: Breeding residents and summer visitors; Canada Goose probable, Turtle Dove, Cuckoo, hirundines, common warblers, Wood Warbler, probably Nightingale. Waders and gulls return from Jul.

Aug-Nov: Greenshank, Common, Green and occasional Wood Sandpipers, peaking Aug; Common Gull; Yellow Wagtail and other small migrants pass Aug-Sep, maybe also Hobby. Most winter visitors return from late Oct, but duck numbers low until winter.

5 Haldon Woods and Little Haldon

(Map 5 and OS Map 192)

Habitat

West of the Exe, Haldon is a conspicuous ridge extending about 6 miles (9½ km) north to south, rising above surrounding farmland to a height of 260 m. The east slope is particularly steep. The flat, sandy top is covered largely by coniferous forestry plantations, with small stands of Beech and other deciduous trees. Many small clearings, with a rich summer growth of ferns, vary the woodland habitat, and a few areas of natural heath remain. The largest open area is the horse-racing track and surrounding heath in the centre of the ridge. Little Haldon is a smaller detached block of similar terrain 2 miles (3 km) farther south, with areas of open heath and a golf course. Both hills afford panoramic views over lowlands and coastline.

The area harbours Roe Deer, often glimpsed in quieter wooded areas, and extensive Badger setts can be found. The clearings hold a variety of moths and butterflies, including Green Hairstreak and White Admiral. Adders and Common Lizards may be seen basking on heaths in warm weather.

Species

The large area of mature conifers means that most birds are those adapted to this specialised habitat. In winter the woods can appear lifeless, although the plentiful local Buzzards soar overhead on fine days, and Woodcocks may be flushed beside the tracks. A thorough search is likely to reveal parties of Siskins and Redpolls moving through treetops. Crossbills can also be found in scattered flocks, swinging silently beneath pine cones or detected by 'chupp' flight calls as parties move about; up to 100 may be present but are hard to locate. In two or three parts of the wood male Crossbills may soon be heard singing, this species being an early breeder, but numbers of pairs are small and irregular. Assorted finches feeding on fallen Beech mast often include Bramblings. Occasional passing raptors or Great Grey Shrikes are seen.

57

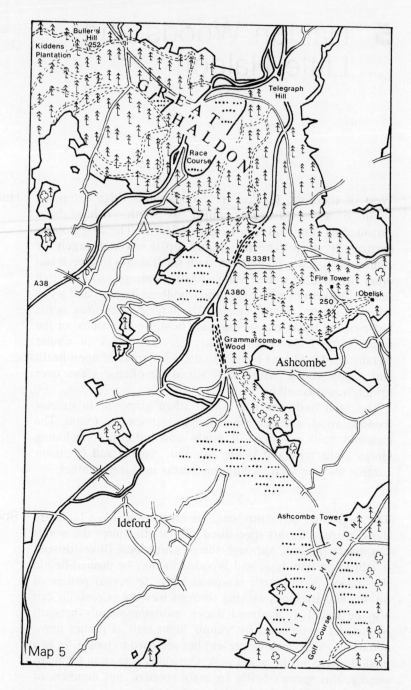

Map 5

As spring comes, resident raptors dive in display overhead, and woodpeckers of all three species seek out nest holes in old timber. Other resident hole-nesters include a very few sooty-headed Willow Tits in damp areas, while Coal Tits and Goldcrests are common in dense conifers. Siskins form pre-migration gatherings of up to 200, but after most of these agile little finches have departed northward there is a gap before many summer visitors become established. Later spring brings a wide variety of breeding species, especially at woodland edges or where clearings or a mixture of tree species give habitat variety; the centres of densest plantations harbour very few species. Apart from commoner warblers such as Willow, there are usually Wood Warblers trilling, especially in Beech groves, while the Grasshopper Warbler occurs on some open heaths and larger clearings. Redstarts are likely in areas of mature deciduous trees, or old pines with small clearings and decayed wood, while Tree Pipits are seen in songflight over younger trees. Redpolls chatter in flight between high nests in mature conifers and lower bushes where they feed. Siskins also tend increasingly to stay into summer: a number of pairs breed although probably fewer than ten. On open heaths, where Cuckoos are fairly common, both Stonechats and Whinchats perch on gorse sprigs; Wheatears have been known to nest but are not regular. Sometimes a migrant raptor, perhaps even a Montagu's Harrier, pauses to feed over the heaths for a few hours on spring passage, and a Honey Buzzard has been seen.

It is usually the end of spring before the most distinctive species are all present. The 30-50 pairs of Nightjars, probably the largest population in the region, have just arrived. Males are active each evening, 'churring' loudly to establish territories in fern-covered clearings and clapping their wings together to deter intruding males; close views may be obtained by a silent watcher as they glide low overhead in pursuit of moths. Occasionally a Hobby is also seen catching moths over open ground. Another late arrival is Turtle Dove, for which Haldon is one of the westernmost regular breeding sites.

When the breeding season is in full swing, dense woods do not permit close views; few birds still sing, although Nightjars continue to churr and the cooing of Turtle Doves may be heard to late summer. At the end of the season, large assorted bands of tits and warblers search the woods for food. Autumn migration is not obvious, but occasionally Haldon's prominent position encourages migrant raptors, including groups of Buzzards from farther north, to circle overhead.

Timing

Most species keep under cover in poor weather; fine conditions without strong winds are best. Mornings and evenings are easier for passerine songbirds; larger raptors do not soar until later morning when the land has warmed. High pressure with light east or southeast winds can bring soaring migrant raptors across from the Continent. Warm summer evenings with moths and insects on the wing are best for Nightjars and other crepuscular species (Nightjars are not usually heard before 21.30 hours).

Access

From Exeter, A38 to Plymouth and A380 to Torquay cross the top of Haldon in parallel. Birds of interest are scattered widely in the extensive woods. The following provide chances of some of the more distinctive species:

Racecourse At the crest of the ridge beside A38. Turn left just before the course if approaching from Exeter side. Drive down a minor road towards A380, but stop after about 100 m and park beside gravel heaps on right. This point overlooks the racetrack perimeter and edge of the woods; raptors may pass here, circling over the steep escarpment, Hobbies sometimes catching moths; Stonechats and Tree or Meadow Pipits are common. From here, return to A38 and turn south (left) again. Cross the dual carriageway after a few metres and take another minor road north towards Dunchideock. Stop by any gate leading into forest on the left, and listen for Nightjars around clearings at last light.

Buller's Hill A mile (1.6 km) farther along Dunchideock road is the Forestry Commission office. Forest trails of general nature interest are marked; leaflets on these are available from the office.

Thorns Valley and the Obelisk From Exeter, take A380 across the ridge and turn left on B3381 towards Starcross and Mamhead. Turtle Doves breed most years near the road junction. Stop by gates to look right across the valley for soaring raptors. Continue ¼ mile (400 m) and turn right at a small crossroads towards Ashcombe. Hillsides on the right have breeding warblers and Tree Pipits. Taller trees left of the road may have Redpolls, Siskins or Crossbills. At the end of the level stretch, park under trees; walk left through woods to Obelisk lookout for extensive views of the east flank of Haldon and Exe valley.

Little Haldon Continue south on A380 beyond Starcross turn. Take B3192 towards Teignmouth. Continue 2 miles (3 km) to a minor road junction with woods to left. Stop and explore along woodland edges. The minor road towards Ashcombe Tower often has Crossbills, and Nightjars are quite numerous in clearings. Try also continuing along B3192 to the heath and car park opposite the golf course, a good vantage point. At migrant seasons, look across golf course from roadsides: Wheatears, pipits and open-ground species may occur and Dotterels have been reported.

Calendar

Resident: Sparrowhawk, Buzzard, Great and Lesser Spotted Woodpeckers, Stonechat, Willow Tit (scarce), common woodland passerines, Crossbill, Redpoll.

Dec-Feb: Occasional Hen Harrier, Woodcock, Snipe, occasional Great Grey Shrike, Siskin, Redpoll, Brambling and other finches, Crossbill (may sing from Jan).

Mar-May: Siskins flock (Mar); from late Apr, Cuckoo, Tree Pipit, common woodland warblers, Wood and probably Grasshopper Warblers, Whinchat, Redstart; Nightjar, Turtle Dove, perhaps Hobby (May), chance of other migrant raptors (chiefly May). Siskins remain to sing in small numbers.

Jun-Jul: Breeding summer visitors as above — Nightjar, Turtle Dove, pipits, warblers, Whinchat, Redstart etc. — plus residents, singing in Jun, quieter in Jul but Nightjars churr; possibly breeding Woodcocks.

Aug-Nov: Nightjars still sing to mid Aug, other migrants leave by mid month; possibly raptors moving (mostly Aug-mid Oct). Woodcocks and winter finches return during Nov.

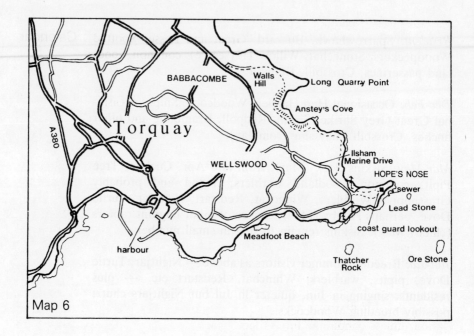

BABBACOMBE

Walls
Hill

Long Quarry Point

Anstey's Cove

Torquay

WELLSWOOD

Ilsham
Marine Drive

HOPE'S NOSE

sewer

Lead Stone

coast guard lookout

harbour

Meadfoot Beach

Thatcher
Rock

Ore Stone

A380

Map 6

6 Hope's Nose, Torquay (Map 6 and OS Map 202)

Habitat

At the north end of Torbay, Hope's Nose is the first promontory beyond Exe estuary mouth, and the low spit at the end curves north into Lyme Bay. Cliff ledges and a small disused quarry face the bay northward. Offshore lie the rocky islets of Lead Stone (nearest, small), Ore Stone (^{1}⁄$_2$ mile/0.8 km out, over 30 m high) and Thatcher Rock (peaked, 45m high, to the south). The peninsula is covered in Bracken, bushes and scrub, with a small pine copse. A sewer outfall is situated near the tip of the point, in front of a Coastguard lookout hut.

Species

Hope's Nose is known mainly as a seawatching point. Birds moving along the coast pass close inshore at times, especially in reduced visibility or when blown by onshore winds; most movement is south out of Lyme Bay. Gulls often stop to feed at the sewer outfall, allowing time for good views, and may remain for several weeks, feeding at the outfall when it is discharging. Other species flying past require swifter identification, unless conditions force them close.

The early part of the year brings least variety, but large flocks of Black-headed Gulls gather at the outfall. It is worth checking for occasional unusual gulls, such as a Little dipping over the sea or a slightly larger Mediterranean Gull among the Black-headed. Gulls not actively feeding may roost on Lead Stone or the rocky beach right of the sewer, where often a dozen Oystercatchers or Turnstones probe the weeds; Purple Sandpipers might also be seen in small numbers. Rock Pipits are always present near the shore, and most years a wintering Black Redstart. Offshore, a few Gannets and Kittiwakes pass; rough weather can bring hundreds of moving auks, and sometimes a burly Great Skua. One or two divers, grebes and seaducks feed in the area, often in the bay on the north side. The most likely diver on the sea is the hardy Great Northern;

Red-throated Divers fly past, although passages of both species can occur. Single Great Crested and Slavonian Grebes come out from Torbay to feed off the end. A local speciality is the stout, long-billed Red-necked Grebe, seen for long periods in most winters, especially after cold east winds. Ducks include a Red-breasted Merganser or two in the north bay and, very often, several brown immature Eiders near Lead Stone.

The start of the spring brings several hundred Kittiwakes calling excitedly on the water below nest ledges, and often unusual gulls as migration begins; Mediterranean and Little Gulls may appear, with a chance of an Iceland or bulky Glaucous dropping in very briefly. Small numbers of Chiffchaffs, Wheatears and perhaps Black Redstarts arrive on land. Later a variety of small migrants feed in the thick bushes, while usually a Lesser Whitethroat gives its brief rattling song. At sea, migrant Whimbrels, Sandwich and a few Common Terns pass north, with a chance of skuas. Northward movements in spring are generally small and not very close to shore; best watches are when onshore winds bring in south-moving birds as in autumn. Such conditions occasionally bring packs of up to 30 skuas, larger groups often being thick-tailed Pomarines, accompanied by scores of Fulmars, Manx Shearwaters, Gannets, terns and auks.

Summer brings thousands of breeding Herring Gulls, especially on Ore Stone and Thatcher Rock, with one or two pairs of Lesser Black-backed. Several pairs of Shags breed, white-thighed Cormorants choosing the highest pinnacles. Up to 500 pairs of Kittiwakes on Ore Stone and mainland cliffs form one of the largest colonies in mainland southern England. Careful inspection of Ore Stone ledges will reveal up to 30 pairs of Guillemots and probably two or three Razorbills. Puffins in groups of up to six are seen on the sea at intervals in late spring and summer, but are not known to nest. Fulmars are not yet established here, but frequently glide past.

Out at sea, parties of dozens of Manx Shearwaters regularly feed low over the waves at dawn and dusk through summer. Very occasionally, rough weather will drive a group of tiny Storm Petrels within view of shore. Gannets and parties of two or three dozen Common Scoters are frequent in midsummer, with a chance of a passing skua. From late summer an increased variety of birds occurs; this season often produces a Mediterranean Gull, which may stay for weeks to moult. Manx Shearwaters are slowly replaced by smaller numbers of the dusky Balearic race, in varying strength according to conditions (average 40-50 sightings per year). One or two of the large Sooty and Cory's Shearwaters are seen most years, in late summer to early autumn.

As autumn progresses, a steady flow of terns moves south past the Nose in early mornings; Sandwich Terns are most evident at close range, up to 100 passing on good days. Common Tern passage fluctuates more, depending on weather, but up to 300 may pass in a morning, often bunching in large groups farther out. Arctic or Roseate Terns are sometimes identified among closer groups by skilled observers. Black Terns, appearing irregularly in parties of up to ten, may stop and feed at the sewer. When terns are passing, there will usually be a skua twisting in high-speed aerial pursuit; over 20 Arctic Skuas may pass on good autumn days, and a peak of over 100 has been reported rarely. Small numbers of Great Skuas are regular, single figures being usual, and one or two Pomarines can be expected; the rare Long-tailed has been seen in several recent years. After most terns have departed, skuas may still be blown in by adverse weather, along with a stray oceanic migrant such as a Grey Phalarope, Sabine's Gull or Little Auk; although virtually annual, these last species are seen in smaller numbers than at watchpoints further west. Parties of Brent Geese and Wigeons flying in to local estuaries, plus a few passing divers, mark the approach of winter.

On shore, a few commoner warblers move through the scrub; later in the season a Firecrest may be detected. Wheatears and sometimes Ring Ouzels flit around the rocks in small numbers, replaced later by Black Redstarts. Overhead, circling local Ravens are often noticed, while Peregrines stay for long periods in autumn, occasionally flying out to attack passing migrants over the sea.

Timing

Seabird movement depends heavily on weather conditions, but largest numbers usually pass in the first three or four hours' daylight; some continue to pass all day if it stays dull, wet or misty but swing away from land once visibility has improved. Days when the horizon is clear, and the coastline is seen well, will not produce many birds. If mist or rain suddenly lifts, there may be a large movement of seabirds out of Lyme Bay past the Nose. Onshore winds (between east and south, especially east) give best birdwatching. Evening watches may prove worthwhile at migration times, and can bring summer sightings of Manx Shearwaters as they move up to feed overnight in Lyme Bay; try the last two or three hours' light.

In fine high-pressure conditions, skuas and terns also tend to move right up to nightfall. For gulls and terns feeding offshore, choose a falling tide when the sewer is discharging. After winter gales, check the bay on the north side for sheltering birds.

Access

From the top of Ilsham Marine Drive in Babbacombe district of Torquay. From Torquay harbour, turn inland up Torwood Street then right at first traffic signals to Meadfoot Beach. Follow the beach and turn sharp right onto winding, scenic Marine Drive at far end. Park by the road at the highest point. In winter check the bay below for divers and grebes. From the road take the public footpath, steep and muddy in places, down the Nose. Check bushes halfway down for warblers at appropriate seasons. Near the bottom, look left into the quarry and bay behind. Wintering grebes may shelter close under the cliff in rough weather. Continue to the end of the spit, where seabirds come in from north parallel with the coast; a few pass directly overhead. To see gulls feeding at the sewer, watch from in front of the Coastguard lookout; in wet weather find shelter under rocks. Try also walking right, overlooking the shore, for gulls and waders.

Behind the pine copse, halfway down the main path, is the north-facing cliff where Kittiwakes breed. Small paths through the bushes lead to the cliff edge. Take care: the clifftop is overgrown and dangerous in places.

Calendar

Resident: Shag, Sparrowhawk, Green Woodpecker, Rock Pipit, Stonechat, Raven.

Dec-Feb: Great Northern, Red-throated and occasional Black-throated Divers, Great Crested, probably Red-necked and Slavonian Grebes, Gannet, Eider (irregular numbers), Common Scoter, Red-breasted Merganser, Oystercatcher, Turnstone, maybe Purple Sandpiper, Black-headed Gull, possibly Little or Mediterranean Gull, rarely Great Skua, auks passing, Black Redstart.

Mar-May: Fulmar, Cormorant, Kittiwake, larger gulls and auks start to breed. Gull passage (Mar) with chance of Little, Mediterranean, Glaucous or Iceland, diver passage starts; Chiffchaff, Wheatear and sometimes Black Redstart late Mar, Sandwich Terns arriving. Manx Shearwater, Whimbrel and most terns after mid Apr, diver passage and most chance of Arctic or Pomarine Skua in first half May. Puffins seen from May. Whitethroat, Lesser Whitethroat and other warblers end Apr-May.

Jun-Jul: Breeding seabirds, Manx Shearwater feeding movements, Gannets pass, chance of Storm Petrel. Common Scoter flocks, often a few Puffins feed offshore; skuas and terns may occur. At end of period, a Little or Mediterranean Gull may arrive with Black-headed, and tern passage starts. Whitethroats breed, Lesser Whitethroats may still sing.

Aug-Nov: Shearwater passage mainly Aug-Sep, with Balearic race, maybe Sooty or Cory's. Terns Aug-mid Oct, mostly Sandwich and Common, maybe Arctic, Roseate or Black, peak end Aug-mid Sep; Arctic, Great and Pomarine Skuas to early Nov, most end Aug-early Oct; Little and Mediterranean Gulls intermittent, mostly Aug-Oct; Peregrine from Sep; a few passage and wintering waders from Sep; warblers, inc. Blackcap, Willow, Chiffchaff, mostly Sep; occasional Firecrest from end Sep, Wheatears stay to Oct, maybe Ring Ouzel. Possibly Storm Petrel, Long-tailed Skua or Sabine's Gull Sep-Oct; first divers, generally Red-throated, end Sep, maybe Grey Phalarope Oct, Little Auk singles Nov. Black Redstart and probably Purple Sandpiper from end Oct.

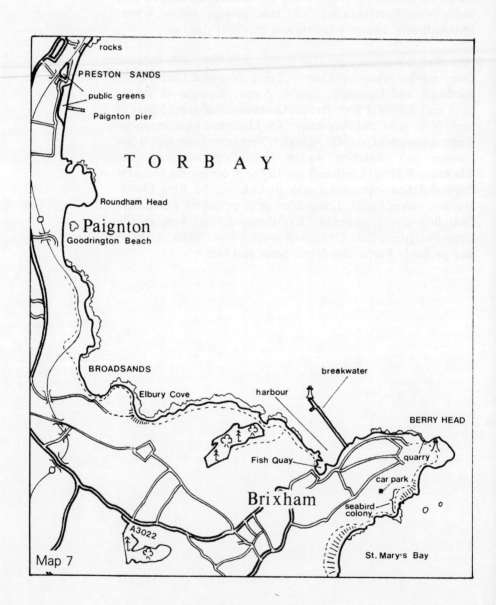

7 Torbay and Berry Head

(Map 7 and OS Map 202)

Habitat

The sea off Torquay, Paignton and Brixham, mainly shallow and sandy, is sheltered from prevailing southwest winds, with Berry Head protruding at the south end. The sea is particularly shallow off Preston-Paignton-Goodrington, a 2-mile (3-km) urban seafront backed by public lawns, with small Roundham Head in the centre. Brixham, under the lee of Berry Head, has a small trawling fleet and fish quay. Berry Head itself, a limestone mass 65 m high, is flat-topped, with a disused quarry facing the sea on the north side: a good area for orchids. The top, a Country Park much used by walkers and tourists, has grass and low thickets. At the end is a small lighthouse, and behind the cliffs lie ruined fortifications.

Species

The bay is one of the best in the region for variety of wintering grebes. Berry Head is known mainly as a seabird colony.

Divers are fairly regular on the sea, with two or three Great Northern usually wintering in the southern half of the bay between Paignton and Brixham, while single Red- and Black-throated occur sporadically. Grebes are more noticeable, although a telescope is helpful for detailed comparisons between species. Twelve to 15 Great Crested, scattered widely at times but favouring Broadsands-Elbury Cove end, form the region's largest regular winter population; the dusky Red-necked is seen only once or twice a year. Preston-Paignton is particularly recommended for Slavonian and Black-necked Grebes on the sea together: Slavonians appear slim and contrasted, while Black-necked have a rounded head and more grey-sided hue; up to ten of either may occur, but five or six is more normal. This is the only bay in our region where Black-necked always winter. Small groups of Eiders and Common Scoters also occur here, while half a dozen Red-breasted Mergansers fish off Elbury or Brixham harbour. All species may be forced to move around by wind, tide or water

Red-necked, Black-necked and Slavonian Grebes (winter plumage)

sports; Torquay end is usually less frequented than the centre and south. Oystercatchers, Turnstones and Purple Sandpipers are seen mostly from Preston south, with up to 20 Purple Sandpipers regular on rocks at the north end of Preston front and similar numbers (perhaps the same birds?) on Brixham breakwater at times. Rock Pipits, sometimes joined by a Black Redstart, feed on tidewrack in sheltered coves. After severe blizzards when most of Devon is snow-covered, the greens behind Preston-Paignton, kept free of snow by salt spray, may provide temporary haven for hundreds of Lapwings, Skylarks, Fieldfares and Redwings.

Brixham fish dock is little watched for birds, but interesting gulls may occur. Offshore, feeding parties of Gannets, Kittiwakes and auks move about all winter, coming closer in poor weather. Guillemots are often found on Torbay beaches as oil-pollution victims (contact RSPCA if live birds are found); the rare northern Black Guillemot has been seen offshore.

In early spring, although most divers and grebes soon leave, parties of Black-necked Grebes may occur, shaking golden cheek-tufts in display on warm days. Seabirds gather to breed on the south side of Berry Head; Guillemots may have returned to ledges on mild winter days, but from now to mid-late summer up to 300 pairs are present on the overhanging cliffs. Several pairs of nesting Fulmars (plus numerous others patrolling past), Shags and Great Black-backed Gulls, over 100 pairs of Kittiwakes and just two or three of Razorbills complete the summer scene. This is now the largest auk colony on the English Channel coast, and birds are easily viewable as they fly to and fro. Herring Gulls breed abundantly around cliffs and quarry; off Torbay beaches a few Sandwich Terns often fish, even in midsummer.

Migration at Berry Head has been little studied, but in spring skuas, including Pomarines, and terns have been seen occasionally, while small migrants in the thickets have included commoner warblers, Redstarts and Whinchat. The lighthouse may attract night migrants: further study could be worthwhile. Shearwaters, skuas and terns have been seen in small numbers off the quarry in autumn, when gales bring large Gannet and Kittiwake flocks. Single Firecrests and Black Redstarts have occurred on the Head late in the season.

Timing

Grebes and other waterbirds in the bay are best picked out when cloudy skies cast pale grey light on the sea. High tides with little wind and calm sea are helpful; east winds usually churn up the surface and make birds hard to watch. On fine Sundays, water sports may cause disturbance unless you arrive early. Heavy blizzards with east winds produce arrivals of sheltering birds on Preston-Paignton greens; the bay is very exposed to such conditions and, if these are prolonged, waterbirds may move off to areas farther west. At Brixham, a weekday visit when trawlers are unloading is likely to be best for gulls. Try a seawatch for passing seabirds off Berry Head quarry in south or southwest winds with mist or rain. For passerine migrants, especially in southeast breezes, try early mornings on the Head before public disturbance is too great. The auk nesting colony can be seen at any time in summer.

Access

A379 runs south from Torquay front through Paignton, with frequent signposts to seafront and beaches; at the hilltop crossroads beyond Goodrington, A3022 is signposted to Brixham. All seafront areas may be worth checking, but main bird viewpoints are:

Preston, between Torquay and Paignton. Follow main road left past traffic lights and under the railway bridge. Turn left immediately onto a small promenade road. You can watch from car windows in bad weather. Slavonian and Black-necked Grebes are regular. Rocks at far left end often have Turnstones and Purple Sandpipers, plus resting gull flocks.

Paignton Pier can be reached by turning left across public greens off the main front road. Black-necked Grebes are seen particularly here. You can walk along the front to Preston (ten minutes) if desired. Car-window views possible. Check lawns after snow. No access onto pier itself in winter.

Goodrington is signposted left off Paignton-Brixham road, at mini-roundabout opposite swimming baths. Grebes and Eiders often present.

Broadsands lies at the end of a suburban road. Turn left at the hilltop 1 mile (1.6 km) south of Goodrington. Walk right across green towards sheltered Elbury Cove for Great Crested Grebe, seaducks, auks.

Brixham Harbour, obvious from town centre, is worth a stop at the left corner near fish quay. For divers and auks in winter try driving right, then first sharp left around the harbour, out to breakwater and walk along.

Berry Head is signposted right as you enter Brixham on main road. Park in car park at top. Walk across right to cove overlooking auk colony (look for Torbay Council sign showing seabirds). Take care near cliff edges. (Do not disturb colony in summer.) For small migrants, check walls and bushes behind. For passing seabirds, walk ahead from car park to the old tarmac access lane into disused quarry. Watch from outer end of quarry floor, or from nearby concrete blockhouse in wet weather.

Calendar

Resident: Shag, Great Black-backed Gull, Rock Pipit.

Dec-Feb: Great Northern, Red-throated and sometimes Black-throated Divers, Great Crested, Slavonian, Black-necked, maybe Red-necked Grebes, Gannet, Eider, Common Scoter, Red-breasted Merganser, Oystercatcher, Turnstone, Purple Sandpiper, gulls, Kittiwakes, Razorbill and Guillemot at sea; irregular Black Redstart. Lapwings, Skylarks, winter thrushes after snow.

Mar-May: Black-necked Grebe to early Apr some years. Fulmars on cliffs from start of period, breeding Shag, larger gulls, Kittiwakes, Guillemot, Razorbill, Stock Dove from late Mar. Possibly migrant passerines late Mar-May; passing seabirds mostly from mid Apr, e.g. Fulmar, Manx Shearwater, maybe skuas, terns.

Jun-Jul: Bay quiet except for odd Sandwich Tern. Berry Head has breeding Fulmars, gulls, Kittiwakes and auks most active to mid Jul; Manx Shearwaters and Gannets pass.

Aug-Nov: Fulmars and gulls still on cliffs in Aug. Chance of migrant Manx and Balearic Shearwaters, skuas, terns, passerines Aug-early Oct, Firecrest or Black Redstart to Nov. First divers and grebes from mid Oct, but often scarce until Nov.

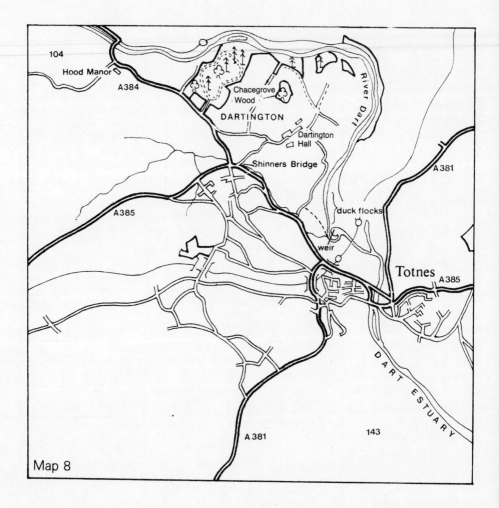

8 Dartington and the Lower Dart

(Map 8 and
OS Map 202)

Habitat

The River Dart flows south in a loop past attractive mixed woods, parkland and farmland of Dartington Estate near Totnes. On the north side, the river is shallow with gravel bars in places, but on the south side a wider slow-flowing stretch lies above Totnes weir. The estuary between Totnes and Dartmouth is scenic and winding, with wooded banks and sheltered creeks used extensively for boating.

Species

The shallower river on the north side is a regular haunt of Dippers and Grey Wagtails bobbing on waterside stones. Early in the year, most birdwatchers focus on wider stretches towards the weir. This area is used by a flock of diving ducks, in cold weather among the largest in Devon; they probably move between here and Slapton. Tufted Ducks are in the majority, well over 100 at times, but the flock attracts small numbers of related species—usually a few Pochards, often Goldeneyes, occasionally scarcer visitors such as American Ring-necked Duck. A scattering of dabbling ducks includes one or two Gadwalls, a species which often frequents diving-duck haunts. When disturbed, flocks may fly to south of the weir, nearer the town. Little Grebes are also usually seen. The varied habitat and sheltered position ensure a wide variety of farm and woodland species, such as woodpeckers, tits, Nuthatch and finches. The district is noted for a few pairs of Woodlarks around copse edges; the males sing their musical descending notes in circular songflights over the meadows from early spring. Summer migrants include wood and hedgerow warblers, e.g. Blackcap, Garden Warbler, White-throat, Willow Warbler and Chiffchaff, with Spotted Fly-catcher and hirundines around buildings. At the end of summer, Kingfishers often spend periods on the river before moving down to the estuary to winter.

The tidal estuary, although scenic, is not rated highly for

75

birdlife. Lack of extensive mudflats or bordering marshes means that wildfowl and waders are never numerous, although small numbers of common species occur. Winding stretches make viewing points difficult. The upper sheltered stretches may hold overwintering Common Sandpipers. Outside the breeding season, Kingfishers are often seen along over-hanging trees, and Cormorants are usually present. There is a heronry near Maypool on the east bank. Shelducks breed, and dozens are seen in spring and early summer; Buzzards and Ravens soar over the wooded banks. In autumn, a few Common Terns follow the tide up the estuary, and there have been several sightings of Ospreys fishing in the middle reaches up to Duncannon.

Timing

Not too critical at Dartington but duck numbers are highest in cold weather, especially when lakes elsewhere are frozen. Spring and summer early mornings are best for songbirds. The estuary has no central high-tide roost for waders: for these, visit at lower tide.

Access

Dartington Estate is just east of A385 Totnes-Buckfastleigh road. To view the south side, turn right to the estate on leaving Totnes northbound, past Swallowfields houses. Stop by estate gates and walk right to the weir along a muddy path. Alternatively, continue by car to the second gateway on right along lane. Park and cross stile to continue upriver on foot for ducks. No access restrictions for individuals, but parties should check with the estate manager before visiting.

To visit the woods and upper riverbank, continue 1 mile (1.6 km) on A385 to Shinners Bridge by A384 road junction. Park in car park on right. Dippers breed along a stream on opposite side of road. From car park, follow signposted woodland trails; the 'woodpecker trail' gives a circular walk of about 3 miles (5 km). Coming back past Chacegrove Wood on the last section, there is a good chance of Woodlark. For those who miss this fine singer, try a roadside stop along the side lane near Hood Barton, 2 miles (3 km) farther up A385, and turn left; pull up after 200 m and listen; do not block gateways.

The estuary is difficult to cover from the banks; many visitors take scenic boat trips between Totnes and Dartmouth, available mainly from April to October (contact local tourist information offices for details).

Resident: Grey Heron, Buzzard, woodpeckers inc. Lesser
Spotted, Woodlark, Grey Wagtail, common woodland passerines, Dipper, Raven.

Calendar

Dec-Feb: Dartington—Little Grebe, Gadwall, Teal, Wigeon,
Tufted Duck, Pochard, Goldeneye, maybe Scaup or other
diving ducks, winter thrushes, Siskin, Redpoll.
Estuary—Cormorant, Shelduck, Water Rail, Common Sand-
piper, maybe Green Sandpiper or Greenshank, Redshank,
Curlew, Snipe, Kingfisher, maybe Chiffchaff.

Mar-May: Most ducks and waders leave by mid Mar. Singing
warblers mostly from mid Apr, perhaps Wood Warbler at
Dartington. A few migrant waders on estuary, Shelducks
present.

Jun-Jul: Woodlarks all summer; common breeding residents
and summer visitors, Shelducks breed.

Aug-Nov: Kingfisher, post-breeding flocks of tits and warblers
(Aug), Osprey, terns and a few waders on estuary (mostly mid
Aug-early Sep), winter visitors from end Oct.

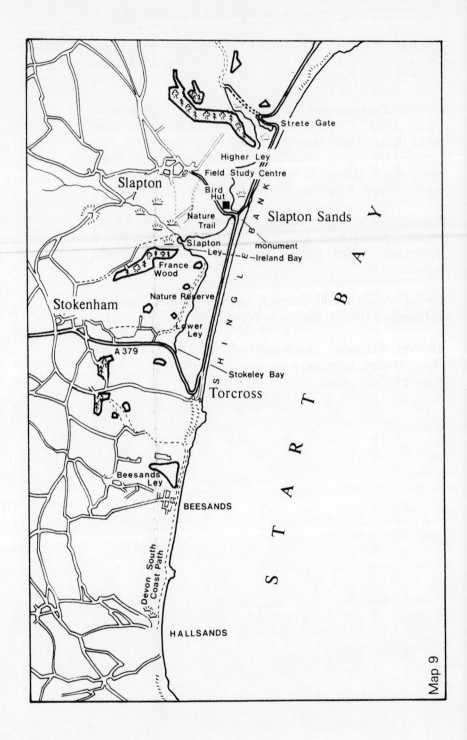

Strete Gate

Higher Ley

Field Study Centre

Bird Hut

Slapton

Slapton Sands

Nature Trail

SHINGLE BANK

monument

Slapton Ley

Ireland Bay

France Wood

Nature Reserve

Stokenham

Lower Ley

A 379

Stokeley Bay

Torcross

Beesands Ley

BEESANDS

Devon South Coast Path

HALLSANDS

S T A R T   B A Y

Map 9

9 Slapton Leys and District (including Beesands and Hallsands)

(Map 9 and OS Map 202)

Habitat

Sheltered from prevailing winds by Start-Prawle promontories and high farmland behind, Start Bay faces eastward. Slapton shingle beach, facing the bay, runs south for 2 miles (3 km). The freshwater lagoon of Slapton Ley lies behind the beach, parallel to the coast; halfway along it is divided by a narrow neck into the northern Higher Ley, reed-choked with encroaching *Salix* scrub and other bushes, and open-water Lower Ley on the south side. Reeds fringe the Lower Ley, and shallow bays at the rear have more extensive reed-beds where streams enter. Opposite Torcross at the south end are water-lily pads. Along the inland side of the shingle ridge, facing the lake, runs a strip of thickets and brambles; the top of the beach is sandy turf, and the main road runs down its length. A ringing hut owned by DBWPS overlooks the bridge between Higher and Lower Leys; a bird logbook is kept in a tin under the left side of the hut. The Field Study Centre in Slapton village manages the Leys as a nature reserve; the area is much visited by anglers, freshwater biologists and botanists. Otters are still seen occasionally; unfortunately, escaped Minks are now resident. Grass Snakes, Adders and Common Lizards can sometimes be seen on the Higher Ley banks.

Shingle beach extends south beyond Slapton towards Start Point, blocking the small, deep, stream valleys of Beesands and North Hallsands. At Beesands an open lagoon, backed by reeds and bushes, forms a sheltered miniature of Slapton lake; at Hallsands a semi-dry reed-bed with scattered bushes extends ¼ mile (400 m) up the valley. Beesands beach is used as a caravan park.

Species

Slapton is well known regionally as an easy area to see winter wildfowl, marsh species and a variety of other birds, especially at migration periods. Beesands and Hallsands are much less watched.

79

In winter one or two Great Northern Divers, Shags, Eiders and Common Scoters are seen regularly from Slapton and Beesands beach, together with a Slavonian Grebe most years and sometimes a Red-necked; a few Grey Plovers and 200-300 Dunlins from nearby estuaries often roost on the shingle at high tide. Large gull flocks, often including hundreds of Great Black-backed and a few Kittiwakes, collect on quieter stretches of beach, flying over into the Lower Ley or the stream entering the sea just beyond Torcross cliff at the south end, to drink and bathe; single Little and Mediterranean Gulls are found among the flock in most years. Several hundred ducks, chiefly diving ducks, use the leys in winter, with largest flocks usually of well over 100 each of Tufted and Pochard on Lower Ley near Torcross. Up to 30 Goldeneyes are scattered along the lake, and at least one Long-tailed Duck is usually present. Single Goosanders and Smews may turn up briefly on sheltered parts of the ley. Small groups of feral Ruddy Ducks have moved down from Somerset reservoirs in recent winters, and odd ornamental wildfowl compete for scraps with Mute Swans and Mallards at Torcross corner. Apparently wild wanderers to this area, the best in the region for diving ducks, have included several Ring-necked Ducks (standing out slightly larger among the Tufted) and Ferruginous Ducks (tending to skulk in Torcross reeds or sometimes the Higher Ley). Dabbling ducks are less regular, but parties of Wigeons moving between estuaries often drop in, and small packs of Teals may be flushed from reedy bays; Gadwalls are increasing, with five or ten usually present. Great Crested Grebes have recently become established; this is one of very few sites in the region where they now breed, although they spread out to neighbouring areas in winter. Single Slavonian and Black-necked Grebes also occur on the ley itself in most years, sometimes joined by a diver after gales, and generally half a dozen Cormorants. Coots are abundant (flocks of up to 500 on open water). The Higher Ley is more difficult to watch, but Cetti's Warblers have become very noticeable among damp vegetation, their loud song carrying far across the ley on mild winter days. Colder weather, which may bring a party of geese or northern ducks, usually produces a skulking Bittern flushed from the reeds, and the metallic 'ping' calls of Bearded Tits are heard irregularly. Up to ten Chiffchaffs and two or three Firecrests stay through the coldest months in sheltered corners at the back of both leys, and many (concealed) Water Rails squeal.

Beesands has similar birds to Slapton: two or three Great

Crested Grebes, dozens of Coots feeding on grassy banks, and parties of Tufted Ducks and Pochards which fly across from the Lower Ley to feed. Close views are possible on this relatively small lake, where a few Goldeneyes are also likely. Rarer ducks such as Ring-necked, which visit Slapton occasionally, may also feed here: try checking Slapton for birds reported at Beesands or vice versa. Cirl Buntings breed in the valley, moving nearer to the beach in winter. Cetti's Warblers are present in waterside vegetation, both here and at Hallsands; the latter has no major attractions in winter, but often a Black Redstart flycatches on the beach.

Spring soon brings a sprinkling of shoreline Wheatears, with the chance of an early Hoopoe on sandy turf near the road at Slapton beach. Normally their arrival coincides with a Scaup, joining the Tufted Ducks temporarily, and several Sand Martins circling over the reeds. Garganeys may appear in marshy bays, and stay for a week or two; this scarce summer duck has bred in the past. Packs of migrant Common Gulls join flocks of other species roosting on the beach. Less usual gulls may be recorded; a Glaucous, perhaps Little or Mediterranean, and once a Ring-billed. Later on a trickle of terns, mostly Sandwich, passes northward, and divers of all three species, mostly singles or pairs, may be seen in breeding plumage off the beach.

From mid spring, migrants are often numerous. Large numbers of hirundines and warblers feed around the leys, many Reed and Sedge Warblers staying to breed in reed-beds, and some Grasshopper Warblers reeling in song from thickets may stay to nest. Falls of migrant passerines cannot always be detected in the thick bushes, but warblers and flycatchers may be seen in Hallsands valley as they filter off nearby Start Point.

Warm winds, which bring main arrivals of summer migrants, also regularly carry overshooting marsh species from the Continent to Slapton. An egret or, more often, a Purple Heron, arrives most springs, the heron often staying for a week or two although tending to skulk among vegetation. Various southern exotics, such as Squacco Heron, Little Bittern and Great Reed Warbler, have turned up; the deep reeling of Savi's Warblers has been heard in the reeds for weeks. In most springs, a brown immature Marsh Harrier quarters the marsh for a few days. Warmer weather encourages three or four pairs of Great Crested Grebes to nest, often performing elaborate 'weed-dance' displays; they have been quite successful in recent seasons, rearing half a dozen or more young, despite predation by Minks. Remaining Goldeneyes on the lake head-jerk in display, and Gadwalls often stay late. Water Rails, although common in winter, are scarce breeders (only one or two pairs in recent years) but Coots generally rear young. Lesser Spotted Woodpeckers nest in France Wood.

Out at sea, seabirds, including strings of Manx Shearwaters, groups of Gannets and Kittiwakes, feed through summer; Kittiwakes often fly in to bathe in the lagoon. Fulmars inhabit the cliffs south of Torcross. Late summer may bring a Sooty Shearwater, feeding with the Manx, and Sandwich Terns fish off the beach. Thousands of Swifts mass over the leys on humid days. Early autumn may produce an Arctic Skua pursuing the terns, and several Black Terns dipping to catch insects over Torcross lily-pads. Waders such as Common Sandpiper and Greenshank feed on lagoon fringe mud if the water level is low. Thousands of Swallows and Starlings roost among Torcross reeds at dusk, swirling flocks forming an attractive target for Sparrowhawks or Hobby as they gather before dropping in. Ringing studies have shown that large numbers of warblers pass through the insect-rich reed fringes at this season, including occasional Aquatic Warblers with prominent 'badger-striped' heads, and other uncommon migrants such as Wryneck and Bluethroat have also been recorded. Owing to the dense vegetation, few of these have been seen without being trapped.

Migrants continue to pass late in the year, with regular sightings of Swallows in November. Meanwhile, gales in the Channel may force a tired phalarope, skua or other stray seabirds into the bay. Cold winds later may bring Snow Bunting, or a passing Hen Harrier.

Timing

Slapton's southerly position encourages large numbers of birds to shelter in winter freeze-ups: Bittern, Goosander and large numbers of winter thrushes might be expected. Strong east winds, although they probably bring birds, create difficult viewing conditions; a seawatch from the beach car park might pay off. Easterlies in autumn will bring Black Terns, and maybe Aquatic Warblers. The area is sheltered from most other winds. Sea conditions need to be calmish to spot divers and grebes from the low beach. For ducks on the ley, avoid high winds, when many shelter among reeds. Feeding movements of shearwaters are most visible during mist with light southerly winds; strays such as phalaropes arrive with prolonged south or southwest gales and rain. Spring migrant arrivals are most noticeable on cloudy, humid days with winds between southeast and southwest; most rarer heron types have arrived in mild southwesterlies. Ducks disturbed by high winds or boat anglers may fly to Beesands. For the autumn hirundines roost, about an hour up to darkness is best.

Slapton beach is very heavily used by the public on fine weekends at any season.

Along coastal A379 between Dartmouth and Kingsbridge. Main areas to watch: **Access**

Strete Gate, at north end of Higher Ley. Park on corner and look off beach for divers or seaducks in winter. Cross road to view Gara Valley reed-bed for possible harrier or herons.

Monument, halfway down the bay, opposite bridge between Higher and Lower Leys. Suitable seawatch point, or alternatively watch from beach car park nearby. Check scrub and gorse across the road for small passerines. Walk south along beach crest for gull roosts and spring Wheatears, maybe Hoopoe.

Ringing Hut Cross bridge from Monument and check logbook for recent news (please insert details of any sightings you make).

Higher Ley Take path in front of ringing hut and walk along back of reed-bed: for rails, Cetti's Warbler, maybe Bittern, a chance of other warblers and migrants at appropriate season.

Ireland Bay Across road opposite ringing hut, take path through gate past fishing boat moorings. Continue on bank path, checking scrub on right for warblers and flycatchers at migration times. View across bay for bathing gulls, and ducks including Goldeneye or Long-tailed in winter. If water level is high, continue along edge of field above. After about 300 m watch across reeds on left for herons, harriers or warblers. Follow lake-shore path until a gated track turns left across the marsh towards France Wood. Check the pool ahead for herons, rails and ducks, including migrant Garganey. Look in the small overgrown quarry on corner for wintering Firecrest and Chiffchaff.

With permit from Field Centre, continue down gated track for herons, harriers, rails, and waterside warblers perhaps including Savi's. Cross the boardwalk towards the wood, which has Buzzards, woodpeckers and Ravens.

Scrub behind beach At migration times, try walking the length of the leys between road and marsh for scattered passerine migrants.

Torcross, at south end of the leys. Ducks are numerous and area is also best for grebes, Little Gull and Black Tern. Divers are seen off the beach, and gulls pass along the shore to drink from the stream beyond the rocks. Fulmars nest farther on. In wet weather the ley can be viewed from roadside car parks. At low tide you can walk south ½ mile (0.8 km) on shingle to Beesands.

Beesands On A379, drive to Stokenham south of Torcross, turn left towards Start Point then left down a steep, narrow road signposted Beeson and Beesands. Walk left to the lake.

Hallsands Continue past Beesands turn, towards Start. Turn left to North Hallsands valley; check beach and nearby reeds.

Calendar

Resident: Great Crested Grebe, Grey Heron, Mallard, Sparrowhawk, Buzzard, probably Water Rail, Coot, perhaps Barn Owl, Lesser Spotted and other woodpeckers, Cetti's Warbler, Stonechat, Cirl Bunting, Reed Bunting, Raven.

Dec-Feb: Great Northern Diver, Slavonian and maybe Black-necked Grebes, Shag, Cormorant, Gadwall, probably Wigeon and Teal, maybe Shoveler, Tufted Duck, Pochard, Eider, Common Scoter, Goldeneye and probably Long-tailed Duck, rarer ducks; Bittern, Goosander, maybe Smew in hard weather; gulls; Kingfisher, Chiffchaff, Firecrest. Waders on beach.

Mar-May: Migrant gulls inc. uncommon species (Mar), Wheatear, Sand Martin, maybe Scaup, Garganey and Hoopoe from mid Mar; Fulmars nesting; divers Apr-May, terns and Whimbrel mostly from mid Apr, auks feed offshore. From mid Apr, wide range of migrants inc. Yellow and probably White Wagtails, hirundines, warblers; chance of a rarer heron or raptor, especially Marsh Harrier.

Jun-Jul: Seabirds feeding, inc. Manx and in Jul maybe Sooty

Shearwaters; breeding residents, Reed and Sedge Warblers; Sandwich Terns return Jul.

Aug-Nov: Sandwich, Common and occasional other sea terns to early Oct, Black Terns from late Aug-Oct; possible skuas to end Oct, Sooty Shearwater to Sep, maybe Sabine's Gull Sep-early Oct, phalaropes Oct (rare). Heavy migration of Swallows, warblers and other passerines including rarer species, mostly Aug-Sep, peaking end Aug. Swallows and maybe other migrants to early Nov.

Note Slapton can easily be combined with a visit to Start-Prawle area at migration seasons, giving a chance to see a very wide range of birds.

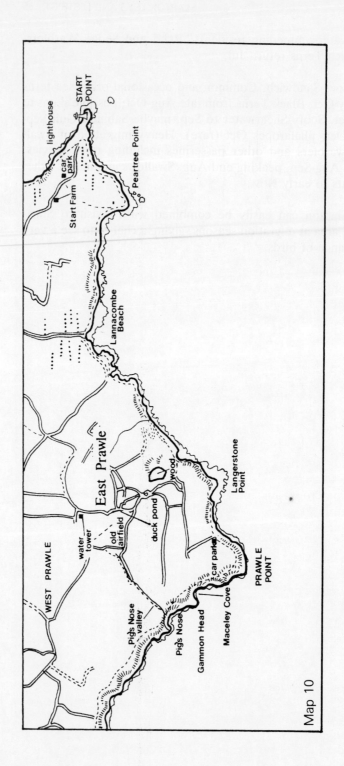

START
POINT

lighthouse

car
park

Start Farm

Peartree Point

Lannacombe
Beach

East Prawle

Langerstone
Point

WEST PRAWLE

water
tower

old airfield

duck pond

wood

Pigs Nose
valley

Pigs Nose

Gammon Head

Maceley Cove

car park

PRAWLE
POINT

Map 10

10 Start and Prawle Points

(Map 10 and
OS Map 202)

This southernmost projection of South Devon comprises
coastal farmland, rocky outcrops, Bracken and cliffs, with
sheltered coves into which flow brooks lined by overhanging
bushes. The coast includes several NT stretches with some of
the county's best cliff scenery. Jagged, Bracken-covered Start
promontory, with a lighthouse and rocky islets at the tip,
projects southeast into Start Bay; the ridge is a spine of rocks,
one side of which is usually sheltered from wind. Among high,
open farmland behind the point lies Start Farm valley,
sheltered from east winds, with trees and bushes. West from
Start to Prawle (about 5 miles/8 km) a low strip of fields
borders rocky Lannacombe Bay, often visited by marine
biologists. Within a few hundred metres inland, the land rises
steeply, with rock outcrops, to flat farmland at about 140 m.

Prawle Point projects southward, reaching slightly farther
seaward than Bolt cliffs, visible to the west. Most of the east
flank is farmland, with stone walls and tall hedges; overgrown
rocky outcrops and wartime bunkers clad with brambles
overlook the shore. The NT car park lies in a sheltered hollow
surrounded by thickets, Hazel and Ash bushes. There is a
dense Sycamore wood on the steep hillside below East Prawle
village, and a tangle of damp vegetation grows behind the
duck-pond, beside the road into the village. The top of the
point, and superb vista of cliffs and coves westward, are
largely covered by rough grass, gorse, Bracken and boulders.
A mile (1.6 km) west is a deep valley, with a stream, trees and
thickets, known as 'Pig's Nose' valley by birdwatchers.
Inland, west of the village, lie flat fields once used as an
airfield.

The sea can produce spectacular sightings of larger creatures
such as massive, but harmless, Basking Sharks, which show
triangular back fins when circling lazily just below the surface
on summer days. Grey Seals often peer up at the intruder
from rocky coves, especially on the west flank of Prawle. Rank

Habitat

vegetation in coves in summer and autumn encourages concentrations of butterflies: residents include Green Hair-streak, and migrants include Clouded Yellow; even the spectacular American Monarch has visited.

Species

Prawle district has recently been recognised as one of the region's top migration watchpoints. Most watchers have concentrated on Prawle rather than Start, partly for convenience of access and partly because birds often stay longer than at Start, where shelter and cover are limited. All counts given below are based on Prawle; anyone watching carefully at Start would probably see many of the same species.

A major attraction for visiting birdwatchers is the resident Cirl Bunting, perhaps commoner here, in thickets and hedges near sea level, than anywhere else in Britain; the flat trilling song of males is a familiar spring sound and up to eight pairs breed in sheltered fields around Prawle, with further sites along the coast to Start. Corn Buntings (rare in Devon) are found occasionally and may breed; they prefer high, open fields near the village. Tree Sparrows have bred at Start, and may still be present nearby. Little Owls are seen frequently around Prawle Point, often perched in daytime on rock outcrops or stone walls. Buzzards and Ravens are common, but large Buzzard-like raptors are worth checking for scarcer species at migration times (beware frequent oddly plumaged Buzzards).

In winter, large numbers of Gannets, Kittiwakes and auks pass at sea, with a few divers, mostly Great Northern. Westward movements of thousands of Great Black-backed Gulls have been seen in gales. Parties of Eiders appear irregularly. Flocks of up to 30-40 Turnstones and smaller numbers of Purple Sandpipers feed on the rocks, together with plentiful Oystercatchers and a few Grey Plovers, Redshanks and Curlews. In sheltered bushes and coves, a Chiffchaff, Firecrest or Black Redstart may remain from the previous autumn. Overhead, a wintering Peregrine often patrols along the coast. Larger fields near the village are worth checking for lark and finch flocks, with occasional Twites among Linnets on the ground. Flocks of up to 1,000 Golden Plovers, which may be joined by other waders, particularly Lapwings, appear irregularly on the aerodrome fields and, in hard weather, large flocks of open-ground species arrive from farther north.

Spring can bring large arrivals of migrants, first usually being Wheatears or Black Redstarts around the beach, rock

Hoopoe

HARRISON 83

outcrops or buildings. Chiffchaffs, Goldcrests and often a Firecrest work their way up hedges and away inland, unless held up by poor weather. The highly distinctive Hoopoe could be encountered from the first warmer March days, probing short turf on Start promontory or the top of Prawle Point near the coastguard lookout. Later, mixed falls of warblers and other small migrants occur in suitable weather, with birds singing and feeding in every bush at dawn, although most soon move on. Willow Warblers are predominant (up to 500 at times), with lesser numbers of Chiffchaffs; up to 50 Blackcaps and Whitethroats may accompany them, with a scattering of Lesser Whitethroats. Three or four Grasshopper Warblers reeling in damp scrub may stay to breed, but Reed and Wood Warblers which sing briefly in sheltered trees are purely migrants; one or two Sedge Warblers nest near streams. A check of either headland on a good spring day is likely to reveal scattered Redstarts, flycatchers and other summer visitors. From mid morning in fine weather, diurnal migrants including hirundines and finches may be seen arriving from France over the cliffs, with a chance of a raptor such as Hobby. Prawle has an exceptional list of raptors: sometimes a Honey Buzzard with barred wings and tail circling over, maybe a harrier, even rarities such as Black Kite. Late spring is best for Turtle Dove, with parties of up to 20 in the fields, and many other interesting migrants such as Tawny Pipit, Serin and Great Reed Warbler have turned up. Poor visibility and onshore winds can bring large parties of commoner seabirds, with a few divers, waders such as Whimbrel, skuas and Sandwich Terns moving through. Manx Shearwaters are present most days, parties sometimes resting on the sea, and hundreds on fine evenings banking low over the waves as they fly up the Channel to feed overnight. The considerably larger Cory's Shearwater from warmer climates has been seen several times in late spring and summer. Storm Petrels, often reported by boatmen around Skerries Bank north of Start, may be driven near headlands by rain or wind.

Other summer birds include breeding Shags, Great Black-backed Gulls and a colony of about 30 pairs of Kittiwakes at Start tip, while one or two pairs of Lesser Black-backed Gulls breed somewhere in the district in most years. Shelducks and Oystercatchers also nest, the former choosing Rabbit burrows near Lannacombe Bay. Density of breeding birds on land, apart from resident specialities, is relatively low, making migrant passerines easy to detect; many common woodland nesters are not normally resident in this exposed area. Late summer brings Sandwich Terns moving westward in twos and threes, often totalling 60 in a morning, while Manx Shear-waters are largely replaced by the Balearic race; this Mediterranean race, lacking the black and white contrast of British birds, is probably as frequent at Prawle as anywhere in Britain, and dozens appear on peak days, together with occasional longer-winged Sooty Shearwaters. When major depressional gales start, hundreds of Gannets and other common seabirds pass west, together with a variety of shearwaters and skuas; Sooty Shearwaters are seen more regularly than elsewhere in Devon, with frequent sightings in rough weather (once over 70 in a day). Skuas have exceeded 100 in a day exceptionally, Great Skuas appearing on most watches, with small numbers of Pomarines. Other pelagic species such as petrels may be seen, and scarcer migrants such as Grey Phalarope or Sabine's Gull may beat past. Most seabirds move straight past against the wind, so views are brief. Later in autumn Kittiwakes and auks pass in thousands, often accompanied by Great Skuas. Most seabird reports come from Prawle, as it is hard to find a convenient sheltered watchpoint at Start.

Early autumn brings peak numbers of migrant passerines, such as warblers, flycatchers and Wheatears, feeding in coves and sheltered farmland. On fine days Yellow Wagtails and

Tree Pipits call frequently overhead, with up to 100 of each passing. Warblers and flycatchers often remain several days feeding in bushy hollows and overgrown hedges, occasionally flicking out to snap up a passing insect; often more are present than at first appears, so wait near suitable cover. Looking stocky among *Phylloscopus* warblers, scarce migrant Icterine and Melodious Warblers, particularly the shorter-winged Melodious, are seen intermittently in most autumns. A seldom-seen visitor is the Corncrake, sadly found dead annually on roads.

From mid autumn, when temperatures start to decline, many diurnal migrants coast overhead. Movements of hundreds of hirundines attract Hobbies, which often patrol the area for weeks to pick off passing birds. Meadow Pipits also move west in hundreds, stopping to feed on open fields and frequently harassed by dashing Merlins. The Merlins often stay all autumn, attracted later by hundreds of Linnets and Goldfinches which swirl in pre-migration flocks on weed and stubble fields. Grey Wagtails, picked out by hard 'chizz' calls, pass southwest, with up to 30 on some days. Among the pipits, wagtails, Skylarks and finches which pour southwest over Prawle on late autumn days, often totalling thousands, calls of northern immigrants such as Brambling and Siskin can often be heard. Peregrines circle over the coast daily, and a passing Hen Harrier or Short-eared Owl might be seen with luck.

As warblers start to thin out, the lively Firecrest is often present on later autumn mornings: usually two or three at favoured locations such as Prawle car park perimeter, and up to 30 in the area on good days. Blackcaps and Chiffchaffs, some of the latter apparently of greyish eastern races, still move through, and Ring Ouzels pass in small groups, favouring rocky outcrops. When strong Atlantic gales blow, there is a chance of sighting a vagrant American passerine such as Blackpoll Warbler or Red-eyed Vireo; Prawle is the only mainland area in the region other than the far tip of Cornwall where these very rare birds have been found. Later, one or two scarce eastern birds such as Yellow-browed Warbler and Red-breasted Flycatcher are found in the lanes; Black Redstarts are frequently seen around coves and coastal buildings, while a few summer visitors put in late appearances. When cold winds bring thousands of Woodpigeons and Starlings across from the Continent, there may even be a tiny yellow-rumped Pallas's Warbler hovering to pick insects from the hedges. Late finch movements sometimes include a Lapland Bunting.

Timing   Dawn and dusk are generally productive for passerines; warblers especially are most active in the morning. After a fall of migrants along the cliffs, warblers may continue to work their way up into areas of cover for another hour or two, so check main patches of vegetation again after this. At Start tip, migrants which have dropped in on barren terrain near the lighthouse on cloudy nights should be watched at first light, as they soon move off the promontory; the valley near the farm may hold small birds later. In spring diurnal coasting migrants such as hirundines and finches arrive from across the Channel four or five hours after daybreak; raptors take longer and may not make landfall until after midday. Departing diurnal migrants in autumn move southwest out to sea, particularly in light to moderate west or southwest winds, and movement often finishes by mid morning. Warblers are most numerous in typical fall conditions; overcast days with cool easterlies can produce rarer species in late autumn. Light southerlies with haze often produce varied migrants, including occasional southern overshoots. Seawatching is usually worthwhile when the horizon is obscured by mist or drizzle, and when gales occur. In the teeth of a really strong southwest wind and rain seabirds do not pass, tending to stay east of Start, moving west past the points when wind or rain slackens. Try also fine high-pressure spring evenings for shearwaters and skuas moving up-Channel. Force 9-10 westerlies in mid-late autumn give best chances of an American vagrant, but little chance for more usual migrants to appear. Short-eared Owls and raptors in late autumn often come on northeasterlies.

To check Prawle car park area, avoid sunny midday periods at weekends or main holiday times, when disturbance by the public occurs. In strong east winds, the sheltered lowest part of Pig's Nose valley often holds interesting migrants; try also Start valley. Try to avoid seawatching in strong sunlight: glare off the water can be a problem.

Access   From A379 Dartmouth-Kingsbridge road, south of Slapton Ley, both points are reached down narrow lanes.

For Start Point, turn sharp left in Stokenham village, just past Slapton area. Drive to car park at top of Point, passing Start Farm valley on right. Walk back and check roadside trees and field edges for migrants; Cirl Buntings are often present. Go through gate into Start lighthouse access lane beyond car park, turning immediately right down the coastal public footpath.

Follow the valley fields down towards the sea. For the Point tip, walk $\frac{1}{2}$ mile (0.8 km) down the lighthouse lane, looking among boulders for rock-loving birds such as Black Redstart at correct seasons. Kestrels and Ravens are usual overhead. The lighthouse compound is open only in daytime public visiting hours. Try a seawatch, or dawn migrant search, from the wall by the compound. Walk up over the ridge to see nesting seabirds.

Some energetic watchers do the Start-Prawle walk by coast footpath, with spectacular scenery, rock-pool waders, scattered migrants and Cirl Buntings en route, but most migrants occur near the headlands.

For Prawle Point, from A379, turn off at Frogmore or Chillington down minor roads to East Prawle village. Approaching the village, the duck-pond and thick bushes lie to the right. For the Point, continue into the village, past the green and keep right down 'no through road' to car park at the bottom. *Car Park:* Check surrounding bushes very thoroughly; many species occur here, the easiest spot to find warblers, Firecrest and flycatchers. Most observers base themselves here and check again at intervals. Also look overhead for diurnal migrants moving towards the Point.

Lower Fields Walk down car park and turn left. Walk east along coast path. Check beach for waders, and gullies for sheltering migrants. Look in scrub around overgrown crags and bunkers on left for warblers and Cirl Buntings. Little Owls or raptors may use crags as vantage points.

Prawle Wood Continue east around corner into next cove. Walk up to wood edge, a very sheltered area for warblers and Cirl Buntings. Watch the edges; the interior is dense and often birdless.

Top Fields From the wood turn left, back up to the lane. Walk back to the Point past open fields with overgrown stone hedges. Look in fields for dove flocks and other seed-eaters. Raptors may pass over. In windy weather, Redstarts and other migrants shelter behind stone walls; Little Owls also sit on them.

Top Track At the first corner of the lane below village, a track branches off right past a large house. Bushes along right of the track are sheltered from northeast winds and often hold warblers; this track leads eventually to Pig's Nose valley.

Point and Coastguard Cottages From car park, walk down towards the sea and turn right uphill past Coastguard cottage gardens. Warblers may shelter here and Black Redstarts sit on buildings. Also try a cliff gully just before the headland for sheltering birds. Cross stile onto heath top and check for pipits, Wheatears, maybe Hoopoe. Daytime migrants pass low overhead here on autumn mornings. *Sea Watch:* From near the memorial seat halfway down the right flank of the Point, or shelter under rocks if it rains.

West Cliffs From the heath, follow the scenic coast footpath west to Gammon Head and Pig's Nose valley. Good for small migrants in strong east winds, Ravens and maybe raptors. Also Grey Seal and spring flowers.

Aerodrome Fields and Pig's Nose valley walk At top end of East Prawle village, take small lane between village corner and duck-pond, turning right if approaching from the north. After 100 m scan fields either side for plover flocks, finches and buntings. Stop after another 200 m near a sharp bend. Park on the right-hand side grass verge. Walk down the tree-lined public footpath to Moorsands Cove, watching for warblers in the trees and possibly raptors passing over. Thickets near the stream can hold numerous warblers, but need patient observation. Great Spotted Woodpeckers and Jays here in autumn often herald a good fall of eastern migrants.

Calendar

Resident: Shag, Sparrowhawk, Buzzard, Partridge, Oystercatcher, Great Black-backed Gull, Stock Dove, Little Owl, Green Woodpecker, Rock Pipit, Stonechat, probably Corn Bunting, Cirl Bunting, Reed Bunting, maybe Tree Sparrow, Raven.

Dec-Feb: Divers (mostly Great Northern), Eider (irregular), Common Scoter; offshore movements of Gannets, gulls, Kittiwakes, auks. Residents flocking on land, Peregrine, Golden and odd Grey Plovers, Turnstone, Purple Sandpiper, Curlew, maybe Chiffchaff, Firecrest or Black Redstart, lark and finch flocks, Twite (irregular), occasional hard-weather influxes.

Mar-May: Chiffchaff, Goldcrest and Firecrest, Wheatear,

Black Redstart from mid Mar, most Firecrests and Black Redstarts passing by early Apr, occasional Hoopoe; chance of migrant raptors from late Mar, but especially Apr-May inc. rarer species, Hobby late Apr-May; wide range of passerines peaking late Apr-early May; Manx Shearwater and Fulmar commonest May, Storm Petrel and Puffin possible May; diver migrants of all three species, Eider, Common Scoter, Red-breasted Merganser, Whimbrel, Bar-tailed Godwit, a few Great, Arctic or Pomarine Skuas, Sandwich Tern, all mostly late Apr-May although odd terns from end Mar; Turtle Dove (May), rarities.

Jun-Jul: Feeding parties of seabirds, Manx Shearwater, maybe Cory's, occasional Storm Petrel, Gannet, Fulmar, breeding Shag, Kittiwakes (Start), occasional late southern overshoots (Jun), breeding specialites; Shelduck; from mid Jul, Balearic and maybe Sooty Shearwaters, a few waders, Sandwich Tern.

Aug-Nov: Seabirds moving throughout: Balearic Shearwaters mostly Aug-Sep, Sooty peak mid-late Sep; odd Arctic and Great Skuas Aug but most Sep-mid Oct when some Pomarine; a few terns to mid Oct. Yellow Wagtail, Tree Pipit, warblers, flycatchers, Wheatear, Whinchat, Redstart peak late Aug-Sep; occasional petrels, Grey Phalarope mid Sep-Oct; chance of larger raptors Sep, from late Sep usually Peregrine and Merlin to Nov, Hobby to mid Oct; Firecrest (late Sep-early Nov), coasting hirundines, pipits, wagtails (late Sep-Oct), possibly Yellow-browed and other scarce warblers or Red-breasted Flycatcher Oct-early Nov, with late Melodious or Icterine to mid Oct; lark and finch passage Oct-Nov, inc. scarcer species. Occasional Hen Harrier and Short-eared Owl; Black Redstart arrivals and winter thrushes (late Oct-Nov), chance of Pallas's Warbler especially early Nov, large pigeon and Starling flocks, divers, ducks, seabird passage inc. many auks, odd late Swallows and summer visitors through Nov.

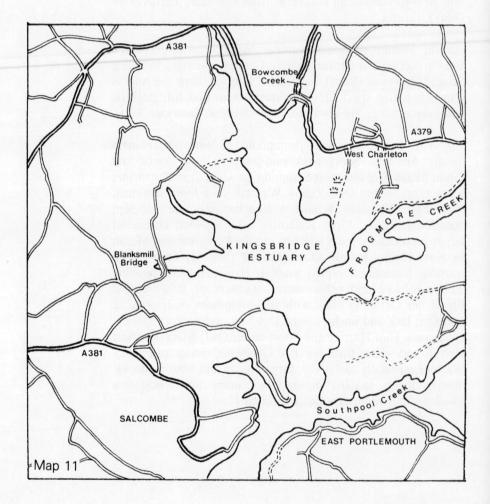

Map 11

11 Kingsbridge Estuary (Map 11 and OS Map 202)

This large South Devon estuary extends from Salcombe at the **Habitat** mouth to Kingsbridge town at the head. Several large, sheltered creeks extend up to a mile (1.6 km) on either side. The central basin of the estuary, over 1 mile (1.6 km) wide in places, is about 2 miles (3 km) long. The waterways are flanked by farmland or houses; this, together with its shape and poor access points, makes easy checking impossible. The estuary is muddy rather than sandy, with weed-covered rocks bordering in places. Some parts are shot over (except on Sundays) during winter.

Because of access difficulties, this estuary is best known for **Species** bigger, more easily seen species, especially grebes, ducks and larger waders. This makes it attractive chiefly in winter, unlike most estuaries where passage waders are seen. An unusual feature is the number of sea-going waterfowl which appear on this estuary system, which is almost land-locked, with a narrow mouth. Divers, mostly Great Northern, are seen, usually singly, perhaps sheltering from bad conditions at sea; a few divers and grebes may occur near the estuary mouth, where up to 100 Shags gather. On the creeks the most numerous grebe is Little, with over 20 commonplace, peaking in mid to late winter. An annual scattering of Great Crested occurs, with ten or more not unusual; three or four Slavonian are usually seen, and one or two Black-necked. Ducks are well represented, Wigeons most numerous with an average peak of over 800 in the New Year, when Shelducks reach about 200; most ducks feed in a mass in the central basin. Other dabbling ducks such as Mallard and Teal are regular, but only in double figures; small parties of less regular species such as Pintail might be expected. Goldeneyes provide the highest numbers of diving ducks, up to 50 at times though averaging about half this, mostly females, perhaps with only one or two males among

97

them. Red-breasted Mergansers average about 15, sometimes reaching 25; there are proportionately more males of this slim-bodied sawbill.

An interesting assortment of further diving ducks, in small numbers throughout the winter period, again includes unexpected species. Pochards, Tufted, Scaup and Goosanders might be found and, after prolonged rough seas, Eiders, Long-tailed Ducks and Common Scoters may turn up inside the estuary, even up narrow muddy creeks, and stay for weeks. Velvet Scoters, and twice the American Surf Scoter, have visited this habitat.

Grey Herons breed in adjacent woods, and there are spring records of the rare Little Egret, which has also wintered. In hard weather, geese will graze the fields of winter corn or grass pastures, where human disturbance is minimal; Brents and White-fronts are most often recorded. Apart from common resident raptors, a Peregrine might appear overhead outside the breeding season, perhaps attracted by flocks of up to 1,000 Golden Plovers which may mass on the central estuary, also feeding in nearby fields. Very hard weather causes plover numbers to rise dramatically. Up to a couple of hundred Oystercatchers and over 400 Dunlins frequent the mudflats; Curlews are generally conspicuous, but numbers are not usually over 150. Small numbers of commoner estuary waders are recorded annually, as passage migrants or winterers. Quiet areas in sheltered creeks regularly produce one or two wintering Spotted Redshanks, Greenshanks and Common Sandpipers. These same areas are favoured by Kingfishers.

The estuary is situated in the midst of the Cirl Bunting's stronghold; thickets and hedgerows around the estuary fringes are home to this decreasing species.

Timing

To watch waders, the tide must be at least partly out. An incoming tide pushes them towards observation points near Kingsbridge. An ebbing tide allows waders to alight on freshly exposed mud in the same areas, enabling you to watch them; at low tide they may be too distant. A neap tide facilitates watching, as the area of exposed mud is less. With scattered high-water roosting areas, however, only a portion of waders present will actually behave in this way. When the tide is fully out, there still remains a substantial main channel stream, used by divers, grebes and diving ducks although they may drift downstream with the tide.

Any daylight hours will suffice for winter visits. During or after prolonged periods of gales and high seas, more sea species may shelter. When severe winter weather is worse in other regions of Britain, and in the 'Low Countries', many birds arrive here seeking milder conditions. Rarer herons and other unusual visitors can be looked for as overshoots in spring southerly winds.

There is much disturbance from people and boats in summer.

Access

A379 runs alongside the estuary adjacent to the town, and crosses Bowcombe Creek by a narrow stone bridge. This same road later, going east towards Slapton, skirts the tip of Frogmore Creek. To check this side of the estuary you can start in the town, although little apart form commoner gulls and a few Redshanks and Dunlins can be expected here. Bowcombe Creek road is on the left immediately before crossing the bridge from Kingsbridge. In winter quite a good mix of ducks can be seen at close range, and there may be Blackcap, Chiffchaffs or Firecrests in roadside bushes.

Just past the bridge the estuary suddenly widens considerably alongside the main road, but there are no·vantage points other than the roadside, where stopping is dangerous. Apart from nearby verges, there are no parking facilities. When the tide is out, one can walk along this side of the estuary for a considerable distance. Take care that the tide is ebbing when setting out; there are low, sandy cliffs in many places bordering the mudflats, and if caught out by a rising tide it may not be easy to find a route back up.

Off A379 at Frogmore, take the Southpool road to look at the Southpool Creek area. From this village at the head of the creek, the road then continues to East Portlemouth near the estuary mouth, running along much of the creek's edge en route, giving intermittent views. The opposite side of the estuary is reached by A381 from Kingsbridge to Malborough, but access is more difficult still. The best checking point is probably from Blanksmill Creek; walk out along the beach when the tide is out until able to see the main estuary. Only roadside parking is available. Checking the area from Salcombe town is easy, as roads run beside the waterfront; since there is more traffic, fewer birds occur, but divers, grebes, seaducks and terns are seen in small numbers.

Calendar

Resident: Cormorant, Shag, Grey Heron, Shelduck, Oystercatcher; in adjacent country, common raptors, Grey Wagtail, Stonechat, Cirl Bunting, Raven.

Dec-Feb: Divers, particularly Great Northern; Little, Black-necked, Slavonian and Great Crested Grebes, probably geese (hard weather); ducks can include Teal, Gadwall, Wigeon, Pintail, Shoveler, Pochard, Tufted, Scaup, Eider, Common Scoter, Long-tailed, Goldeneye, Red-breasted Merganser, occasional Goosander. Peregrine, Coot, Golden Plover, Grey Plover, Turnstone, Dunlin, Common Sandpiper, Spotted Redshank, Greenshank, Bar-tailed Godwit, Kingfisher. Maybe wintering warblers, Firecrest or Black Redstart, Water Pipit.

Mar-May: Most of above depart by end Mar; apart from a few regular migrants such as Whimbrel, little happens. More watching could produce better records: Apr-May could bring rarer herons, or wader passage.

Jun-Jul: Breeding species. Heavy human disturbance.

Aug-Nov: The estuary is not usually watched until later part of season. Better coverage would almost certainly turn up more interesting species among commoner returning waders.

12 Thurlestone Area

(Map 12 and
OS Map 202)

Situated in a mild and locally drier part of South Devon, three **Habitat**
major habitat zones are found in this interesting area: at *South
Milton Ley, South Huish Water Meadow*, and *Thurlestone
Bay*.

South Milton Ley is a reserve, comprising 40 acres (16 ha)
mostly of *Phragmites*, the second largest reed-bed in Devon;
there is no open standing water. Facing east-west, the reed-
bed lies in a shallow valley, the narrow mouth of the marsh at
the west and facing Thurlestone Bay. It is surrounded by
arable farmland, and, apart from narrow strips of hedgerow
and some larger trees at its upper end, supporting cover is
minimal. The uncommon Harvest Mouse uses unkempt
growth on the side of the ley to build its summer nest.

South Huish Water Meadow is at least 40 acres (16 ha) of flat,
easily flooded rough pasture, lying in a shallow open-sided
valley among arable farmland. Running east-west and facing
the sea, parallel to South Milton Ley which lies over the ridge
to the north, it is separated from the bay by about 20 m of low
sand dunes, recently reclaimed by NT for use as a car park.
The meadow is interspersed with drainage ditches, linked to
an outflow on the beach; heavy winter rain partially floods it.

Thurlestone Bay is dominated by remarkably shaped Thurlestone Rock, which projects from an otherwise mostly sandy
shoreline.
   Two other areas worth checking at certain times are the golf
course, and trees and hedgerows in the general area. All
summer the beach is a major tourist venue.

South Milton Ley Because reed density is great, many species **Species**
present, including occasional rarities such as Aquatic Warbler

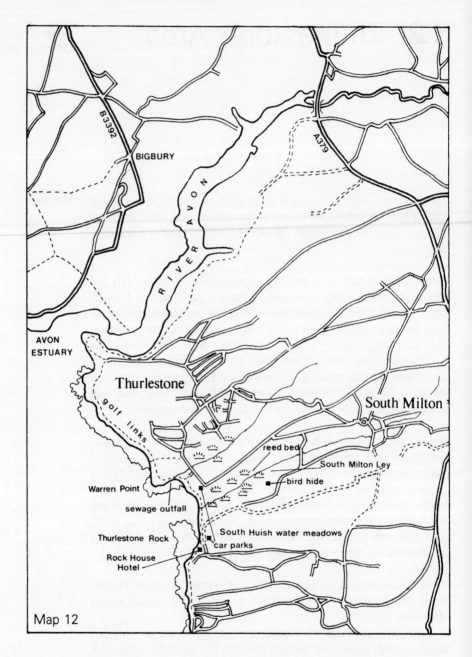

Map 12

and Bluethroat, are often seen only when removed from a mist net by ringers. Bearded Tits sometimes visit the ley in winter and, especially on calm days, can be watched moving through reed tops giving their distinctive twanging calls. Even at this season, one of the resident Cetti's Warblers may burst into song. Water Rails may also be heard, rather than seen, though Reed Buntings present less problem.

Through the later spring, Reed and Sedge Warblers sing from reed-tops. Cuckoos, which parasitise reed-bed dwellers, are evident during the day, even in the height of summer, as are first-brood Reed and Sedge Warbler fledglings.

South Huish Water Meadow A hard spell in winter when there are areas of standing water is especially attractive to dabbling ducks such as Mallard, Teal and Wigeon; numbers vary but 500 Teals and 1,000 grazing Wigeons are not infrequent, and two American Wigeons were recently found with the flock. Geese, usually White-front or Brent, sometimes visit in hard weather, and often stay for several weeks. Gulls come to rest, bathe and preen by pools; unusual species should be looked for (see Thurlestone Bay for likely visitors). Migrant Lesser Black-backed Gulls often number 100 or so in mid-late winter, and may include individuals of the darker Scandinavian race. Peregrines are frequent, and an occasional Hen Harrier or Merlin stops briefly, attracted by the large numbers of prey.

In spring, returning waders such as Bar-tailed Godwit, seen in small groups of three or four, are often in summer plumage. Similar numbers of Whimbrels may stay several days, though flocks of up to 50 pass over. If water is lying on the meadow in late spring, even if only shallow pools, two or three Garganeys may be attracted. Early Wheatears can be looked for from the first spring days. When the meadow dries out, there is little of unusual interest.

Thurlestone Bay The bay is exposed to westerly winds. A sewer close to shore off Leysfoot beach, below the golf course, is attractive to gulls: Little, Mediterranean, Sabine's, Glaucous and Iceland have all been seen. Along the winter shoreline, Turnstones and a few Purple Sandpipers are present, while Rock Pipits and Pied and Grey Wagtails feed together among the tidewrack. Grassy cliffs and buildings near Rock House Hotel are favourite haunts of Black Redstarts. Divers, mostly Black-throated or Great Northern, and grebes, particularly Slavonian, occur occasionally offshore.

From early spring, Fulmars pass by the bay and the first Sandwich Terns are usually noted, often pausing to fish. Later, smaller numbers of Common Terns, and sometimes Arctic or Little, may do the same. By late spring, the colony of some five or so pairs of Sand Martins is nesting in the low, sandy cliffside, usually at the entrance to the ley. In autumn unusual waders may use the beach, but are usually frightened off by disturbance; Kentish and Little Ringed Plovers have been seen. Gales can produce unusual gulls off the sewer, especially Little or Mediterranean.

The golf course, though busy, is a specialised habitat used regularly by a few waders, pipits, wagtails and Wheatears, particularly in spring and autumn; a Buff-breasted Sandpiper has been seen. Hedgerows and trees hold small numbers of passerine migrants, as well as Cirl Buntings, and barns in the area may well hold Little Owls. Interesting species turn up in the whole complex around Thurlestone; for example, Hoopoe is recorded nearly every spring, and both Great Reed and Icterine Warblers have been found exceptionally late in the year in sheltered vegetation.

Timing

Not critical during winter. There is no shooting over the water meadow, but occasional shooting over areas of the ley. The sewer operates only on outgoing tides. In spring and autumn an early morning visit is best, partly because there is less disturbance and partly because bird movement is usually greater, or at least more observable, then. Late afternoon and evening checks, however, have been productive, especially for seabirds and waders; at dusk in early autumn, hirundines and wagtails fly in to roost at the South Milton reed-bed. In summer, most breeding birds in the reed-bed are active in early mornings. Try the water meadow when flooded, or containing pools, after rain.

Access

Approaching from Plymouth side, follow A379 to the top of steep Aveton Gifford hill, then follow Thurlestone signs at the roundabout a few hundred metres after the hilltop. Take the first right off B3197 after the roundabout, down narrow minor roads to the village. Either park beside the road in Thurlestone (often congested at popular times), or preferably drive through it, past the golf course. On the brow of the hill towards South Milton, the road curves left; at this point there is a sharp right turn (about 1 mile (1.6 km) past Thurlestone village). This entrance leads to a car park overlooking the bay, a good place for checking it.

If approaching from Kingsbridge, take A381 towards Salcombe then branch off to Thurlestone (this same road is also initially taken for South Milton or South Huish); either route will bring you to the car park overlooking both water meadow and bay. From here, for South Milton Ley or Thurlestone village and golf course, walk north along the car park; a public footpath opposite public toilets leads across a footbridge over the mouth of the ley. From this point there are good views of the reed-bed. The path continues past a small area of sand dunes before meeting the road which adjoins the first-mentioned Thurlestone car park.

Access into South Milton Ley reserve is normally by permit obtainable from DBWPS. There is no access onto the water meadow, but birds can be seen well from the NT car park, especially with a telescope. The perimeter of the golf course has open access, and closely overlooks the sewer.

Calendar

Resident: Sparrowhawk, Buzzard, Little Owl, Rock Pipit, Cetti's Warbler, Stonechat, Cirl Bunting, Reed Bunting, Raven.

Dec-Feb: Possibly one or two divers, grebes, auks on sea. Geese may visit water meadow, large numbers of Teals and Wigeons, a few Pintails, Shovelers and Gadwalls. Snipe in hundreds, Ruffs in ones and twos. Bearded Tits in ley (some years); sheltered places may have wintering Blackcap, Chiffchaff, Firecrest. Hen Harrier, Peregrine, Merlin may hunt over area. Unusual gulls, e.g. Glaucous or Iceland.

Mar-May: Garganey may visit water meadow from Apr, also Whimbrel and godwits. Sandwich and other terns from Apr. Possibly Hoopoe from Mar, Wheatear from mid Mar; Sedge and Reed Warblers in ley from mid Apr. Mediterranean Gull may pass through early in period. Commoner migrants may include unusual species.

Grey Phalaropes

Jun-Jul: Breeding species include Sand Martin; reed-bed roost begins to be used by hirundines, wagtails and Starlings late Jul.

Aug-Nov: Roost still heavily used to mid Sep, when White Wagtails become more evident. Return passage of migrants represented by all main families: raptors, waders, seabirds, passerines, and always species of unusual interest. Grey Phalarope and Snow Bunting irregularly from Oct, Black Redstarts arrive late Oct. Mediterranean, Little or other unusual gulls.

13 Wembury and Bovisand

(Map 13 and OS Map 201)

Habitat

This section of the South Devon coast follows from near where Plymouth coast walk (Jennycliff) ends.

The Wembury side of the Yealm estuary has quite high cliffs, quickly losing height westward, dropping almost to sea level near Wembury village. From then until Bovisand Bay, cliffs remain mostly only 4-5 m high, rising at Bovisand in one place (for a short distance only) to about 20 m. As the immediate coastal land is low-lying, the vegetation is generally taller. Bushes and trees away from the shoreline are abundant, offering good cover. A good range of butterflies includes Green Hairstreak and Marbled White.

The whole coastline is rocky and holds a varied shoreline and rock-pool fauna; it is a marine sanctuary. This walk can offer something of interest all year, with hedgerows, brakes and arable fields forming an intermittent backdrop.

Species

Probably the most interesting area along this walk during autumn and winter is that used by waders at Wembury Point. Owing to high tides and wind motion, large quantities of rotting seaweed are washed ashore, providing rich feeding areas for myriads of tiny animals. Among waders foraging here, Turnstones are found not only during winter, hundreds strong, but unusually as 'residents'; non-breeding individuals attain full summer plumage, numbers dropping to 30 or so in midsummer. During autumn, 30-40 Ringed Plovers may be present. Purple Sandpipers are winter regulars, usually about 15 around rocks at the Point. Waders seen occasionally, particularly in autumn, include Little Stints and Curlew Sandpipers, but only ones and twos. Sanderlings, Common Sandpipers and Bar-tailed Godwits are regular in slightly larger numbers. Whimbrels pass through in spring and autumn in small groups.

Leaving the immediate shoreline, a third speciality is the

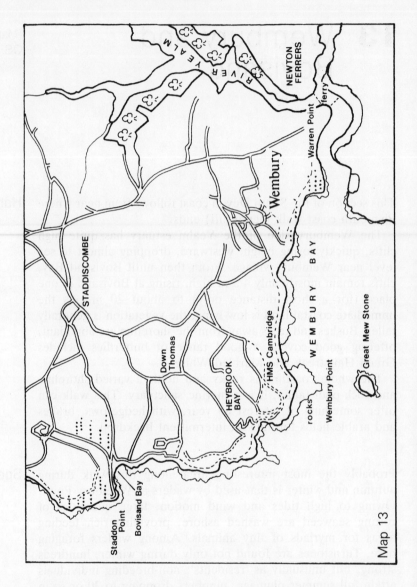

Map 13

resident Cirl Buntings among brakes and hedgerows, or feeding perhaps in the company of Yellowhammers in stubble fields, especially near the Point. A wide variety of migrant birds often arrives when time of year and conditions allow, the habitat encouraging them to linger, common warblers especially. Black Redstarts are frequent from later autumn, feeding in sheltered coves, particularly near Bovisand, and also around Wembury church.

Few interesting species are seen on the sea, although

Cormorants, Shags, Fulmars, Shelducks, Herring and Great Black-backed Gulls breed on Great Mewstone rock, 1 mile (1.6 km) off the Point. This rock also acts as the major winter night roost for thousands of Herring Gulls which scavenge the tips and estuaries of Plymouth. Five or six pairs of Fulmars breed on the higher cliffs at Bovisand.

Scarcer visitors to the area have included Iceland Gull, Black Guillemot and Hoopoe.

Timing

A rising tide is required to force waders off rocks and coastline, concentrating them onto the beach at the Point; on morning high tides there is less human disturbance. The naval gunnery school, HMS Cambridge, situated at the Point, causes disturbance to birds unused to firing; a red flag warns of the danger of approaching within several hundred metres either side (thus interrupting the cliff walk) while firing is in progress. Firing is infrequent, and not undertaken at all at weekends. Disturbance by the general public can be a problem on sunny weekend afternoons.

Access

A379 Plymouth-Kingsbridge road is the best starting point. From Plymouth, turn right at Elburton roundabout on the edge of the city (opposite Elburton Inn), through the village, along narrow country lanes. Head towards Staddiscombe for Bovisand and Wembury Point, or direct from Elburton to Wembury village. Continue through village to NT car park.

At Bovisand there is a car park, then walk left towards Wembury. At Wembury Point, parking may be more difficult on weekends, as the public road to HMS Cambridge stops at its entrance, with no real parking facilities. Limited parking is allowed along roadside verges. A public footpath opposite the gunnery school entrance leads down through a brake. This area is often very good for birds. The brakes are best checked either by walking along their edges or by penetrating narrow paths through them. The Green Hairstreak butterfly favours areas near the bottom. The path continues beside a field to the coast path. Views from the roadside are magnificent, the Mewstone taking your eye seawards.

The main wader area at the Point is viewed very easily from the public footpath which runs adjacent to the cliff edge throughout. Total length of walk is about 2 miles (3 km); access is unrestricted at any time. Eastward, the coast path leads towards the Yealm estuary.

Strictly no access is allowed on Great Mewstone without special permission from HMS Cambridge.

Calendar

Resident: Cormorant, Shag, Shelduck, Sparrowhawk, Buzzard, Oystercatcher, Turnstone, Rock Pipit, Meadow Pipit, Stonechat, Cirl Bunting, Raven.

Dec-Feb: Grey Plover, Purple Sandpiper, Curlew, occasional Black Redstart and Brambling.

Mar-May: Mar often produces early Chiffchaff and Wheatear, first Sandwich Terns often late Mar, also Willow Warbler. From Apr, other passerine migrants increasing, waders e.g. Whimbrel from mid month, Hoopoe possible.

Jun-Jul: Breeding species, inc. Fulmar, Cuckoo, Grasshopper Warbler, Blackcap, Whitethroat, Spotted Flycatcher.

Aug-Nov: Possibly a moving Peregrine. Waders, inc. Ringed Plover, Whimbrel (especially Sep), Dunlin, Redshank. Sandwich and Common Tern, less frequently other terns, Aug-Sep. General passage of departing summer migrants such as warblers, Wheatear, then Black Redstarts Oct-Nov and early morning coasting movements of Skylarks, Chaffinches, Linnets.

Cirl Bunting

14 Dartmoor Area: General Introduction

(Maps 14(i)-14(v) and OS Map 191/202 or National Park Map)

Habitat

Dartmoor is the only major area of high open moor in southern England, with about 400 square miles (1036 km^2) of rough grassland, heather, stones, bog, streams and woodland, standing out above surrounding fertile Devon lowlands. Underlying granite shows through characteristically as 'tor' rocks on exposed moorland hilltops. The moor forms a steep-sided plateau from which many rivers and torrents flow, running down through deep scenic wooded valleys around the fringes of the area. The highest hills and main peat bogs, from which most of Devon's rivers originate within a few miles of each other, are on the northern half of the moor, with High Willhays (627 m) and Yes Tor forming a twin high point near Okehampton. The southern moors, south of Princetown, are characteristically 100 m lower than those in the north, with less peat bog and more rough grassland. Gorse grows freely on better-drained slopes, with extensive Bracken in summer. Most open ground on the central moor is relatively gently sloping, with broad marshy valleys and rolling hillsides.

Rainfall on high ground averages 80 inches (2030 mm) per year, substantially higher than in the lowlands, resulting in waterlogged acidic soil. A light covering of snow is common in midwinter, although it often thaws in a day or two as mild depressional air arrives from the sea. Gales are frequently recorded on open hillsides in autumn and winter, combining with cold and damp to give a high 'exposure factor', preventing natural deciduous tree growth over 400 m altitude. A few Hawthorn and Rowan bushes, often stunted and twisted by winds, grow along sheltered stream banks; the Forestry Commission has well-matured conifer plantations on the centre and southwest moor. Some rivers have been dammed on the plateau edge to form reservoirs. Parts of the moor, particularly on remoter northern sections, are used as Army firing ranges for a portion of the year.

This whole open area, and much high farmland and valley

111

woods on the flanks, is incorporated into Dartmoor National Park. The moor acts as a centre for relatively undisturbed wildlife, with many Badger setts on better-drained and wooded slopes, while Foxes are met even in high bog zones. Adders are often encountered on sunny hillsides among gorse and Bracken in summer. Feral moor ponies are widespread (**Note** Do not attract ponies near roadsides as serious accidents can occur), and hardy sheep and beef cattle range over the unfenced hills. Many visitors come in summer and hiking activities have increased in recent seasons; parties now visit even remotest areas. The National Park authorities arrange guided walks over more accessible sections in summer.

Species

Open moorland holds many small breeding passerines in summer, although the number of species is limited. Skylarks and Meadow Pipits sing constantly overhead and Wheatears are seen on many rocky slopes; Stonechats and Whinchats are encountered on gorse and Bracken tops. Highest moors have very small, scattered numbers of specialised birds such as Red Grouse and Ring Ouzel, with a few breeding waders such as Golden Plover. Steep valley woods on moor fringes hold many breeding summer visitors, including widespread Wood Warblers, and Pied Flycatchers are becoming firmly established, especially where nestboxes are provided. Moorland conifer plantations have encouraged specialised feeders such as a few Crossbills and Siskins, although the peaty waters of adjacent reservoirs are too barren to attract much birdlife except a few fish-eating Goosanders. Dippers and Grey Wagtails feed along many swift-flowing streams running off the moor, while Buzzards and Ravens sail overhead. Migration times can bring large flocks of Golden Plovers, halting on open slopes, and sometimes a passing raptor; even lost seabirds (once a Long-tailed Skua) have turned up. In winter, hardy Red Grouse, occasional crows, Ravens or raptors such as Hen Harrier and Merlin may be encountered on open moors. Winter visitors such as Fieldfares and finches tend to feed in less exposed moor valleys and fringes of high farmland.

Of the many sites on Dartmoor, the major birdwatching areas are given below.

Haytor and Yarner Wood

(Map 14(i)
and
OS Map 191)

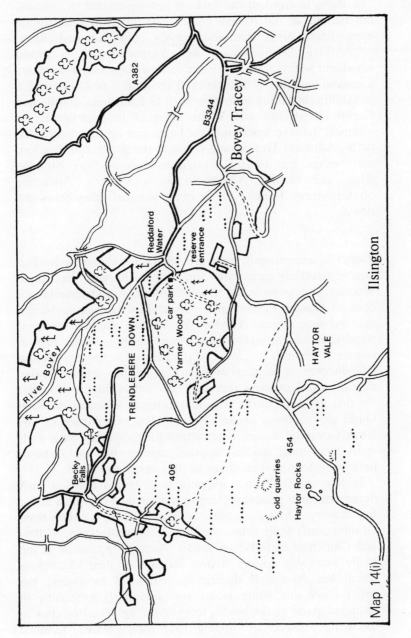

A382

Bovey Tracey

B3344

Reddaford
Water

reserve
entrance

car park

Ilsington

Yarner Wood

TRENDLEBERE DOWN

River Bovey

HAYTOR
VALE

Becky
Falls

406

old quarries

454

Haytor Rocks

Map 14(i)

Habitat

At the southeast edge of Dartmoor, the land rises very steeply from coastal lowlands. The most prominent landmark is Haytor Rocks (459 m), with wide views over South Devon. The down in front of the rocks is heavily eroded by tourists, but behind lie old mining gullies and relatively undisturbed open heath with scattered bushes. On the east flank, overlooking Bovey valley, lies Yarner Wood, a mixed woodland National Nature Reserve with many oak trees above a ground covering of Bilberries. The wood is particularly rich in wildlife, including butterflies such as Brimstone, Purple and Green Hairstreaks and White Admiral in open glades in summer; massive wood ant nest heaps can be seen beside the paths. Adjacent Trendlebere Down to the north, with Bracken and bushes, has unusual butterflies such as Silver-Studded Blue, and basking Adders in warm weather. Attractive boulder-strewn Becky Falls lie in the wooded valley below the down.

Species

Yarner is exceptionally rich in summer woodland birds. The area is relatively quiet early and late in the year, but single Woodcocks may be found in woodland rides, and sometimes a flock of Golden Plovers or a passing Hen Harrier or Merlin may be seen around Haytor. Yarner can provide views of woodland resident birds perhaps more easily in winter than in summer, when leaf cover is thicker, with Lesser Spotted Woodpecker as regular as anywhere in the region. Spring migrant warblers arrive relatively late in these high woods, but the first good migration days may bring in Wheatear or Ring Ouzel on the moor around Haytor. The prominence of this latter viewpoint makes it an attraction to soaring birds and, apart from local species, migrant raptors such as Goshawk have been seen several times circling north overhead.

In late spring Yarner abounds with bird activity, a high density of small passerines singing and feeding overhead in the tree canopy. The trilling song of Wood Warblers comes from all directions, while other warblers such as Blackcap, Willow and Chiffchaff can also be found. A major attraction is the easily watchable colony of over 20 pairs of Pied Flycatchers which has flourished through provision of nestboxes; the smart black and white males are particularly noticeable in sheltered parts of the wood, looping through the branches to catch tiny insects or singing from twigs above occupied nestboxes. Spotted Flycatchers are also present. Redstarts, up to 20 pairs, and commoner tits have also made good use of

Raven

HARRISON 83

boxes. More open areas at the top and edges of the wood attract a different range of species, with Tree Pipits frequently song flighting from the treetops while larger species such as Buzzard and Raven circle overhead.

The semi-open heathland bordering the wood has its own distinctive birds. In most years a pair or two of Nightjars can be found, although their neighbour, the Grasshopper Warbler, is very variable in numbers from year to year; Stonechats, Whinchats and Tree Pipits are also regular here. Higher up, there is likely to be a pair of Ring Ouzels in old quarry workings behind Haytor, although some old nest sites are now occupied by Blackbirds. Three hundred metres below, characteristic hill-stream birds such as Dippers and Grey Wagtails may be seen close to tourist paths past Becky Falls.

Timing

For migrants arriving at Haytor, fine high-pressure conditions with light east or southeast winds are needed. Yarner Wood can be watched in most weathers owing to its sheltered position and thick summer leaf canopy, but sunny mornings are best for watching small birds, as leaf cover cuts down available light on dull days. For Nightjar and Grasshopper Warbler, a late dusk visit to Trendlebere on a warm day should be planned.

Avoid Haytor when heavily congested with tourists on peak

summer weekends and holiday periods, unless an early morning start is planned.

Access

From A38 Exeter-Plymouth road, turn north on A382 to Bovey Tracey. Take the first major road left when you reach Bovey Tracey, heading towards Haytor and Widecombe on B3344. After 1 mile (1.6 km), fork left for Haytor, or continue on B road towards Manaton for Yarner Wood. From this fork:

Haytor After about 5 miles (8 km) stop in roadside car parks below the tor and walk up to the right; cross to rear of the hill for heathland and old quarries.

Yarner After about 2 miles (3 km) the road dips through Reddaford valley, then climbs sharp right onto the moor. Turn left immediately on the bend, on a tarmac lane into the wood. Pass the warden's cottages, and park beyond. There are prepared nature trails and ecology displays (see notice board beside car park).

The wood is wardened full-time by the Nature Conservancy Council. Free access is given to individual visitors, provided that they abide by the instructions posted and keep to paths. Parties should book with the warden to avoid clashes; May and June weekends are often booked well in advance.

A minor road through Reddaford, just below the reserve, connects with Haytor route. Trendlebere Down can be watched from roadsides on the moor above the wood entrance, or by taking paths leading out from the wood itself. For Becky Falls continue up Manaton road for another 2 miles (3km), park and walk down to falls on the right.

Calendar

Resident: Sparrowhawk, Buzzard, Kestrel, woodpeckers inc. Lesser Spotted, Tawny Owl, Dipper, common woodland passerines, Grey Wagtail, Raven.

Dec-Feb: Possibly Hen Harrier or Merlin over open land, Golden Plover, Woodcock, feeding parties of small birds.

Mar-May: Occasional migrant raptors, Wheatear and Ring Ouzel (mid Mar on); from late Apr many summer visitors, e.g. Cuckoo, Pied and Spotted Flycatchers, warblers inc. many Wood and probably Grasshopper, Redstart, Stonechat, Whinchat, good numbers of Tree and Meadow Pipits; late May, Nightjar.

Jun-Jul: Nightjars active, singing passerines in wood, mainly Jun, quieter in Jul when busy feeding young. One or two pairs of Ring Ouzels near Haytor.

Aug-Nov: Most summer visitors leave in Aug. Generally quiet period.

Soussons and Postbridge District

(Map 14 (ii) and OS Map 191)

Habitat

Near Warren House Inn on the east side of the moors, West Webburn brook runs south down a sheltered valley over-looked by 450-m heather-covered hillsides and old overgrown tin-mining gullies. Scattered Hawthorn bushes and ruins of old settlements stand along the stream banks. The lower valley is occupied by Soussons forestry plantation, and the mine-furrowed hillside is known as Vitifer. Mine gullies extend east across the ridge to Grimspound in the next valley. Unpolluted brook water contains abundant aquatic life in summer, and deep heather on nearby slopes provides cover for wild animals such as Foxes and Stoats.

West of Soussons lies Postbridge, a small community on the upper East Dart river. North and west of the village are boggy riverside pastures, overlooked by high moorland behind. Sundew plants grow in the wet soil and Beech and *Salix* trees line the riverbanks. Across the river is the large mature Bellever forestry plantation.

Species

Soussons area is one of the most productive moorland birdwatching sites in winter, valley and plantation acting as a central gathering ground and roost for many species. Wood-pigeons, Fieldfares, Redwings and finches pass the night here in large numbers; Sparrowhawks and Merlins often chase roosting flocks as they arrive. Hen Harriers (often ashy-grey males) are a regular midwinter feature, attracting many local birdwatchers; they hunt widely over the hills, and towards dusk may glide to roost in deep heather near the top of the valley; up to six are seen together. Along thorn bushes near the stream, or on telegraph wires, a Great Grey Shrike often

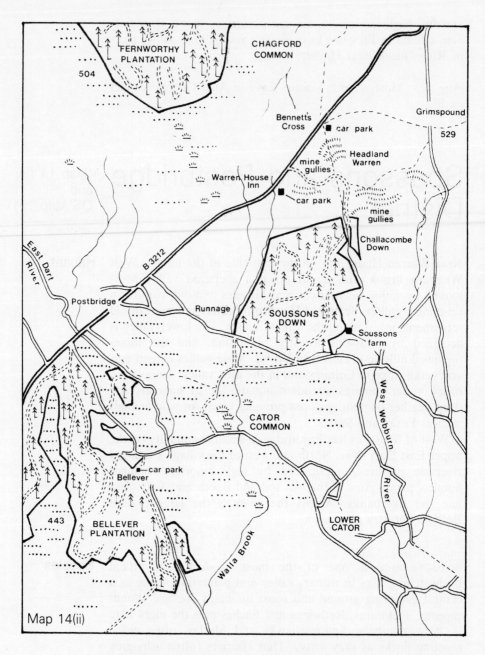

Map 14(ii)

perches alertly waiting for prey. Walking eastward across the Headland Warren hillside, you may flush a pack of Red Grouse from the heather; there is a small breeding population in the district.

Soussons plantation is often quiet on winter days except for a few Goldcrests and Coal Tits. Occasional Woodcocks may rise from the side of tracks, or flight out in late afternoon to feed on open boggy ground, while Snipe can be flushed near the stream. Larger residents such as Buzzard and Raven are usually visible circling overhead. On farmland edges south of the plantation the population is more varied, with flocks of Chaffinches and Bramblings often appearing. Bellever can usually be relied on for parties of Crossbills, flying around high treetops above the visitors' car park or nearby rides with characteristic hard 'chip' calls. In winter, Short-eared Owls and other predators sometimes hunt boggy pastures behind Postbridge.

Early spring, while snow still lies in some years, brings Wheatears and Ring Ouzels back to their territories. Warren House-Vitifer area is perhaps the easiest on Dartmoor for finding Ring Ouzels, with probably half a dozen pairs, the harsh 'tack' alarm call or piping song showing their presence along heather-clad gullies. Open slopes support many Meadow Pipits in the breeding season, while Whinchats perch on Bracken along the valley floor. Snipe perform drumming display flights over rushy pasture below the plantation, and higher up towards the main road a pair of Curlews may be found. Both species, together with Lapwing, also nest in the Dart valley pastures above Postbridge, and Grey Herons, Dippers and Grey Wagtails can be seen along the Dart river; a pair or two of herons often nest nearby, an unusually high site.

Migrants passing up Soussons valley in later spring sometimes include a raptor such as Montagu's Harrier or Hobby. Cuckoos are often abundant, scouring slopes for pipit nests to parasitise. In Soussons wood-clearings Redstarts occur in small numbers, while metallic trills overhead draw attention to several pairs of Redpolls nesting in fir tree tops; these diminutive finches fly out to feed in bushes overhanging nearby streams. Redstarts are also likely along riverbank trees near Postbridge, where the rippling song of Willow Warblers can be heard. Stock Doves nest in the rocky areas and old mines, and in some years Siskins breed in Bellever.

Late summer sees parties of young birds foraging along Soussons valley, while occasional post-breeding flocks of Crossbills from Bellever visit the taller trees. When most other species have departed, Ring Ouzels may still be feeding on Rowan berries beside the stream; by the time frost returns to open slopes, the first Hen Harriers have taken up residence in the valley again.

Male Ring Ouzel

HARRISON 83

Timing

On fine days, most winter roost species spread widely to feed. Although a Great Grey Shrike may be present at any time (perhaps moving up the hillside telegraph wires if disturbed), most birdwatchers concentrate on afternoons to see birds gathering in Soussons valley before roosting. Hen Harriers tend to hunt the valley above the plantation in the last two hours' light. In the last hour before nightfall, especially on frosty evenings, pigeons, thrushes and other mass-roost species fly to the south end of the plantation behind Soussons farm; at this time Woodcocks may fly out. Short-eared Owls, if present, are most likely to hunt near Postbridge in the afternoons. Breeding waders call and display over territory in early mornings, also the best time for songbirds.

On fine weekends and at the peak summer season, there is often disturbance by walkers over all Soussons-Vitifer area.

Access

B3212 Moretonhampstead-Postbridge road crosses the head of West Webburn valley above Soussons. Birdwatchers seeking roosting Hen Harriers often park by Bennett's Cross (ancient stone monument), in the dip immediately east of Warren House Inn, for pre-dusk views down the valley without needing to walk. To cover the valley and Vitifer gullies, walk down across the moor from here, or down the gravel track near the Inn. Where telegraph wires cross the stream halfway along the valley is a good starting point to look for the shrike in winter. If energetic, follow the wires east across the ridge for grouse, or in summer for Stock Doves and Ring Ouzels; alternatively, continue to Soussons plantation and explore clearings. If Ring Ouzels have not been seen, try the hillside in front of the Inn when returning. For the lower end of the plantation continue west towards Postbridge by road, turning very sharply left just before the village; this minor road follows the plantation side. At the minor crossroads near Soussons farm, turn left to watch over boggy ground to the wood edge.

At Postbridge, cross the river on B3212 westward and park near road for views right over boggy pastures. There are footpaths along riverbanks south past the stone clapper bridge. To reach Bellever, take the signposted lane left adjacent to the plantation, following this for 1 mile (1.6 km) to the car park; park under trees and wait nearby for Crossbills calling.

Calendar

Resident: Grey Heron, Sparrowhawk, Buzzard, Kestrel, Red Grouse, Stock Dove, Grey Wagtail, Goldcrest, Coal Tit, Dipper, Crossbill.

Dec-Feb: Hen Harrier, Merlin, Woodcock, Snipe, perhaps Short-eared Owl (Postbridge); roosting Woodpigeon, Fieldfare, Redwing, Starling (some years), finches inc. Brambling.

Mar-May: Most winter visitors leave by mid Mar, Great Grey Shrike may stay to mid Apr. Breeding Lapwing, Snipe and Curlew arrive. Wheatear and Ring Ouzel by late Mar. Cuckoo, Whinchat and Redstart late Apr. Redpolls active in May, possibly Siskin (Bellever). Occasional migrant raptors late Apr-May.

Jun-Jul: Breeding residents and summer visitors as above, family parties in Jul.

Aug-Nov: Summer migrants move out during Aug. A few Wheatears and Ring Ouzels to Oct. Passing Hen Harrier, Merlin, sometimes Peregrine from Oct, winterers become established from late Nov.

(Maps 14(iii)
and 14(iv) and
OS Map 191)

Okehampton Area: High Moors around Cranmere, and Okement Valley Woods

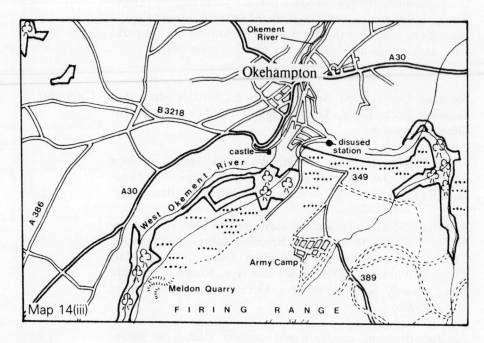

Habitat

The highest part of Dartmoor forms a unique area in southern England. Uninhabited terrain stretches for over 10 miles (16 km) south of Okehampton. Rolling open moorland and peat bogs form a desolate landscape, relieved by a few protruding tors and the white tufted seed heads of bog cotton in summer. The ground, mostly 550-600 m in altitude, is wet and uneven to walk over. Most of Devon's rivers originate here. The 'Pool' itself is a small hollow in the centre, forming a landmark for hikers. A number of shaggy long-horned Highland cattle graze in the shelter of peat banks. On the edge of the high moor plateau, steep escarpments have rock scree and gorse thickets. The open moor is used as an Army firing range for part of the year. Foxes are often encountered in early mornings.

At the foot of the northern escarpment, the East and West

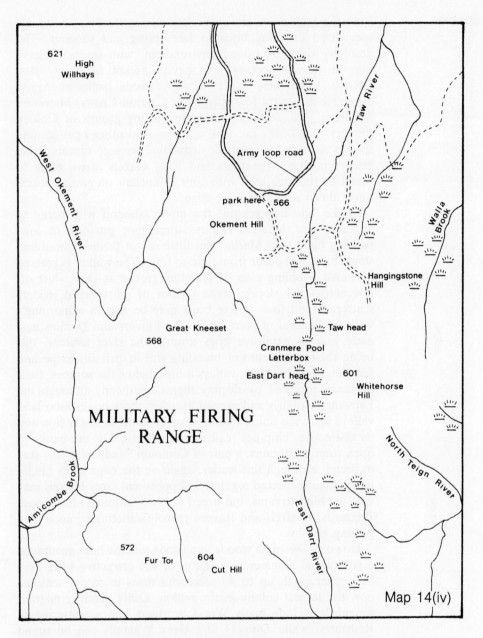

621
High
Willhays

Taw River

West Okement River

Army loop road

Walla Brook

park here 566

Okement Hill

Hangingstone
Hill

Great Kneeset

568

Taw head

Cranmere Pool
Letterbox

East Dart head

601

Whitehorse
Hill

MILITARY FIRING
RANGE

North Teign River

Amicombe Brook

East Dart River

572

Fur Tor

604

Cut Hill

Map 14(iv)

Okement rivers flow close past Okehampton, through a deep,
sheltered valley with oak woods, and carpets of Bluebells in
spring.

Species

Both the high moor and the valley woods are best known for specialised breeding birds in late spring and summer. The desolate winter moorland environment, with frequent heavy rain or snow, supports few species except for hardy Red Grouse, which may shelter along roadside banks by Army-range roads, and a few Ravens or Carrion Crows. Migration has been little studied, but large passing groups of Golden Plovers wheel over the tors at times, and other open-ground species such as Dotterel, or occasional passage raptors, have been reported. Wheatears and Ring Ouzels arrive early to breed on the high tors, with later Whinchats on gorse thickets lower down near the moor edge.

In the breeding season, the moors abound with breeding Skylarks and Meadow Pipits, sometimes pursued in low, twisting flight by a Merlin; this little raptor formerly bred and single birds still occur from time to time. The walker is greeted by harsh gobbling calls of breeding grouse as they whirr off low across the slopes; some dozens of pairs breed, widely scattered, and four or five birds may be met in a morning's walk. A handful of pairs of Golden Plovers and Dunlins nest each year in extensive bogs around the river sources, this being their southernmost breeding site in Britain. Snipe and Lapwings inhabit rushy valleys a little below the sources, their presence revealed by display flights overhead; although the Lapwing is a fairly widespread breeder, these boggy moorland valleys form the Snipe's main summer home in the region and its distinctive 'chip-per' call is often heard. On the banks of open running streams, a pair of Common Sandpipers may stay to breed, although this wader, again on the edge of its range, is no longer expected regularly. Dippers and Grey Herons may visit the high streams, but breed at lower altitudes. Overhead, Buzzards, Kestrels and Ravens patrol, sometimes joined by a passing Hobby.

Down in Okement woods, a nestbox scheme has encouraged a substantial summer population of the attractive little Pied Flycatcher, with up to 40 successful nests in recent seasons, now the largest colony in the region. Other summer migrant songbirds include many Wood Warblers and a scattering of Redstarts, while Dippers and Grey Wagtails can be found along the riversides.

Breeding species, apart from a few larger birds, soon abandon the open moors once young have been reared, and summer woodland visitors move back towards the coast. Although high moors are generally quiet at this period, passage birds might be seen, including a wandering Peregrine, moving flocks of Ring Ouzels, or, as in spring, waders such as Golden Plover flocks. There is a chance of other strays such as Snow Bunting on open, rocky stretches in late autumn.

Timing

Fine weather is essential to cover the moors properly: accurate weather forecasts should be sought. Do not attempt to walk across the high moor in severe winter conditions or fog; every year walkers become ill with exposure (some die), and emergency rescues are needed. Allow sufficient time to reach civilisation before nightfall. Most birds on high ground can be seen at any time of day, but waders are most easily seen in the first three or four hours of daylight when display flights occur. The moor is best avoided on days when large-scale hiking events such as 'Ten Tors' (around mid May) are planned. See also Access section for Army-range restrictions.

Mornings are best for singing Pied Flycatchers and other breeding birds in the valley, which can be fitted in after an early moorland trip.

Access

From A377 through Okehampton, turn left in the town centre along a minor road signposted 'Dartmoor National Park' and 'Battle Camp'. For the moors, drive up a steep hill, past the Army camp and through a gate onto the roughly tarmaced military road. (**Note** Army firing ranges operate some weeks; red flags fly from tors when firing commences. Do not continue beyond the gate before checking. Advance-warning notices are published in local newspapers or at police stations. Do not touch metal objects found on the ranges.) Continue to the farthest point of the 'loop' road at Okement Hill, then explore southward across the bogs. Carry a compass and let someone know where you are going. Try also walking up larger tors and screes for rocky-ground species. Boots and waterproof clothes are needed. The best area to cover for a range of species is between Okement Hill and Fur Tor (south of Cranmere), and around the upper Taw and Dart. A circular walk around these points could be interesting, although very arduous. Try to avoid flushing birds from nest sites.

For woodland species, visit either Okehampton Castle (NT property) on the West Okement, or the East Okement near the railway station. To reach the castle, start off from Okehampton centre along the Army-camp road, soon turning right with NT signposts. Try wooded slopes behind the castle ruins and the woodland edge. For East Okement, continue up the moor access road for $\frac{1}{2}$ mile (0.8 km), park near the railway and take the public footpath eastward along the valley. (**Note** A new bypass is planned this side of Okehampton.)

Calendar

Resident: Red Grouse, Carrion Crow, Raven on moors. Buzzard and Kestrel range over area. Dipper, Grey Wagtail and common woodland passerines in valley.

Dec-Feb: Generally very quiet. Possibly Woodcock in woods or a passing raptor on moors.

Mar-May: Wheatear and Ring Ouzel return from late Mar. Most other migrants from late Apr — Whinchat and breeding waders (Lapwing, Golden Plover, Dunlin, maybe Common Sandpiper, Snipe), passage plovers and maybe Dotterel (latter most likely May), passing Merlin or Hobby; in valley woods, Pied Flycatcher, Wood and other warblers; Redstarts arrive same period.

Jun-Jul: Breeding species as arrived above, active through Jun but most finished song and display by Jul when young being fed and post-breeding flocks start to form.

Aug-Nov: Summer breeding visitors departing. Possibly passing Peregrine or other raptors, e.g. Hen Harrier and Merlin (mostly Oct on). Chance of Snow Bunting near end. Passing plover flocks again.

(Map 14(v) and OS Map 202/201)

Burrator Reservoir and Woodlands

Habitat

Near Yelverton, on the southwest edge of Dartmoor, this 150-acre (60-ha) reservoir lies in a steep-sided valley, overlooked by scree-covered tors reaching over 300 m altitude. The lower slopes are tree-clad, mostly with Forestry Commission conifers; many trees are now reaching maturity, and large tracts are being felled. Small areas of broadleaf, mostly Beech remain, and many Rowan (Mountain Ash) trees are found, with bunches of scarlet fruits in autumn.

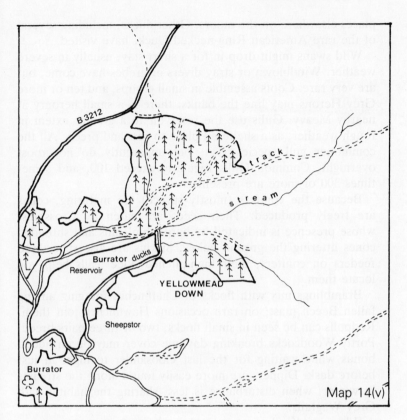

Map 14(v)

None of the Dartmoor reservoirs is very attractive to plant or animal life, being steep-sided and exposed. They lack muddy margins, unless water levels are exceptionally low, and peaty acidic water prevents many plants from growing. Burrator, however, has more varied habitat than other moor reservoirs, and also attracts more public visitors.

Species

Ducks are the main birds found on the lake in winter. Mallard (a few of which breed) and Teal often exceed 50, while Tufted and Pochard remain fairly constant at about 20 each, and Goldeneyes visit in twos and threes. Goosanders are the most interesting ducks seen regularly. This attractive sawbill has reached over 20 on occasions, though about half that number is more usual. The ratio of males to females has also been much higher than normal recently: often an equal proportion or even a majority of males, conspicuous with pinkish-white sides, occurs. Goosanders use the lake as a night roost, flighting in late on winter afternoons from scattered feeding places elsewhere on the moors. Other ducks, including several of the rare American Ring-necked Duck, have visited.

Wild swans might drop in for a short stay, usually in severe weather. Windblown or stray divers or grebes have come, but are very rare. Coots assemble in small groups, and ten or more Grey Herons may line the banks; there is a small heronry at nearby Meavy. Gulls use the reservoir to a greater extent in rough weather, as a sheltered place to rest and preen. All the commoner gull species visit, but apparently do not roost overnight. Common Gulls regularly exceed 100, and sometimes 300 or more are present.

Because the conifers (mostly spruce) are maturing, cones are freely produced. Their seeds are eaten by Crossbills, whose presence is indicated by hard 'chip' calls and shredded cones littering the ground below. Siskins are also specialised feeders on conifers; their high-pitched 'klee' calls help you locate them.

Bramblings mix with flocks of Chaffinches foraging among fallen Beech mast; on rare occasions Hawfinches join them. Redpolls can be seen in small flocks; two or three pairs breed. Portly Woodcocks breaking daytime cover may be an added bonus while waiting for the last Goosander to flight in just before dusk. Dippers are more easily found along the streams in winter, when disturbance is less, sharing the habitat with Grey Wagtails.

When wildfowl depart northward as spring commences, there is little to see on the reservoir save for a rare visit from the odd duck, late diver or grebe. Attention now centres on surrounding woodlands. By mid spring both Chiffchaffs and Willow Warblers are singing, the latter the commonest local warbler. Blackcaps and Garden Warblers breed, and up to ten pairs of Wood Warblers inhabit the tall deciduous trees. A population of some 20 pairs of Redstarts can be found nesting among dry-stone walls and ruined farm buildings. Cuckoos call, and Tree Pipits song flight from perches on small moorland-fringe trees. The sparrow-sized, scarce Lesser Spotted Woodpecker may be heard drumming; it is much less easy to see than the commoner Great Spotted or abundant Green Woodpecker.

Summer finds both Sparrowhawk and Buzzard soaring overhead, ever watchful for prey. Family parties of residents such as Coal Tit and Nuthatch may include Siskins and their broods. These roving flocks are soon joined by earlier-breeding summer visitors and their first-brood fledglings. Goldcrests can be abundant, especially if winters have been mild and their stocks have remained high. An irruption of Scandinavian-bred Crossbills may occur, when restless groups arrive.

After a long dry spell in early autumn, the area farthest from the dam may have exposed mud. Very small numbers of waders such as Common and Green Sandpipers may then pass through. Ring Ouzels, moving off the high moor, can be watched feeding on Rowan and Hawthorn berries. By late autumn, waterfowl, including the first Goosanders, are returning.

Timing

Human activity around perimeter roads and verges on fine weekends, even in winter, can be substantial; in late spring and summer, worse still. Fortunately, the vast majority of trippers do not wander far from their cars. The few anglers are not a real disturbance.

In winter, mornings or late afternoons are not only quieter, but there is also a better chance of seeing larger numbers of Goosanders.

Access

Leave A386 at Yelverton and take B3212 to Dousland, 1 mile (1.6 km) or so farther. At the village crossroads, follow signs to Burrator, taking a minor road. Roads surround the lake and there are several car-parking and pull-in spots. Permits are required if you wish to enter the reservoir banks; these are obtainable from an office near the dam. There is, however, no need to buy them as the water can be checked from the roadside (at least when leaves are off the trees). Best views are from the road running along the south (Sheepstor) side; about halfway along is probably best for Goosanders.

Surrounding woods and moorland have open access. Dogs must be kept on leads to prevent them chasing sheep. Tracks at the top end of the lake (farthest from dam) lead off left and right. The right hand is probably better. Along this track, among walls and ruined buildings, watch for Redstarts. Most other species present in the area can be seen along here.

Calendar

Resident: Grey Heron, Mallard, Sparrowhawk, Buzzard, Kestrel, Barn Owl (a pair may breed), Tawny Owl, Dipper, woodpeckers inc. a pair or two of Lesser Spotted, Grey Wagtail, Goldcrest, Coat Tit, Raven, Redpoll, Siskin, Crossbill (some years).

Dec-Feb: Possible appearance of a diver, grebe or wild swan. Teal, Pochard, Tufted Duck, Goldeneye, Goosander; singles of other ducks, especially in severe weather. Gulls inc. Common. Brambling.

Mar-May: By mid Mar, wildfowl have departed except stragglers or passage birds. Maybe a diver or grebe. Cuckoo, House Martin, Tree Pipit, Redstart, Wheatear, Garden Warbler, Blackcap, Wood Warbler, Chiffchaff, Willow Warbler and Spotted Flycatcher arrive to breed, most from late Apr but Spotted Flycatcher mid May.

Jun-Jul: Breeding species, possibly Crossbill influx in Jul.

Aug-Nov: If any exposed mud, waders include Green and Common Sandpipers. Sep-Oct, Ring Ouzel. Waterfowl begin to return by end Nov.

15 Plymbridge Wood

(Map 15 and
OS Map 201)

On the northern outskirts of Plymouth, this large mixed
(mainly broadleaved) woodland, through which the River
Plym flows, is owned by the NT. Adjoining the Trust land is a
conifer plantation owned by the Forestry Commission. The
NT part of the wood, particularly the lower section at
Plymbridge, is an extremely popular picnic and recreation area
for local residents. The woods, though dense in parts, have
open glades and border onto rough meadows. The mixture
of trees is great, with good numbers of oak and Beech
supporting many forms of wildlife. Other fruiting trees, such
as Chestnut, Hazel and Rowan, are abundant. Open glades
with bushy fringes, the river and its banks and damp meadows
ensure a range of specialised natural history subjects to study.

Commoner wild animals are present in very good numbers
and include those associated with water, such as Water Voles,
toads and frogs. Both Grass Snake and Adder are present.
Deer are best seen very early in the morning or at dusk. There
are several species of bat, and one of the authors has seen 23
species of butterfly here, including Purple Hairstreak, Silver-
washed Fritillary and White Admiral.

Habitat

This is a good area to 'learn your birds', as all the commoner
passerine families are represented. During winter the so-called
'winter thrushes' can be watched stripping Rowan and other
berries from trees, or searching among the understorey for
food. Woodcocks and Snipe may be flushed from wetter areas,
and white-rumped Bramblings identified among a flock of
Chaffinches feeding on fallen Beech mast. Among conifers
there is a possibility of wintering Crossbills. Along the
riverbanks, Redpolls and Siskins swing upside-down on Alder
trees, while on the river Dippers and Grey Wagtails are
commonly seen. The less turbulent stretches are favourite
haunts of Kingfishers, which with luck may be seen for more

Species

131

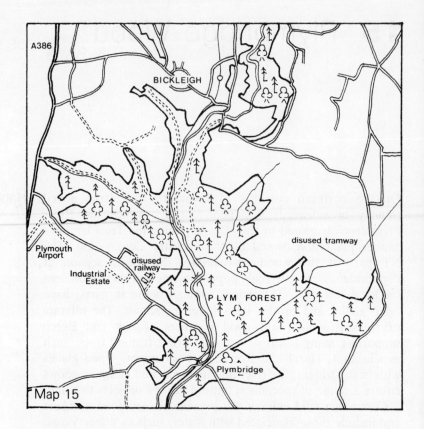

Map 15

than the usual few seconds of blue and orange blur. Spring brings the return to the wood of less common migrants, such as Garden and Wood Warblers. In summer, especially if an early start is made, breeding species can be watched feeding young, offering a further chance to widen your knowledge. At the end of summer, the phenomenon of irrupting Crossbills has resulted in flocks of these fascinating and colourful birds frequenting the woods. Autumn provides increasingly less hindered views of resident species, as deciduous trees reveal birds among them.

Timing

During summer all woodland birds become more secretive, as they have nests and families to protect. Early morning is by far the most productive time. Later in the day, places where many birds were seen earlier may now appear almost birdless save for the occasional call. Human disturbance can be chronic around the bridge area on fine summer days, but a mile (1.6

Dipper

km) or so upstream lies a wealth of interesting flora and fauna, relatively free of disturbance.

During winter, there is more or less constant daylight activity by birds, and far less disturbance by humans.

Access

At Estover roundabout, Plymouth (situated near Wrigley company factory), take the narrow, rather steep Plymbridge Road. At the bottom of the hill at the bridge area there are recognised parking spaces. Approaching from Plympton, you can pick up Plymbridge Road from either Plymouth Road or Glen Road. Your starting point for the walk will again be the bridge. From here, follow the woodland path or disused railway track, usually heading north. Length of walk from the bridge to Yelverton Halt is about 4 miles ($6^{1}2$ km).

Calendar

Resident: Sparrowhawk, Buzzard, Kestrel, Stock Dove, Tawny Owl, Lesser Spotted and other woodpeckers, Grey Wagtail, Dipper, Goldcrest, common woodland passerines, Raven.

Dec-Feb: Grey Heron, Woodcock, Snipe, Kingfisher, winter thrushes, Brambling, Siskin, Redpoll, possibly Crossbills.

Mar-May: Late Apr, first migrant Cuckoos, possibly Tree Pipits; Garden Warbler, Blackcap, Whitethroat, Wood Warbler and Redstart returning.

Jun-Jul: Possibly Nightjar towards the moors; maybe irrupting Crossbills end Jul.

Aug-Nov: Maybe Kingfisher; Redwings and Fieldfares return from Oct; feeding parties of small passerines (mixed species) move through woods early on.

16 Plymouth Area

(Map 16 and
OS Map 201)

Plymouth city lies on the Devon/Cornwall border, on the confluence of four rivers: Lynher, Tamar, Tavy and Plym, all discharging into Plymouth Sound. The city's waterfront has a rocky foreshore, enclosed in a large bay (the Sound), protected from all but roughest seas by a breakwater across the bay mouth; at several points along the waterfront are sewage outfalls. Tiny Drake's Island is situated in the Sound, surrounded by shallowly submerged rocks covered in seaweed. Trawlers unload fish catches at several points, main quays being the Barbican and Millbay.

On the coastline at the eastern side of the bay, at Jennycliff, rocky cliffs and brakes reach a height of some 90 m. The bay here is sheltered from north and east winds. The Tamar and Tavy unite at their mouths, forming extensive mudflats, and are less disturbed than Plym estuary on the city's eastern boundaries.

Habitat

The coastal areas produce most of the interesting and rare birds. Every winter, through to early spring, one or two divers and grebes are found in the bay. After prolonged gales or in very harsh icy conditions, numbers and variety often increase as sheltering birds arrive. Up to ten or more divers (mostly Great Northern) and similar numbers of grebes appear. Normally Slavonian is the most regular grebe, with one or two present, but cold-weather influxes are mostly of Great Crested and up to three or four Red-necked Grebes; favourite areas are around Jennycliff and Drake's Island, especially Jennycliff in easterlies and the lee of the island in westerlies. During very mild winters the bay is virtually ignored by these species, but occasional sightings are made of Eider, Common Scoter and Long-tailed Duck, which may stay for weeks.

Severe weather conditions do not really influence the occurrence of uncommon gull species, for which Plymouth has

Species

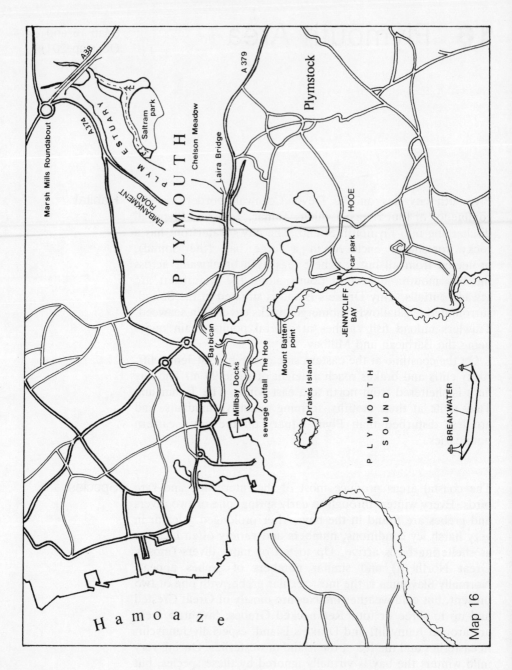

Map 16

an enviable record. Thousands of gulls gather throughout the area in winter. One of the best places to watch them is at the sewer off West Hoe, where they scavenge for edible waste. The fish quays, especially when trawlers are offloading, attract them like magnets. Among their swirling, noisy hordes may be one or two of special interest. Patience and expertise have resulted in many sightings of uncommon, and a few rare, kinds being made. Mediterranean, Little, Iceland and Glaucous Gulls are now seen annually, the two latter mostly between late winter and early spring. Within the last few seasons, expert birders have been finding the once unexpected, exceptionally difficult-to-identify, Ring-billed Gull; these are usually among flocks of migrant Common Gulls, from late winter. Other American rarities found have been Franklin's and Kumlien's Gulls.

Few waders are able to inhabit the bay's narrow, rocky shoreline. Oystercatchers commonly feed on limpet-strewn rocks, accompanied by Turnstones and a few Purple Sandpipers, and small parties of Whimbrels are brief spring visitors.

Among the bay's first spring migrants are Sandwich Terns, the most numerous tern species here. Terns use the bay in small numbers, pausing to rest and feed on both migrations. Spring sightings of other terns are unpredictable, usually only in ones and twos. On return passage Sandwich are often first to arrive again, now accompanied by their still semi-dependent juveniles. Common Terns are usually next. Arctic, mostly juveniles, are latest to arrive (as in spring); numbers are always higher than in spring. Black Terns are seen in ones and twos, while Roseate and Little are very irregular.

The Plym estuary, open to frequent disturbance, does not regularly attract interesting waders or ducks. Teals are present in very small numbers; other ducks, perhaps a few Wigeons or one or two Goldeneyes, are only spasmodic visitors. Mallards and Shelducks, which both breed, are the commonest wildfowl, the former reaching 100 at times outside the breeding season. Black-tailed Godwits can reach 30 or 40, and flocks of several hundred Golden Plovers may visit. Dunlin flocks may exceed 1,000. Small numbers of Common Sandpipers and Greenshanks pass through in autumn and one or two often overwinter, but there is a very poor autumn passage of the more interesting waders; other common species overwinter in unremarkable figures. Grey Herons and Kingfishers, both breeding locally, are resident.

The Plym is very good for gulls, many using it to loaf during the day when the tide is out. In winter over 1,000 Great Black-backed Gulls may assemble. Several hundred Common Gulls may include a Ring-billed Gull, this being a favourite haunt. Glaucous, Iceland and Mediterranean Gulls are all relatively frequent visitors, usually singly.

The wide Tamar-Tavy estuary is more difficult to watch, but many of its birds are similar. Ducks are more numerous, with a few Goldeneyes, Tufted and Pochards annual. Occasional grebes visit, usually Slavonian or Great Crested, more rarely Black-necked or Red-necked. Sometimes a small group of Avocets breaks away from the upper Tamar population, and may stay for much of the winter. One or two Spotted Redshanks, Greenshanks and Common Sandpipers regularly overwinter. Every winter, at irregular intervals, a Peregrine spends time hunting in the area, concentrating over the estuaries.

Timing

Tides are of little consequence if checking the bay and waterfront, but an outgoing tide is essential for discharging sewers. Trawlers unloading in winter attract clouds of gulls to the fish quays. Otherwise, times of day are normally unimportant in the bay. Low winter sunlight, however, can make a check of the main sewers very difficult; an overcast day with good but flat light is ideal. Prolonged northerly winds, especially from midwinter onwards, often produce Glaucous Gulls. Gale-force southerly winds in early autumn can cause numbers of terns to shelter in the bay, perhaps accompanied by Little Gulls.

To check the estuaries for waders, it is essential that mud is exposed. The main channels always flow, attracting ducks or grebes. The head of the Plym is less disturbed, though boating and bait-digging are year-round activities. Gulls in particular gather here, where they bathe and preen in fresh river water when the tide is out. Waders on the Plym cluster in the same upper area when an incoming tide pushes them up the estuary; it is also a good time to check just as the tide is ebbing, as birds are again forced to congregate in a restricted space. There are no central high-tide roosts on either estuary. Severe weather can increase all populations.

Access

The seafront is well signposted throughout the city centre, from which it is less than $\frac{1}{2}$ mile (0.8 km). Barbican fish quay is a tourist spot. Apart from gulls, occasional divers, grebes or seaducks venture into this area, where very close views can be obtained. Millbay docks is also well signposted; though privately owned, access is allowed without permit. Several sewage outlets can be watched for gulls. The best and largest, at the west end of the Hoe, is only some 200 m offshore; it is easily watched from a public walkway off the road, where it bends down towards nearby Millbay, and is also a good place to check the sea for divers and grebes around Drake's Island.

To reach Jennycliff from Plymouth city take A379 to Plymstock, where you take the Hooe road (pronounced 'who', a southeastern outlier of Plymouth, not to be confused with the Hoe). Hooe adjoins Jennycliff, where there is a large car park. From here, a scan of the sea takes in the whole eastern part of the Sound. Divers, grebes and seaducks can often be best seen from here.

Plym estuary is very accessible, easily watched, and can be checked from both sides. Immediately across Laira bridge on A379, in Plymstock direction, is a sharp left-hand turn marked to Saltram. There are parking places along the entrance to the estuary, allowing you to walk its entire length, taking in the edge of the NT wood at Saltram. Kingfishers may be seen sitting on branches overhanging the estuary, or a Lesser Spotted Woodpecker among the trees if you are very lucky. Sunlight is always at your back, and the surroundings are more pleasant than on the opposite bank. If checking from the Embankment side, there are several car pull-in spots, and a pavement runs along its length.

To reach the Tavy estuary at Warren Point, take A38 to St Budeaux then the Budshead road on your left. Walk between factories on an industrial estate, along public footpaths to the point area. Access at Warleigh Point, opposite across the creek, is restricted.

Calendar

Resident: Mallard, Shelduck, Sparrowhawk, Buzzard, Stock Dove, Lesser Spotted Woodpecker, Kingfisher, Grey Wagtail, Stonechat, Raven.

Dec-Feb: (Waterfront and Sound) Occasional Black-throated Divers, especially towards end of period, Great Northern annually, Red-throated rarely; all grebe species occasionally, Slavonian most frequent; occasional seaducks. Gulls, inc. rarer species. (Estuaries) Apart from gulls, also Goldeneye, Pochard, Tufted Duck, Goosander and Red-breasted Merganser, probably Peregrine, Golden Plover, Black-tailed

Godwit, possible Avocets on Tavy. Black Redstart in coastal gardens.

Mar-May: All above seabird species may be present in gradually reducing numbers, except Fulmars arriving and Black-throated Diver possible through early part of period; waders and ducks depart from early Mar. Uncommon gulls still pass through in Mar-early Apr, particularly Iceland and Ring-billed. Sandwich Terns from end Mar. Chiffchaff and Wheatear from mid Mar. Early Apr on, in favourable conditions, passerine migrants at Jennycliff. Common Tern may pass. Breeding summer visitors arrive in woods, where Blackcap and Chiffchaff might have overwintered.

Jun-Jul: Mostly only breeding species.

Aug-Nov: Mostly waders reappear on estuaries early Aug onwards, gradually increasing in number and variety. Possible Osprey Aug or Sep on Tavy. Terns reappear in the bay: Sandwich from early Aug, Common a little later, Arctic and Black from Sep. Passerine migrants at Jennycliff. Black Redstarts from Oct. Uncommon gulls, especially Little and Mediterranean, can occur throughout period.

17 St John's and Millbrook Lakes, Lynher and Tamar Estuaries: General Introduction

Habitat

This complex of tidal waterways is situated at the extreme southeast of Cornwall. All are interconnected by the wide, ill-defined Hamoaze channel, between Torpoint on the Cornish bank and Devonport naval dockyards on the east bank. The Devon side of the Tamar-Tavy confluence is described under Plymouth. All sites form mudflats at low tide, with St John's Lake nearest to the sea, directly linked to Plymouth Sound. Both St John's and the Lynher are wide and difficult to observe thoroughly.

All these sites are essentially interesting for waders and waterfowl in autumn and, particularly, winter, with relatively little bird activity in summer. Together they form the region's most important estuary habitat after the Exe.

Main Birdwatching Zones

As these sites are close together, it is usual for birdwatchers to check several of them in one day. Each site has its own interest: ease of viewing, particular species expected, etc. We have split them into three headings: *St John's Lake and Millbrook Lake; The Lynher; The Tamar.*

St John's Lake and Millbrook Lake

(Map 17(i))

Habitat

St John's Lake is a large area of open water and mudflats, forming a semi-sheltered basin between Plymouth Sound and river estuaries upstream; Millbrook Lake is an estuary backwater providing further shelter from the wind.

141

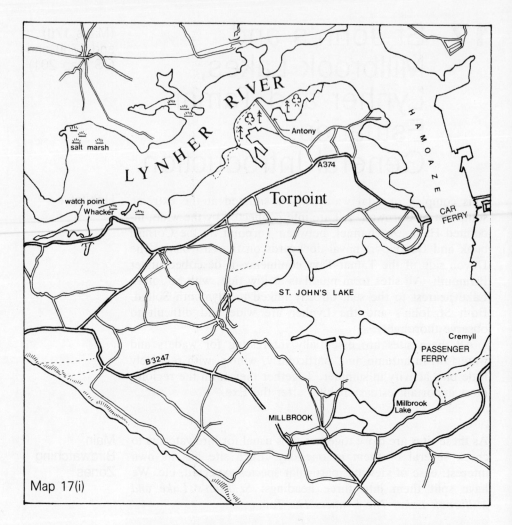

LYNHER RIVER

salt marsh

Antony

HAMOAZE

A374

watch point
Whacker

Torpoint

CAR
FERRY

ST. JOHN'S LAKE

Cremyll
PASSENGER
FERRY

B 3247

Millbrook
Lake

MILLBROOK

Map 17(i)

Species

Because of the proximity of the sea, St John's Lake tends to harbour more marine species, perhaps when blown in by rough weather, while Millbrook is used more by strictly estuarine birds and marsh birds. Divers are annual and regular, mostly Great Northern in ones and twos; single Black-throated may also occur, but Red-throated are very irregular. The most common grebe is the Little, but small numbers of Slavonian and Great Crested are also seen. Mute Swans number over 50 in autumn, more than anywhere else in Cornwall, although only a pair or two breed locally. Parties of Brent Geese, seen in most winters, rarely exceed ten. Shelducks are scattered across the mudflats, 200-300 each winter. The most numerous dabbling duck is the Wigeon: the

rafts of up to 5,000 which occur here are by far the largest in
the county; the flock may move to the Lynher if disturbed.
200-300 Teals winter, and first-class views can be obtained of
this tiny duck, along with other estuary birds, at Millbrook. A
wide range of other ducks in small numbers, including less
common visitors such as Velvet Scoter and Long-tailed Duck,
is noted annually.

Outside the breeding season, Peregrines are occasional lone
visitors. Waders are well represented, with an interesting
spread of species. Very small numbers of Little Stints and
Curlew Sandpipers normally visit Millbrook in autumn.
Turnstones are common, with groups totalling 100 or so; good
views are obtained beside roads at Torpoint. Both godwit
species are seen, usually more Black-tailed, but both normally
only attaining 50-60. Flocks of about 300 Redshanks and
Knots can also be expected. Whimbrels, passing northward in
spring, may rest for a day or so; they are seen again in autumn
on their return journey, numbers being highly variable but
averaging ten. Spotted Redshanks, Greenshanks, Green and
Common Sandpipers all use the area, chiefly in autumn,
although every year a couple of each elect to see winter
through. Millbrook is popular with them.

Among Black-headed and Common Gulls, one or two
Mediterranean Gulls may be present, although they are hard
to pick out, especially in immature plumages. Even more
difficult to identify are the three or four Ring-billed Gulls now
reported here. Little Gulls are more obvious visitors in ones
and twos, largely in autumn or early winter, juveniles being
most usual. Terns frequently feed here, all the British sea
terns being noted most years in spring and/or autumn. Roseate
and Little are seen the least, mostly in autumn. Higher tern
numbers are expected in autumn, but not usually over ten of
any single species; Sandwich and Common are most numerous, with a scattering of Arctic, mostly juveniles, and an
occasional Black Tern, which favours sheltered areas such as
Millbrook. Auks drift in from the Sound, usually in late winter
when they begin to come closer to shore, instinctively, at the
start of their breeding cycle.

(Map 17(i)) # The Lynher

Habitat

This estuary is wide at its mouth into the Hamoaze, narrowing sharply farther upstream near Antony village. There is a small saltmarsh on the opposite bank to Antony, together with several narrow creeks. The main river, forming a long, narrow tidal creek above here, itself splits into three: the first creek ends at Polbathic, the second at Tideford, and the third near Trematon, just outside Saltash. All these creeks have saltmarsh, mostly towards their heads, little visited by birdwatchers.

Species

In the main estuary in winter, small numbers of divers and grebes, including an occasional Red-necked, may be seen; possibly the same birds move up from St John's Lake. Ducks certainly move from site to site, notably Wigeon flocks, and at times of disturbance there may be wholesale interchange between sites. Pintails, however, are the Lynher's speciality; the flock, usually located around the main estuary saltmarsh, reaches about 50 birds. Occasionally a Spoonbill favours this area, and may remain through winter. Migrating Spotted Redshanks and Greenshanks find the creeks ideal, and may overwinter in above-normal numbers, the former reaching ten or more. Green and Common Sandpipers are also passage migrants which spend winter here in ones and twos. Recently a Forster's Tern visited from America, only the second ever British record. Commoner species are the same as at adjoining St John's Lake, but generally in lower numbers.

(Map 17(ii)) # The Tamar

Habitat

This estuary forms the boundary between Devon and Cornwall. From the Tamar road bridge upstream to Kingsmill creek is a wide area of rather unproductive mudflats. From Landulph on the Cornish side, the estuary becomes narrower, but more productive. It is mostly flanked by pasture farmland, and groups of trees meet near the water's edge.

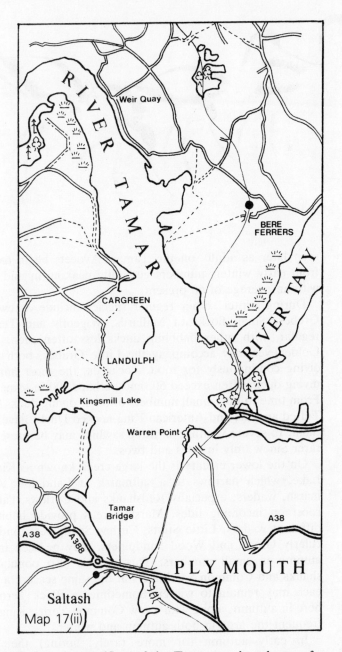

Map 17(ii)

Above all else, the mudflats of the Tamar are best known for that graceful wader the Avocet, adopted and made famous by the RSPB as their national emblem. Evidence exists linking at least some Tamar birds with those raised on RSPB reserves: some chicks marked with coloured plastic leg-rings have been

Species

Avocets

seen later as adults on the Tamar. Avocets begin to arrive from early winter, numbers generally peaking in mid season with an average of 60 present.

During winter, other regular species include a few Little Grebes. Small flocks of Mallards, Wigeons and Teals are regular, with other dabbling ducks less often seen. A few Goldeneyes may accompany the Little Grebes, both species diving continuously for food. Pochards, the most numerous diving duck, often exceed 50, and perhaps 100 in some years. From time to time small numbers of other diving ducks such as Tufted appear, and American Ring-necked Ducks have joined them. In severe weather all three sawbills may be present, the rarer Smew only in ones and twos.

On the lower estuary is the large creek known as Kingsmill Lake, which narrows to a saltmarsh at Landulph. At this marsh, waders, especially Redshanks and Curlews, gather to roost on incoming tides. Marshy areas provide habitat for different waders: Little Stints, Curlew Sandpipers, and particularly Green and Wood Sandpipers, may be seen in early autumn in small numbers. This area is also popular with shanks and Common Sandpipers at the same season; a few of each may remain to winter. Sometimes a Black Tern feeds here in autumn, along with a few Common Terns. Kingfishers frequent the area in both autumn and winter.

In early autumn (or more rarely, spring) the Tamar sometimes plays host to an Osprey. This exciting raptor may establish temporary residence for a couple of weeks during autumn, before again setting off southward. Outside the breeding season, a Peregrine might be watched flashing over the mud pursuing a luckless wader.

The severity of winter weather will influence variety and numbers of species: the harder the weather, the greater the numbers. Any daylight hours are suitable, but it will depend whether a high or low tide is required. For example, for watching waders across the mudflats the tide must be out, as there are no easily checked roosting points. Most waders either drop into saltmarshes at high tide, where they are impossible to see, or move away to inaccessible roosts. When the tide is out, main deepwater channels remain at all sites, used by divers, grebes and ducks.

Wader roosts at St John's Lake are also scattered and difficult to observe. Areas around Millbrook are utilised but suffer from disturbance by dogs and the public, so are not reliable.

Some shooting takes place on all sites, which disrupts normal flock behaviour, especially on the Lynher and St John's Lake.

Timing
(all sites)

From Saltash, the *Tamar* is checked by taking A388, turning right to Landulph. Park near the church, then walk left along a narrow tarmac road until you reach a wooden gate and stile. This leads through a small rough pasture meadow, with a small marshy area to your right (which may contain interesting waders). This public path then leads to an embankment, from where you check Kingsmill Lake area. If the tide is out (preferably now incoming), you can walk along the beach to a point which brings you level with the marshy area in the field. From here, check the saltmarsh where waders gather at its edges before dispersing at high tide. On higher tides you can, with care, walk along the concrete embankment.

The same turn off A388 for Landulph takes you to Cargreen for Avocets, this being one of their favourite feeding sites. You are likely to see at least part of the flock, if not all. Views are reasonably close and they can be seen from your car, as there are parking spaces near the waterfront.

The Lynher is reached from Torpoint by A374 to about 1 mile (1.6 km) past Antony to a well-signposted picnic area and parking place at Whacker Creek. Here you are opposite the saltmarsh and overlooking the best part of the estuary for birds. A telescope is essential, especially when checking birds on the opposite shore (where there are no public access points). Higher creeks are not easily checked; several roads pass near their edges at various points, where parking is very

Access
(all sites)

difficult and vision restricted by tree growth. Stretches are probably best tackled on foot.

St John's Lake is checked from Torpoint where there are roads along the waterfront. Many birds congregate here, though mostly in mid channel, or along the relatively undisturbed opposite shore, when a telescope will be necessary. The B3247 is taken to Millbrook village, which has waterside roads throughout its length.

Calendar (all sites)

Resident: Cormorant, Grey Heron, Shelduck.

Dec-Feb: Divers, particularly Great Northern; commoner grebes, at intervals. Possible wintering Spoonbill, occasional Brent Geese, Wigeon, small numbers of all dabbling ducks, also diving and seaducks at times. Peregrine, Turnstone, Knot, Spotted Redshank, Greenshank, Green Sandpiper, Common Sandpiper, Black-tailed Godwit, Bar-tailed Godwit; Avocets peak late Dec; possible Mediterranean Gull.

Mar-May: Most of above depart from early Mar. By Apr first migrants are arriving, inc. a trickle of returning waders, notably Whimbrel. Sandwich and a few Common Terns. Possible Osprey.

Jun-Jul: Very little other than odd late spring or early autumn passage migrants. Resident species.

Aug-Nov: Early on, possible Osprey. First returning commoner waders may be in summer plumage, joined by Little Stint, Curlew Sandpiper, Green Sandpiper, Wood Sandpiper, Spotted Redshank, Greenshank; possibility of uncommon or rare waders from Europe or America; Avocets return from late Nov. Terns pass through, mostly Sandwich and Common, in larger numbers Aug-Sep with Arctic from mid Sep to mid Oct. Possible Little, Mediterranean and other uncommon or rare gulls.

18 Rame Head, Whitesand Bay and Looe

(Maps 18(i)-18(iii) and OS Map 201)

On the southeast coast of Cornwall, Rame faces south, the **Habitat** closest mainland point to Eddystone Lighthouse, 6 miles ($9\frac{1}{2}$ km) seaward. Rame peninsula includes Penlee Point, at the western entrance to Plymouth Sound. West of Rame sweeps wide Whitesand Bay, terminating in narrow, steep-sided Looe estuary mouth. Along the steeply sloping coastline, gorse and Bracken brakes are interspersed with Blackthorn, small clumps of trees and small rough grazing fields. Flatter fields above are used for arable farming. The area around Rame Church and Farm affords more shelter, with groups of trees, mostly Sycamore, a few gardens, and hedgerows. A small road runs from the church to an old fortification above Penlee Point, overgrown with brambles and Ash trees. Habitat along this road is varied, with a wide, dense copse, mainly Blackthorn, providing shelter and cover. Alongside this lie demolished buildings, where wild flowers grow, including various umbellifers; teazels and brambles have also colonised. Adders are common. Fallow Deer from Mount Edgecumbe park may be seen from the road between the church and Penlee fort, especially in autumn and winter.

The scenic coast road from Rame to Looe, following the escarpment edge overlooking the coastline, affords panoramic views. The air in spring can be heavily scented by countless gorse flowers.

The chief interest for birdwatchers visiting Rame will probably **Species** be spring and autumn migrants. Two distinct groups occur. The first is landbirds, mostly small passerines, such as Swallows and warblers; raptors, a harrier perhaps, occasionally pass through, and Honey Buzzard has been seen. The second group is seabirds. Rame formerly received scant attention from seawatchers; recent years have witnessed better coverage, producing for instance a spring Long-tailed Skua,

149

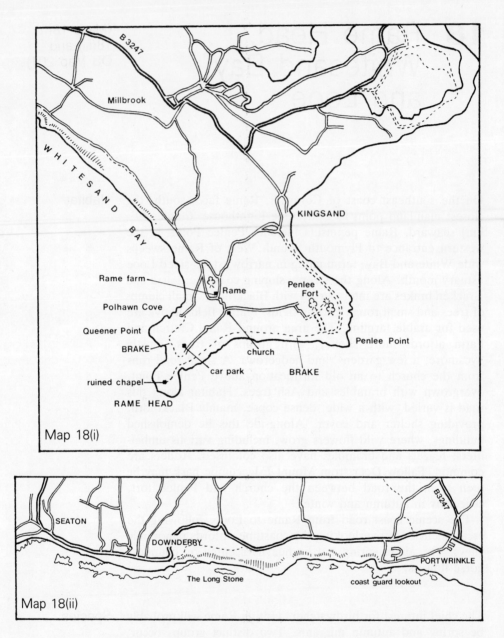

Map 18(i)

Map 18(ii)

and showing that a variety of seabirds occurs in both seasons, although in smaller numbers, usually, than at some southwest seawatching venues.

Resident species are mostly unremarkable, with one exception. Dartford Warblers have recently been discovered.

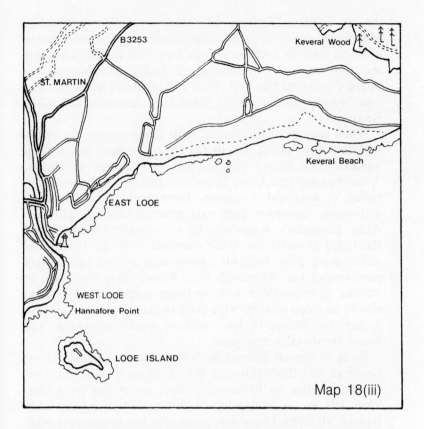

B 3253

Keveral Wood

ST. MARTIN

Keveral Beach

EAST LOOE

WEST LOOE

Hannafore Point

LOOE ISLAND

Map 18(iii)

Extremely elusive, four or five pairs may be found (with difficulty) skulking among low, scrubby bushes such as gorse, anywhere between Tregantle and Penlee.

Most passerine migrants do not linger on exposed heathland, quickly working towards sheltered areas. Trees and hedgerows around the church and farm are favourite places, as are hedges and scattered groups of small trees around Polhawn Cove on the west side of the headland. Small fields among or near the brakes form yet another habitat. Resident Skylarks and Meadow Pipits in the fields are joined by migrant flocks of the same species. Also sharing this habitat are common migrants, including Tree Pipits, Yellow Wagtails and Wheatears. Occasionally Turtle Doves are seen, often in cereal fields, among foraging feral pigeons. Linnets are resident, increased in autumn by migrants; a few less common finches or buntings, such as Brambling or Snow Bunting, may join them. Trees and bushes provide vital food and shelter, even if only for a few hours during early morning for overnight migrants. More common species, such as Blackcap, Whitethroat, Garden Warbler, Chiffchaff and Willow Warbler, sometimes occur in quite large numbers, and uncommon warblers such as Melodious may visit with them. Goldcrests are most numerous in autumn, as always outnumbering the brightly coloured Firecrest. Pied and Spotted Flycatchers also visit in both seasons, as do Whinchats, Redstarts and Black Redstarts.

When seawatching in spring, most likely species are Black-throated and Great Northern Divers, sometimes several hundred Manx Shearwaters and perhaps hundreds of Gannets. A few Pomarine or Arctic Skuas occasionally coast eastward in spring, or westward in autumn. Terns, particularly Sandwich, with some Common, pass east towards breeding grounds. Auks, particularly Razorbills, fly to and fro. Whimbrels and Bar-tailed Godwits also coast eastward in flocks, the former often giving their diagnostic, seven-note contact call as they pass; one or two Whimbrels often winter along this coast. In autumn all species can occur in larger numbers. Great Skuas should be more evident, with more seaducks such as Common Scoter; the chance of less common species is greater; and Sooty Shearwaters may pass.

Birds of special interest in Whitesand Bay include Great Northern and Black-throated Divers, often in small scattered groups totalling up to ten at a time, sometimes twice that. From late winter into spring Black-throated Divers gradually replace wintering Great Northerns; the few late-staying birds may attain summer plumage. Black-necked, Slavonian, Red-necked and Great Crested Grebes may visit in winter, usually in ones and twos, Slavonian most frequently. Seaducks such as Eiders and Common Scoters visit in small groups, possibly attracting a Velvet Scoter.

On Looe beach in winter you can expect good views of Grey Plovers, Turnstones and Purple Sandpipers; search through rocky areas, as they usually gather in small flocks, camouflaged among seaweed. In the narrow estuary, especially opposite Looe railway station, gulls assemble in large numbers, including many hundreds of Common Gulls, particularly in late winter and early spring when they accompany migrant Lesser Black-backs; check among them for unusual gulls, such as Glaucous and, less frequently, Iceland. Higher up the estuary, less common overwintering waders may be found along marshy fringes. These might include Spotted Redshank, Greenshank, Green and Common Sandpipers. This area is also popular with wintering Kingfishers. In the hilltop trees, across the estuary from the railway station, is a heronry.

Activity is visible from the station in early spring, before leaves fully clothe the trees.

The whole area is heavily used by tourists in summer. Morning visits to Rame area in spring or autumn, especially in southerly or southeast winds during fall conditions, will almost certainly give you interesting species among commoner migrant birds. You could try any time of day, in any winds, in migration seasons.

    Seawatching in spring or autumn could be attempted in similar conditions to those for passerine fall arrivals, and in the same winds. Provided there is visibility of at least 1 mile (1.6 km), winds from south and west also give good results; neither direction has to be strong to produce birds. Southwest gales have never given worthwhile results. Onshore winds induce birds to fly close to shore. As shelter is lacking, waterproof clothing should be taken on seawatches.

Timing

From Torpoint, for Rame, take A374 to Antony. Take B3247 to Tregantle, turning right onto the coast road to Rame. Along this route check Whitesand Bay and seaward brakes; there are frequent pull-ins. There is a car park at Rame. Public footpaths along the coastline allow you to cover all the best bird spots around Rame. From the car park you can follow the coast path to Penlee, or out to the headland. Another good route is to Polhawn, where bushes surrounding the old fort (now private) can be overlooked from the footpath. Following the above track will bring you back to Rame Farm and Church. The narrow road from the church towards Penlee and the overgrown fort should be checked for migrants. A path leads from the fort to connect with the coastal track at Penlee. From Tregantle, continue west along B3247 coast road to Portwrinkle; you can detour down to the village waterfront, where divers or grebes may be offshore. The main road is high above the sea, and a telescope is essential for checking waterbirds.

    The next stop westward is Downderry, with the possibility of seeing any of the bay species. Drive through to adjoining Seaton. Beside the beach is a car park, adjacent to which are Alder trees and Sallows standing by a stream; check these for wintering Blackcaps, Chiffchaffs or Firecrests, or for passing migrants. Walk from the car park up the hill on your left. From this road look seaward through groups of pines; watch in

Access

particular for Great Northern and Black-throated Divers, which gather in groups here.

Drive up this same hill, continuing along it before joining B3253 for Looe. After checking the estuary and gulls in Looe harbour, proceed to the seafront at West Looe, where parking on the waterfront road is allowed. Check the whole seashore and bay along this road, to where it becomes a dead end. Divers and grebes often shelter from winds in the lee of Looe Island, and can be seen from the road.

For seawatching from Rame Head, find what shelter you can among low rocks. Watch from near the bottom of the slope, directly in line with the old chapel at the tip of the headland.

Calendar

Resident: Cormorant, Grey Heron, Shelduck, Sparrowhawk, Buzzard, Grey Wagtail, Dartford Warbler, Stonechat, Cirl Bunting (a few scattered pairs), Raven.

Dec-Feb: Mostly Black-throated and Great Northern Divers, Slavonian and Great Crested Grebes, occasional Black-necked and Red-necked; Little Grebe Looe estuary. Eider, Common Scoter, occasional Velvet Scoter, Grey Plover, Turnstone, Purple Sandpiper, possible Spotted Redshank, Greenshank, Green and Common Sandpipers. Possible Glaucous, Iceland, or Mediterranean Gulls.

Mar-May: More Black-throated than Great Northern Divers, many fewer of each late in period; declining chance of grebes after mid Apr. Glaucous or Iceland Gull possible throughout period. Terns, especially Sandwich, pass throughout, peak Apr when other terns coast by. Shearwaters (Manx), skuas, Whimbrel, godwits, all from Apr on. First migrant passerines mid-late Mar, e.g. Black Redstart, Chiffchaff, Wheatear; wider range of migrants later spring inc. possible raptors (e.g. Hobby), hirundines, wagtails, pipits, warblers, flycatchers and Redstart.

Jun-Jul: Crowds of holidaymakers. Mostly resident and breeding birds, inc. Fulmar, Cuckoo, Grasshopper Warbler, Blackcap, Whitethroat, Willow Warbler, Chiffchaff, Goldcrest, Spotted Flycatcher.

Aug-Nov: Return passage of seabirds, birds of prey and passerines from early Aug. Most seabirds, e.g. shearwaters,

skuas, terns, late Aug-Oct. Harriers or Merlin seen mostly mid
Sep-Oct. Passerine movement peaks same months.

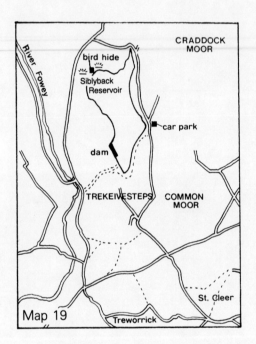

Map 19

19 Siblyback Reservoir (Map 19 and OS Map 201)

Habitat

A 140-acre (57-ha) reservoir on the southeast edge of Bodmin Moor. The flooded valley is set among moorland and rough sheep pasture. The northern shore is shallow, with mud exposed as water levels drop, becoming extensive in dry autumns. Along this perimeter are narrow areas of marshy vegetation, mostly rank grasses, Bracken and bramble. As in all moorland reservoirs, the water is acidic, preventing a wider range of plants from growing. As the area is exposed, tall trees do not grow, but there are scattered Sallows, Hawthorns and Rowans.

Trout are the main fish stocked, the lake being extremely popular with anglers. Windsurfers and small sailing craft also use it.

Species

The lake is noted chiefly for autumn waders and winter wildfowl, including some scarcer species. During winter one of the most numerous birds is probably Mallard, usually 100 or so; a few breed. Coots reach 150 in most winters, with a few breeding pairs. Smews are rare visitors to Britain, little seen in the Southwest, where they are only casual visitors in severe cold. Siblyback is an exception: three to five, mostly brownheads, are annual visitors. Surprisingly, other ducks are rather few, even diving ducks. Pochards may number 30, and Tufted half that. Goosanders, mostly brownheads, are annual in twos and threes, and one or two Goldeneyes seen regularly are also typically brownheads. Other diving ducks, usually singles, visit occasionally. The few dabbling ducks include an average of 25 Teals, perhaps 150 Wigeons, and others infrequently. Grebes have included Red-necked, and equally unexpectedly both Great Northern and Black-throated Divers have appeared here — well inland. Small parties of Bewick's Swans very occasionally visit, as do White-fronted Geese, arrivals usually coinciding with hard weather elsewhere.

157

Because exposed mud cannot usually be found in winter, when water level is higher, most waders are then absent, but 100 or more Snipe frequent boggy margins and field edges, accompanied regularly by one or two Jack Snipe. Flocks of Golden Plovers and Lapwings crowd nearby fields, both often exceeding 1,000. Raptors wintering on the moor visit the area, no doubt attracted by the plovers; Peregrine, Merlin and Hen Harrier are regular, and a Red Kite was once seen.

As spring approaches, the avian population declines and changes. There are far fewer wildfowl, although Cormorants and Grey Herons still visit. Hirundines, especially Sand and House Martins, pause on passage, often in large feeding flocks, while Swifts scream and fly over the water in hundreds. A marsh tern, usually Black, could appear in summer plumage, or some other unexpected visitor may occur.

An ornithologically quiet summer gives way to returning migrant waders; mudflats now exposed attract them to stop. Numbers are never large, but apart from regular migrants, less common (e.g. Temminck's Stint and Red-necked Phalarope, easterly species seen very little in our region), and even rare vagrants such as Wilson's Phalarope are found each year. More routine annual visitors include Ringed Plovers, Little Stints, Dunlins, Curlew Sandpipers, Ruffs, Spotted Redshanks, Redshanks, Green Sandpipers, Wood Sandpipers, Common Sandpipers, Curlews. Little Gulls, usually first-winter birds with blackish 'W' markings across the wings, pass through in ones and twos. Black Terns, in dowdy grey-brown autumn plumage, also in very small numbers, sometimes include a flock of six or more.

Timing

Not critical, although mornings and evenings should have less human disturbance. Hard winter weather may bring further interesting species.

Access

From A38 in Liskeard, take A390 from the town centre to the outer edge of town. Branch off onto B3254 (where signposted to Siblyback Lake) for about 1 mile (1.6 km). Leave the B road and take the road to St Cleer (also signposted for Siblyback). Just past the village turn right. At the road junction, about 1 mile (1.6 km) on, take the minor road opposite which leads to the lake (again signposted). From the large car park you can scan over the lake. You can walk to the dam, continuing along this path on the opposite shore.

Alternatively, walk past dinghies on the lower edge of the car park, over a stile, and continue around this boundary. Both routes lead to the shallower north end, which has difficult terrain and areas of soft mud, requiring wellington boots. A bird hide has been erected by SWWA in this vicinity.

Windsurfers and boats are officially restricted from entry to the shallow end, but fishermen are not. Most birdwatchers approach this area, most used by ducks and waders, from the car park side. Entry permits can be obtained from the warden.

Resident: Little Grebe, Coot.   Calendar

Dec-Feb: Little Grebe; geese, probably White-fronted, and wild swans in hard weather. Teal, Wigeon, Pochard, Tufted, Goldeneye, Smew, Goosander, occasional other dabbling and diving ducks, possibly a 'sea' grebe or diver. Maybe wintering raptors from moors. Snipe and Jack Snipe. In surrounding fields, Golden Plover and Lapwing. Gulls, mainly Black-headed.

Mar-May: Winter visitors mainly depart by end Mar. Perhaps a stray passage diver, grebe or duck. Late Apr and especially May, perhaps a marsh tern, hirundines, Swifts.

Jun-Jul: Breeding species, inc. Sedge Warbler (a few pairs).

Aug-Nov: Waders arrive from early Aug on, peak late Aug and Sep. Little Gull and Black Tern from late Aug. Golden Plovers begin arrival from mid Sep. Waterfowl return from mid Nov.

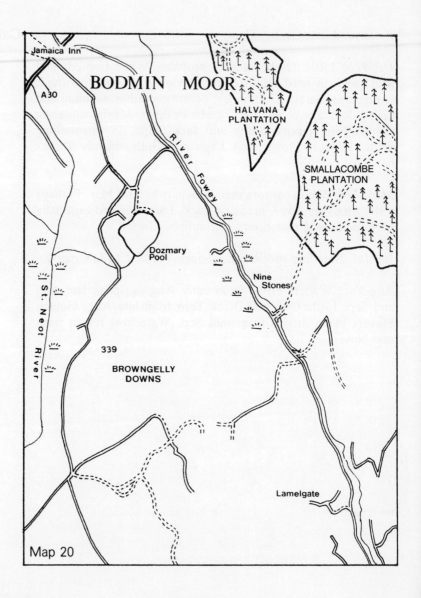

Jamaica Inn

A30

BODMIN MOOR

HALVANA
PLANTATION

River Fowey

SMALLACOMBE
PLANTATION

St. Neot River

Dozmary
Pool

Nine
Stones

339

BROWNGELLY
DOWNS

Lamelgate

Map 20

20 Upper Fowey Valley, Dozmary Pool and Moorland

(Map 20 and OS Map 201)

On the southeast fringe of Bodmin Moor, Upper Fowey Valley, sometimes known as Lamelgate or Bolventor, is near the head of the long Fowey river. The valley is mostly shallow-sided and forms several different habitats in miniature. Localised and uncommon wild flowers include Pale Butterwort, Lesser Bladderwort and Ivy-leaved Bellflower. The fast-flowing river is lined by Alder, *Salix* and Blackthorn trees. Conditions are suitable for trout. You will be extremely lucky to see an Otter, although Minks (unfortunately) are also present. Large areas of peat bog, including some small, deep pools, make walking nearby rather treacherous; sundews, including Long-leaved, thrive. Local butterflies such as Marsh Fritillaries are found. Drier areas support rank grasses, various heathers, and patches of gorse. Lichen growth (harmless to its hosts) is varied and luxuriant in the moist, clean air. Surrounding farmland is mostly rough sheep pasture. Groups of large trees in the valley are mostly Beech. The huge Smallacombe forestry plantations can be seen above the hill crest.

Dozmary Pool, over the hilltop westward, is naturally formed, circular, deep in the middle, with open perimeters. Higher moorland surrounding Dozmary has much the same vegetation as drier parts of Fowey valley. Lower-lying areas remain wetter, with patches of *Salix* in the centre. The pool lies within sight of Brown Willy (423 m), highest point on Bodmin Moor.

Habitat

There are no large numbers of birds, save for the hordes of wintering Starlings noisily searching for worms and leather-jackets on short sheep pasture; they are usually joined by winter thrushes, in particular several hundred Fieldfares. Resident specialities in the valley are Dipper and Willow Tit, while Ravens can be seen in groups of ten or more in winter.

Species

161

Male Hen Harrier

Kingfishers possibly breed; one or two remain through winter, but may be killed off in severe weather, when breeding may lapse for a year or two. Many common lowland passerines such as Treecreeper can be found in this moorland valley, alongside species such as summering Grasshopper Warbler. This mix enables you to see many kinds of birds in a small area.

In winter fewer species inhabit the valley, but birds of prey (e.g. Hen Harrier or Merlin) might pass through on hunting trips, and occasionally a Great Grey Shrike is seen. Moorland surrounding Dozmary Pool supports interesting winter raptors, regularly including up to five Hen Harriers, a Peregrine, one or two Merlins, and a few Short-eared Owls; a Goshawk was seen recently. The pool is uninviting to most wildfowl, but small numbers of ducks come and go throughout winter, and a dozen or so Pochards are regular, as are twice that number of Mallards. Goosanders and Goldeneyes occasionally visit, as do small numbers of dabbling ducks, mostly Wigeons and Teals. Tufted Ducks are casual visitors, and other scarcer ducks such as Smew and Long-tailed Duck have turned up, almost certainly having moved off Siblyback Reservoir. Coots are often present, and a small party of Bewick's or, more rarely, Whooper Swans may visit irregularly. Snipe inhabit boggy margins and small numbers of commoner gulls usually roost; unusual for the region, there is a winter night roost of 50-100 Lesser Black-backed Gulls, arriving from late afternoon.

Spring in the valley echoes with cascading notes of Willow Warbler song. Similar Chiffchaffs are many fewer, their song enabling a ready distinction between the two. Tree Pipits, Blackcaps and Grasshopper Warblers breed in quite good numbers. Spotted Flycatchers, Wheatears, Redstarts and Whinchats usually breed, but are somewhat sporadic. A small number of Sand Martins may nest in suitable riverbank, while Cuckoos parasitise nesting Meadow Pipits. Snipe, present throughout the year, probably breed in ones and twos, along with Curlews and Lapwings. Some Redpolls breed in Smalla-combe plantation, ranging into the valley to feed. Marshy areas and scrubby trees around Dozmary Pool are inhabited by Tree and Meadow Pipits, attended by Cuckoos. Willow Warblers and Chiffchaffs also nest. Summer becomes quieter, as birds settle into a more secretive breeding routine: lush marsh growth aids the naturally furtive behaviour of breeding waders.

At the end of summer, families of young birds move around the area. Soon most summer visitors move off, and autumn may bring a few migrants, perhaps with an uncommon raptor such as Montagu's Harrier.

Timing

For a general visit any time of the day will suffice, although in late spring and summer the earlier the better, avoiding disturbance from trippers. Birds have to be very active in the morning, ensuring for themselves and their dependent mates or young a plentiful food supply very quickly, to replace energy lost overnight, and therefore are more easily seen then. There is also a last flurry of activity before nightfall, when the crepuscular hunting Barn Owl and singing Grasshopper Warbler are more active.

Hard weather may produce more or different birds on Dozmary Pool, such as wild swans. Raptors are best seen an hour or two before dusk, as they begin to congregate near roosting areas, becoming active again, attempting to kill and feed before nightfall.

Access

From A390 at Liskeard take the same route as for Siblyback Lake (see that section). At the crossroads to the lake, follow the road signposted to Launceston. A few hundred metres farther, a sharp turn is signposted to Draynes, Bolventor and Launceston. Follow this road until the hamlet of Lamelgate; on crossing the humpbacked bridge you have entered the valley, which is 3 miles (5 km) long. A road runs the entire length, with several pull-ins. Most of the valley can be seen from, or near, a car.

Access to Smallacombe plantation is from the track at Nine Stones bridge in the valley. The Bolventor road will also take you to the new Colyford Reservoir, now completed. Approach the valley from A30 to Bolventor, directly opposite Jamaica Inn public house. For Dozmary, turn off A30 at Bolventor on the opposite side of the Inn, along a minor road for about $1\frac{1}{2}$ miles ($2\frac{1}{2}$ km) alongside rough moorland. The road skirts the pool; a rather rough track can be walked to the water's edge. Any areas allowing a good view over moors either side of the pool are suitable for passing raptors.

Calendar

Resident: Sparrowhawk, Buzzard, Snipe, Barn Owl, all three woodpeckers (Lesser Spotted very scarce), Grey Wagtail, Dipper, Marsh Tit, Willow Tit, Coal Tit, Raven, Reed Bunting, Redpoll.

Dec-Feb: Possibly wild swans. Teal, Wigeon, Tufted Duck, Pochard, possible Smew and Goosander, Hen Harrier, Peregrine, Merlin, Coot, possible Great Grey Shrike, winter thrushes.

Mar-May: A few of above raptors may linger into Apr. Curlew, possible Lapwing, Cuckoo, Sand Martin, Tree Pipit, Grasshopper Warbler, Blackcap, Willow Warbler and Chiffchaff, Spotted Flycatcher, Wheatear, Whinchat, probable in small numbers.

Jun-Jul: Breeding species.

Aug-Nov: Breeding species flock early in period, migrants begin departure in Aug. Passage migrants may occur. Towards end of period, winter visitors start to return.

21 Crowdy Reservoir and Davidstow Airfield

(Map 21 and OS Map 200/201)

Habitat

Near Camelford town, these exposed moorland sites are close together, separated in parts by maturing Forestry Commission conifers, now being felled. The disused airfield consists of poorly drained short turf, grazed by sheep, with temporary surface water after rain. Remnants of tarmac runways are still passable, and the control tower, although ruined, still stands. The 115-acre (47-ha) reservoir has a greater area of marginal bog than other moorland reservoirs, even when water levels are high. Large areas of mud are exposed when levels are lower. There are several small islands near the shallow end (farthest from the dam), where Sundew, Long-leaved Sundew and Pale Butterwort grow in profusion. The area, prone to high winds and thick mists, is often inhospitable in winter.

Species

The main attraction to birdwatchers is the chance of good views of ducks, waders and raptors, including rarer species. During late autumn and winter flocks of up to 5,000 Golden Plovers regularly occur; Lapwings (usually totalling 1,000 or more) can be equally numerous, especially when hard weather persists elsewhere. Apart from high numbers of these plovers, few waders winter, except perhaps a Ruff. This species is also a spring migrant, and five or six at a time are present each autumn. Only a few Curlews are present at any season. A winter Woodcock may be flushed from the road near the reservoir and small numbers of Snipe may be seen most times of year. Jack Snipe occur only in ones and twos.

Little Grebes are resident in small numbers, a pair or two breeding irregularly. Other grebes and divers are very rare (fewer than Siblyback) and several years may elapse without any. Two or three Cormorants and Grey Herons are usual. Duck species and numbers are also quite restricted. Mallards and Teals both peak at about 300 in autumn (a few pairs of Mallards breed), and about 100 of each in winter. Numbers of

165

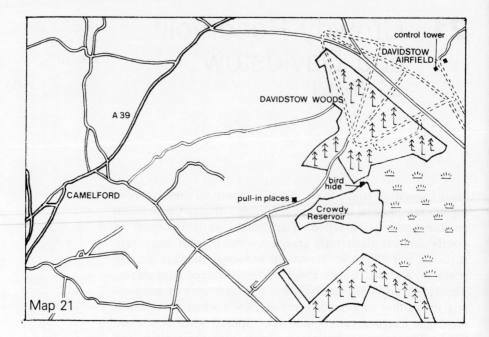

Map 21

most other ducks are tiny. Gadwalls are annual with up to five present, Wigeons vary greatly from 20 to 100 or more, and other dabbling ducks visit sporadically, mostly in ones and twos. Pochards annually peak at not much more than 20 or 30, and Tufted only half that. Goldeneyes are regular, usually three to five brownheads. More casual visitors are Goosanders, averaging even fewer, and Smews, occurring rarely in ones and twos. Other diving ducks are occasionally noted, including the rare Ring-necked Duck from America. Wild swans, usually Bewick's, have been recorded from time to time. Coots usually reach 100-200 in winter and two or three pairs may breed.

Unlike most reservoirs in the region, where spring sees the disappearance of most birds, several arrive and breed. A few pairs of Reed and Sedge Warblers are summer residents. Most numerous breeders are Black-headed Gulls; up to 50 young have fledged at this irregular colony. Other commoner gulls bathe and preen, 200 Herring Gulls being about normal most of the year. Small numbers of waders pass through in spring. Regular, distinctive and easily seen are Whimbrels. Not so regular are mountain-nesting Dotterels, small parties of which have been found on the airfield for a few days. They might also be seen on return passage in autumn in ones and twos, often among Golden Plovers. Montagu's Harriers have visited on spring passage.

Autumn draws the region's more active birdwatchers, often finding interesting migrants and rarities. One of the earliest flocks of Golden Plovers in the region congregates here, acting as decoys and attracting other related species. Rare, but regular in recent years, is the American Lesser Golden Plover, occurring mostly singly; difficult to identify unless you are fairly expert, they often resemble Grey Plovers, which also occasionally turn up! Another American wader, the smaller Buff-breasted Sandpiper, is not seen annually; when present, it often associates with plover flocks on the airfield. Unfortunately Buff-breasteds closely resemble small female Ruffs (Reeves), which also mingle with Golden Plovers.

Small numbers of commoner migrant waders drop in on the reservoir's muddy margins, including a few Ringed Plovers, while Dunlins attain small flocks of 30-40. Spotted Redshanks, Redshanks and Greenshanks are seen in groups of three or four apiece, while fewer Green, Wood and Common Sandpipers, Black- and Bar-tailed Godwits occur. Little Stints and Curlew Sandpipers are noted most autumns in ones and twos, though peaks of five or six are not unusual. The reservoir has its share of American waders: Pectoral Sandpiper, Wilson's Phalarope and Long-billed Dowitcher have all graced its mud. (It should be noted that there is often interchange by many species between the two sites, if there is particular disturbance at one or conditions become more favourable at the other; birds do not necessarily stick to their normal habitat.) Black Terns are annual autumn visitors to the lake, often singly or in small numbers, and have passed through in spring.

Another group of species which ranges over both sites, as well as surrounding moorland, is birds of prey. Food supplies, in the form of flocking birds, are an obvious attraction. All three common resident raptors are here, with others particularly during autumn and winter. Several reliable records of the often misidentified Goshawk have come from here, with adults, immatures, males and females accurately described. Hen Harriers, present on moorland around, occasionally overfly the area, wings held in a shallow 'V' as they glide; females and immatures are the more common. Peregrines arrive in early autumn and may not depart until late spring. Dashing Merlins arrive later and normally depart earlier, ranging more widely. The Hobby has been seen in spring and autumn as an irregular passage migrant.

Numbers of resident or breeding passerines in autumn are

swollen by migrants — Meadow Pipits and Skylarks for example. Other open-ground species such as Wheatears, which breed in small numbers nearby, become more numerous. Two uncommon open-ground buntings, Snow and Lapland, are occasional visitors in ones and twos in late autumn.

Timing

On fine weekends the airfield often suffers disturbance from model aircraft and gliders, so a morning visit is preferable. Individuals of smaller American waders are unconcerned: neither of these activities scares them off. Other birds move to a quieter corner, while some leave the vicinity completely, a few alighting by the reservoir. Plovers normally leave completely. Towards evening in autumn, disturbed birds, including plovers and associated species, or those which have fed elsewhere, often return to roost. This can be a rewarding time, with raptors also more active now. Vast flocks of Starlings return to roost at dusk in autumn and winter.

Winds or thick mist may be localised here, or worse than elsewhere, and until your arrival you may have no real indication of conditions. Hard weather elsewhere may increase species and numbers, but, if conditions are really bad, almost certainly there will be a marked decrease. Windsurfing, towards the dam end of the reservoir, normally does not affect waders.

Access

From A39 at Camelford, minor roads lead to the site. A road runs lengthways through the airfield (with several places where you can pull off). From A30 take Altarnun turn, following minor roads after that village. From A395, several minor roads will bring you to the road running the length of the airfield; the route from A30 also leads to this same airfield road. The slightly raised road, along the flat airfield area (beware of wandering sheep), has several pull-off places on either side which lead onto the old runways across the grass; you will need these to cover the whole area adequately.

Drive along both sides of all runways slowly, stopping every 100 m or so to scan for birds; this allows close approach to species which would never permit such closeness on foot. On finding your quarry, watch from the car; you will obtain good views without disturbing them, or preventing others from seeing them. If on foot, extreme caution is needed in approaching birds, being prepared to watch most species from a greater distance. Areas near the old control tower appear favourite for many birds. Pools are attractive for some species. Raptors may be seen anywhere.

For the reservoir, from the airfield road, follow the signpost. Where the road begins to overlook the reservoir on the edge of the forestry plantation there is a pull-in. A track here leads to a hide on the water's edge at the marshy end. The reservoir can be checked from this road for waterfowl, or birds flying over, which are seen reasonably well especially with a telescope. For close access, walk to the water's edge via the track; you will need to do this when checking for waders.

Apart from use of the hide, this site, though bleak in winter, lends itself very well to visits by elderly or disabled people. The hide is kept locked; keys and permits needed for entry are available from SWWA.

Calendar

Resident: Little Grebe, Grey Heron, Sparrowhawk, Buzzard, Coot, Black-headed Gull, Coal Tit, Raven.

Dec-Feb: Possibly wild swans. Teal, Wigeon, probably Gadwall, Pochard, Tufted Duck, Goldeneye, possibly Smew or Goosander. Dabbling and other diving ducks in ones and twos, sporadically. Hen Harrier, Peregrine, Merlin, Golden Plover, Lapwing, possible Ruff and Woodcock, Snipe, maybe Jack Snipe. Fieldfare, Redwing, millions of Starlings roost.

Mar-May: Most above visitors have departed by Apr. Wheatear from mid Mar, Whimbrel from mid Apr. Possible Dotterel (late Apr-May) and Ruff. From end of Apr on, possible Montagu's Harrier or Hobby, and marsh tern, e.g. Black. Cuckoo.

Jun-Jul: Breeding species, may inc. Black-headed Gull, Reed and Sedge Warblers. First returning waders, e.g. Spotted Redshank, towards end of period.

Aug-Nov: Waders gradually increase in number and species; most are seen on the reservoir at the beginning, e.g. shanks and sandpipers. Early Sep, a few hundred Golden Plovers. Most other waders begin to reach peak numbers through Sep. Uncommon and rare waders appear. Black Terns. Peregrine and Goshawk may appear. Early Oct, Merlins arrive, also Snow and Lapland Buntings perhaps. Towards end of period

most waders have departed. Golden Plovers, Lapwings and
Snipe increase. Winter thrushes begin arriving, as do Hen
Harriers.

22 Gerrans Bay

(Map 22 and OS Map 204)

Habitat

A southerly-facing bay on the south coast of Cornwall, east from Carrick Roads waterway system (near Falmouth). The bay has no apparent unique habitat features; a rocky coast extends its length, unprotected from heavy seas from most wind directions. Gerrans Bay runs from Nare Head at the east end west to Portscatho. The exposed and scenic Nare headland itself is under NT control with public footpaths. These paths run eastward far beyond Nare, and are continuous westward to Portscatho and beyond.

Species

The bay's real claim to fame emanates from one species, the Black-throated Diver. The area holds numbers unequalled anywhere else in Cornwall, peak counts regularly exceeding 50. The population can fluctuate wildly throughout winter and spring months, even during the period when they are traditionally present in good numbers. This may arise through genuine absence or because they have moved farther out to sea; some may move to another area (they visit adjacent Veryan Bay). The Black-throated usually form several groups, scattered across the area. At times they feed very close to shore, among rocky gullies densely covered in seaweed, searching out small crabs and fish. Later in April a few may attain immaculate summer plumage: the white foreneck is lost, as are the white flanks, but they still lack any trace of tail, an important distinction from either Shag or Cormorant.

The next most numerous diver, Great Northern, struggles to muster ten individuals at a time, five being average. The Red-throated Diver, as elsewhere in Cornwall (apart from passage birds at one or two localities) is a scarce, irregular visitor, usually singly. Grebes are annual winter or early spring visitors, most numerous being Slavonian, though numbers rarely exceed six at once. The Black-necked Grebe, confusingly similar, and the larger Red-necked Grebe, which has

171

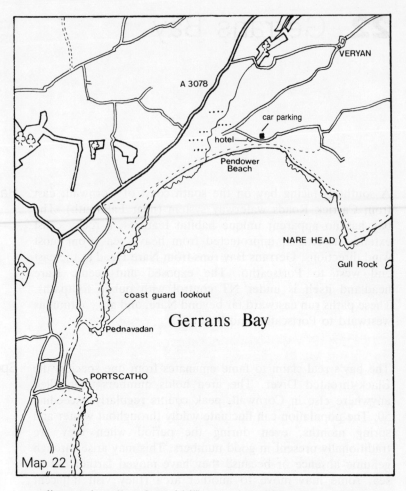

VERYAN

A 3078

car parking

hotel

Pendower
Beach

NARE HEAD

Gull Rock

coast guard lookout

Gerrans Bay

Pednavadan

PORTSCATHO

Map 22

a diagnostic yellow-based bill, are annual but scarce: only ones and twos are normally recorded, staying usually only a week or two. Great Crested Grebes are very spasmodic in occurrence. Seaducks are poorly represented, only groups of up to 20 Common Scoters visiting with any regularity. There is a possibility of the odd Velvet Scoter, or a few Eiders, usually brown females or pied immature males. Guillemots and Razorbills breed on Gull Rock (off Nare Head), although numbers of both fluctuate each year: up to 30 or so pairs of Razorbills may nest, with Guillemots sometimes attaining over 75 pairs; a few individuals of both species are present throughout the year. Several pairs of Lesser Black-backed Gulls also breed. Sandwich Terns can be watched heading eastward from early spring, or west in autumn. Other terns, such as Common or Arctic, are also seen, but less predictably.

Whimbrels pass, usually in small flocks, and Fulmars cruise by en route to nearby breeding ledges.

Any daylight hours should suffice. Flatter light reduces glare and shadow caused by low winter sunlight. An incoming tide may induce birds to drift closer to shore. Calmer seas enhance chances of picking out smaller birds such as grebes.

Timing

Leave A3078 when signposted to Pendower Beach and Hotel. The road runs beside the hotel, and adjacent to the cliff edge (more or less beside the hotel) are roadside parking spaces for several cars. This is probably the best vantage point in the bay, with at least a few divers and particularly grebes always present in winter; it is not unusual to find the largest flocks off here. From Pendower, rejoin the A road at the point where you left it. Next checking place is at Pednavadan (near the village of Tregassa). Park carefully, beside the narrow road, taking care not to block farmers' access into fields. Walk out to the point along public footpaths. A concrete bunker marks an appropriate place to stop and look. The coastline here is low, thus reducing distance between you and the sea, with close divers often an added bonus.

Access

To check around Portscatho, park near the western edge of the village. At the west point of the village, watch from along coastal public footpath. Rarely are large numbers seen from here, but divers, grebes and seaducks are recorded, so a visit could pay off.

Resident: Cormorant, Shag, Guillemot, Razorbill.

Calendar

Dec-Feb: Up to early Feb, low numbers of Black-throated and Great Northern Divers, Slavonian Grebes; Common Scoter often present. Possible Red-throated Diver, Black- and Red-

Red-throated Diver

Great Northern Diver

HARRISON 83

Black-throated Diver

necked Grebes. Divers increase towards end.

Mar-May: Mar-early Apr, peak numbers of Black-throated Divers, especially beginning Apr. Late Apr, most divers and grebes have left, few remaining early May, perhaps in summer plumage. Sandwich Tern from early Apr, Common Tern and Whimbrel from mid Apr, possibly Arctic Tern May.

Jun-Jul: Breeding species.

Aug-Nov: From end May-Nov, little normally present; late Oct, first divers, probably increasing by late Nov; from Nov, grebes and seaducks.

23 Fal Estuary-Carrick Roads Complex

Habitat

The Truro and Fal rivers, joining to form Carrick Roads waterway, have their combined entrance at Falmouth Bay, between the headlands of St Anthony on the east side and Pendennis on the west. Nearby is Falmouth town (see next article). Although tidal, deep water remains in the Roads, which at the widest point are about ³⁄₄ mile (1.2 km) wide: there are no sand- or mudbanks. On the east side of Carrick Roads a high steep bank, forming a brake, terminates in a low rocky cliff, shelving abruptly into deep water. On the west side land is more level, and villages such as Mylor, or individual houses, are scattered along.

Extensive creeks lead off both sides of the Roads, the largest being Restronguet, sheltered from rough weather. It is mostly narrow, however, and suffers from human disturbance along both banks; there is a quieter, very narrow area towards Devoran. Tresillian is a very narrow, tree-lined river with a small saltmarsh; it is extremely sheltered from high winds. Many of the trees lining the banks are Alder. Ruan Lanihorne is the wide upper reaches of the Fal estuary; here the surroundings are more open, and, with human habitation lacking, much less disturbance occurs.

Species

The habitat and underwater-diet preferences of diving ducks are reflected by their concentrations on the Roads: Goldeneyes regularly peak at more than 40, while Red-breasted Mergansers average higher, often exceeding 50. This is the two species' stronghold in Cornwall. Females predominate, especially in Goldeneye. All three divers visit, Great Northern being most frequent, with two or three present for much of the winter, and often six or more together. Black-throated tend to appear later in the winter, when three to five is not unusual. Although recorded annually, the smaller Red-throated Diver is least common, very irregular, and usually seen singly.

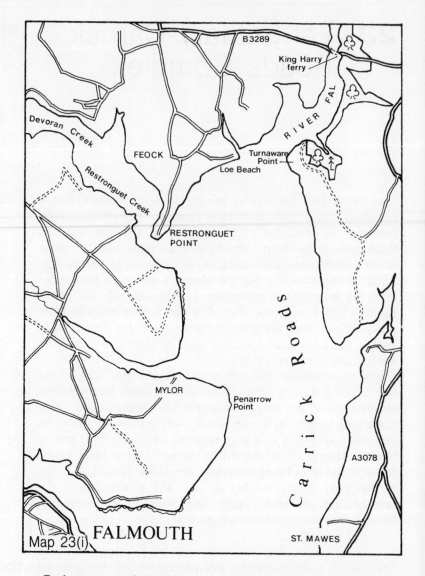

Map 23(i)

Grebes are regular visitors, most frequently Great Crested and Slavonian, with at least five of each present at a time most years; Black-necked and Red-necked Grebes are annual but irregular, in ones and twos. Eiders and Common Scoters visit most winters, with up to ten of each sometimes, and single visits are occasionally made by Velvet Scoters, Long-tailed Ducks and Goosanders. Among the few Razorbills and Guillemots seen in winter are now almost annual sightings of single Black Guillemots; later sightings may find them in full black and white summer plumage. Why this largely sedentary northern auk should turn up here is a mystery. Both Shags and Cormorants are common, their preferred habitats overlapping in the Roads.

Restronguet Creek seems to attract only unexceptional numbers of commoner waders, many of which feed along deepish freshwater channels which flow across these mudflats. When the channels are filled by the incoming tide, waders begin to fly to Devoran roost, as remaining mudflats are rapidly covered. Up to 500 Dunlins and 200 Redshanks form the bulk of birds at the roost. A few Greenshanks and Spotted Redshanks pass through in autumn, as do Little Stints and Curlew Sandpipers. Two or three of both migrant shanks stay to winter. Little Grebes frequent the main stream, remaining in the creek even when the tide is out. Surrounding sheltered gardens and hedgerows provide habitat for a few over-wintering Blackcaps, Chiffchaffs, Firecrests and Black Red-starts.

Tresillian River, with dense bush and tree cover in places, provides winter quarters not only for the same passerines as those found around Restronguet, but also for small flocks of Siskins which find here their favourite food, Alder seeds. Grey Herons are resident and several pairs breed, as do Shelducks. Probably two pairs of Kingfishers also nest. Autumn brings a good passage of Spotted Redshanks and the larger Green-shanks, with more than 25 of each some years at peak times; about six of each may overwinter. Greenshanks have slow, graceful wingbeats, their dark upperwing contrasting with white underparts; their ringing 'choo-choo' call also readily identifies them. Green and Common Sandpipers pass through in small numbers in autumn, but neither appears to stay regularly in winter. Black-tailed Godwits peak at about 50 most autumns, some still with rich chestnut underparts of summer plumage.

On the ornithologically important mudflats at Ruan Lanihorne, waders attract most attention. Apart from high numbers of common waders in autumn and winter, a small number of less common visitors to Cornwall are regularly noted, mostly in autumn. These include Wood Sandpipers, and rarities such as American waders; Baird's and Pectoral Sandpipers have been seen. Among commoner waders, both Dunlins and Curlews can attain 1,000 each; Curlews usually peak in autumn, when about 800 is normal, whereas Dunlin numbers remain high throughout winter, sometimes reaching over 2,000. Oystercatchers may exceed 300. Black-tailed Godwits in autumn are over 200, one of the region's larger

Little Egret

HARRISON 83

gatherings of this localised species, but only about 100 overwinter. Ringed Plovers often reach 100 or so in autumn, but, as usual in southwest England, few remain to winter. A regular feature in early autumn is the number of Spotted Redshanks which gather, up to 30 or more at a time in some years. Elegant birds, they wade belly-deep while sweeping their long, straight bills sideways through the water; several of the earliest arrivals may still be in their jet-black and silver-spotted breeding plumage. Greenshanks can reach a similar number in autumn, and up to five of each species regularly winter. Little Stints and Curlew Sandpipers are annual autumn visitors, but numbers are never much over five apiece, often not even that. Ruffs and Green Sandpipers are annual in ones and twos, as are Avocets, which sometimes stay to winter. Gulls roost and loaf in the area, Black-headed often exceeding 5,000, especially in autumn. Common Gulls average about 100 during winter. From late winter the largest gatherings of Lesser Black-backed Gulls take place, with several hundred sometimes present.

On the Fal complex, dabbling ducks are generally restricted to the most common kinds. Average peak numbers around Ruan area, where most are seen, are 200 Teals and Mallards, 400 Wigeons and about 100 Shelducks. Other ducks visit, sporadically in ones and twos, and include all diving species.

Grey Herons, like Mallards and Shelducks, breed near Ruan, where up to 20 nests have been counted. One or two pairs of Kingfishers also breed. The Osprey, usually singly, passes through in autumn, often staying several days, sometimes weeks. Peregrines are frequent visitors which menace and panic Ruan's avian occupants throughout autumn and winter. A Spoonbill may arrive during autumn or early winter, possibly staying for a month or two.

Lower or incoming tides are required for waders on mudflats such as Devoran Creek and Ruan; rising tides concentrate previously scattered birds, and those feeding in deep channels, into reasonably defined areas. There is no one consistent high-tide wader roost at any of the sites. Very high tides (over 5 m) cover all mud and saltmarsh, and waders are forced into fields or split up to roost until tides begin to drop, exposing some mud. **Timing**

From the hide near Ruan, waders are best seen an hour or so after the tide begins to rise, driving them out of gullies and main channels (which fill first) across still exposed mudflats. This enables you to watch waders for several hours, before high tide moves them off altogether. At high water in winter, diving ducks, such as Red-breasted Mergansers and Golden-eyes, may follow the tide up, swimming close to the hide. If tides are not particularly high, waders at Ruan will roost towards the right-hand side of the hide.

It is pointless checking Devoran at low tide. As with Ruan, waders are forced out from deep channels and other hidden areas by rising tides. For about three hours before high tide, waders fly into Devoran Creek, and close views are obtained. On very high tides (over 5 m), roosting areas are flooded, and the birds disperse. Greenshanks and Spotted Redshanks do not usually appear until almost high tide. At low tide on Carrick Roads, some birds drift downstream towards the mouth, returning when waters rise; many, however, stay around the wider middle reaches at all times. Hard weather, as with other similarly sheltered areas in the Southwest, brings a short-term increase in many species as they flee worse conditions elsewhere. Boating activities in the Roads become quite busy from April onwards, and this, combined with a traditionally early departure by many waterfowl wintering in southwest England, means that few birds remain from that date.

Access

To check Carrick Roads, leave A39 Truro-Falmouth road at St Gluvias and drive to Mylor village, where there are parking facilities. Walk along the beach on the south side of the creek to Penarrow Point overlooking the Roads. This widest area is usually one of the best for concentrations of most species. A good telescope is essential for a complete check.

For the best area at Tresillian, mostly for close views of waders at low tide, leave A39 where signposted to Pencalenick, north of Truro as you leave towards St Austell. Leave your car beside the road at Pencalenick as near as possible to the public footpath. Take this good path, which follows the riverbank to St Clement, just outside Truro. The track passes Tresemple Pool, which often provides first-class views of Kingfishers. This walk is about ³₄ mile (1.2 km).

Access to Devoran Creek is gained by taking a right turn from the direction of Carnon Downs on A39 south of Truro, along Greenbank Road, just before the main road crosses the creek and before reaching a garage. After entering Quay Road, drive at least 50 m past a very sharp bend (for safety), parking beside the road. Walk along this narrow road, adjacent to the creek. After about ³₄ mile (1.2 km), you can obtain close views of assembled waders, before and after high tides.

Access to the hide near Ruan Lanihorne is by leaving A3078 Truro-St Mawes road at Ruan High Lanes. Drive a couple of hundred metres along the road signposted to Philleigh, then take a minor road to Trelonk Farm. (Please note: the hide is on private farmland. Access throughout the Fal complex is difficult, often impossible, because of private land, so please respect this farmer's stipulations.) Near the farm entrance the farmer has provided car-parking space which is marked, or enquire at the farm. Follow two fields leading from the car park to the hide. As there are no hedges or other cover near the hide for further concealment, the farmer insists that the hide *must* be used if a visit is made. Keys are obtainable only from Mr S Gay at Lower Farm, Trewithian, near Portscatho: all enquiries should be addressed to him.

Calendar

Resident: Cormorant and Shag present all year. Grey Heron, Sparrowhawk, Buzzard, Kingfisher, Raven.

Dec-Feb: Divers of all three species; Little, Black-necked, Slavonian and Great Crested Grebes, probable Red-necked Grebe; Teal, Wigeon and other dabbling or diving ducks irregularly visit; seaducks — Eider, Common, Scoter, possible Velvet Scoter, Long-tailed Duck — and Goosander. Golden-eye, Red-breasted Merganser. Dunlin, Spotted Redshank, Redshank, Greenshank, Black-tailed and Bar-tailed Godwits, Curlew, Snipe, probable Avocet, possible Spoonbill. Lesser Black-backed Gull numbers rise from Feb. Probable Blackcap, Chiffchaff, Firecrest, Black Redstart, Siskin.

Mar-May: By mid Apr, most waders and waterbirds departed. Possible rare species, e.g. Little Egret, from mid Apr.

Jun-Jul: Breeding species. By mid Jul returning waders, inc. Spotted Redshank and Green Sandpiper.

Aug-Nov: Most wader numbers and species increase through Aug and Sep, inc. Ringed Plover, Greenshank and Black-tailed Godwit. From Sep-Oct waders include Little Stint, Curlew Sandpiper, probable Wood Sandpiper, Ruff; also raptors — possible Osprey, probable Peregrine. By end of period divers, grebes and seaducks returning.

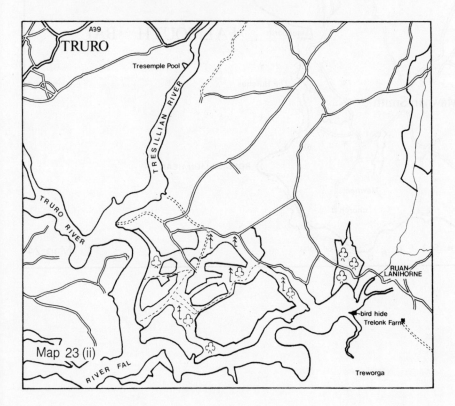

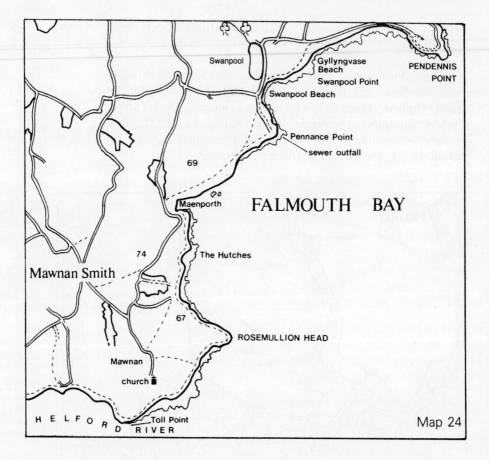

Swanpool

Gyllyngvase
Beach

PENDENNIS
POINT

Swanpool Point

Swanpool Beach

Pennance Point

sewer outfall

69

Maenporth

FALMOUTH BAY

74

The Hutches

Mawnan Smith

67

ROSEMULLION HEAD

Mawnan
church

Toll Point

H E L F O R D   R I V E R

Map 24

24 Falmouth, the Bay and Rosemullion

(Map 24 and OS Map 204)

Habitat

On the west side of the large Carrick Roads-Fal estuary complex, at the mouth, lies the town of Falmouth. Eastward, docks face back towards Carrick Roads (see previous description); southward, the town looks onto a deep but sheltered bay. A mile (1.6 km) of mainly rocky shoreline with small shingle beaches extends between Pendennis Castle promontory, by the estuary mouth, and wooded Pennance Point at the west. The tip of Pennance Point has a sewer outfall. A marshy wooded valley runs down the west side of the town, culminating in Swanpool, a ¼-mile (400-m) long park lake with reedy fringes and Alder trees immediately behind the beach. The town has large gardens with mature trees and bushes, including palms and other exotics.

West of Pennance Point, the high rocky coast of Falmouth Bay curves south towards Lizard peninsula, interrupted by the deep mouth of Helford River (known as the Passage). Overlooking the Passage is the open downland NT property of Rosemullion Head, with wide coastal views, projecting eastward into the bay. The only gap in the cliffs between Falmouth and Helford Passage is at Maenporth, a deep sheltered cove and stream valley 1 mile (1.6 km) south of Pennance Point.

Water Voles are common in Swanpool.

Species

Falmouth has gained a reputation in recent winters as a feeding area for large numbers of gulls, including regular occurrences of scarcer species, making it one of the best areas in our region for studying this group of birds. The town has overwintering warblers in the sheltered valley behind Swanpool, with the chance of an uncommon migrant at the lake.

The sharp rise in gull sightings off Falmouth is probably due partly to increased careful watching, and especially to large trawlers and fish-factory ships which now base themselves in

183

the bay for the winter. Thousands of gulls wheel screaming over the ships, generally too distant to watch, or rest in large numbers along seafront rocks, where they can be checked closely. Swanpool lake and Maenporth Cove serve as drinking, bathing and preening areas, with a steady stream of gulls commuting in and out to boats. The majority of gulls following trawlers are Herring Gulls, with brown immatures numerous. The more slender Iceland Gull, with long white wingtips, might be picked out among a resting flock; often they sit on flat rocks just east of Swanpool beach. Iceland Gulls are as regular here as anywhere in southern Britain, especially in late winter, although rarely are more than two or three of these scarce birds in the bay at one time. Care should be taken in distinguishing them from the other northern gull: the burly thick-billed Glaucous, also a regular visitor, with sometimes up to ten in the district, often seen resting on Maenporth beach where many larger gulls including Great Black-backed gather. Wind and tide drift fish scraps onto the seashore, giving a chance for agile Black-headed Gulls hovering over the tideline, sometimes joined by a Little Gull. The smaller gull species can also be seen feeding at Pennance sewer. Mediterranean Gulls are present most winters, particularly late in the autumn, with a chance of further individuals passing through, in a variety of plumages from young birds resembling patchy young Common Gulls to snow-white winter adults. Common Gulls move through in flocks towards spring. Kittiwakes, normally oceanic feeders in winter, gather in thousands to feed on easy food sources here.

In early spring most larger gulls soon move off, but one or two Glaucous or Iceland may linger late, fresh individuals appearing with passage groups of gulls moving up the coast. Black-headed and Common Gulls move through, with the chance of a rare transatlantic visitor such as a Bonaparte's Gull, or the now increasingly detected Ring-billed Gull, among them. Identification of the varying plumages of the many gulls present requires patient and meticulous watching.

Although most birdwatching visitors expect to see gulls, other species of interest may be found. Parties of several Great Northern and Black-throated Divers, and one or two Slavonian Grebes, are seen offshore. Small groups of Eiders are irregular off the rocks, where Turnstones and Purple Sandpipers forage busily; a Black Redstart is likely in a sheltered corner of the shoreline or around seafront buildings. Auks are scattered on the sea in small numbers, and the rare Black Guillemot has been reported in the bay several times.

The deep waters off Rosemullion and Helford Passage may also be used by feeding divers, seaducks, including often a Velvet Scoter or two, and auks. A Red-necked Grebe is seen most years, seeming to favour deep, rocky bays more than other grebes; this species and Velvet Scoter are also seen intermittently off Falmouth front, presumably the same individuals moving along the coast. Sometimes coastal ducks such as a single Long-tailed take up residence, along with Pochards and Tufted Ducks, on Swanpool, where close views are possible; Water Rails lurk in the margins.

Moving inland, sheltered trees near the stream behind Swanpool often hold a wintering Blackcap, Firecrest or Chiffchaff, also seen in well-vegetated gardens around the town. Chiffchaffs can be quite numerous, over 40 wintering birds having been counted in the district. Siskins in twos and threes use the waterside Alders.

Early spring warblers and hirundines appear in sheltered coves. Groups of up to half a dozen Black-throated Divers pass through the bay, where the odd Slavonian Grebe may linger and acquire breeding dress, and Sandwich Terns are seen in small numbers. A variety of passerine species may be seen around Swanpool, including one or two Sedge and Reed Warblers later in spring, which are likely to stay and breed, as do Little Grebes most years. Other 'marsh' species have included overshooting rarities such as Little Bittern, surprisingly hard to see when not in flight, even in this thin fringe of reeds.

In later spring, and through to early autumn, seawatching off Rosemullion promontory can be worthwhile, with a chance of Manx Shearwaters, skuas and terns passing south offshore after being pushed into Falmouth Bay in poor weather. Although numbers have not been high (three or four skuas in a watch) and few birdwatchers spend time here, interesting observations such as feeding parties of tiny Storm Petrels or a non-breeding summer flock of Pomarine Skuas have been made. Falmouth is busy with tourists through summer and relatively little visited by birders until the end of the year, when gull numbers start to build up again. In one recent winter Britain's first Forster's Tern, from the Americas, spent several weeks fishing off the seafront. Late autumn gales may blow in a tired Grey Phalarope or Little Auk to rest on Swanpool lake.

In peak winter periods, gulls are constantly moving in and out **Timing** from the beaches to ships, so give yourself time to wait (two or three hours at least) at strategic points such as Swanpool and Maenporth for incoming birds. Falling tides attract birds, mostly smaller gulls, to Pennance sewer, where larger species may be seen passing en route to favoured areas. For resting gulls on shoreline rocks and beaches, a dropping tide leaving more exposed landing space is best. Time of day is not critical; afternoon is usually best at Swanpool lake for gulls, but avoid very late afternoon when fading light will not permit detailed watching. East and southeast winds bring most fish debris onto the beaches.

Swanpool valley is most likely to hold interesting spring migrants and overshoot species when they funnel in on south and southwest winds. Wintering passerines are most numerous in years without heavy frost. Seawatching at Rosemullion seems best in winds between south and east in early morning, tending to drift seabirds nearer shore, and in poor visibility or drizzle, especially after anticyclonic spells. Strong depressional southwesterlies do not seem to produce much here, but may force individuals in to shelter on Swanpool in late autumn.

Access

Falmouth lies at the south end of A39 from Truro. For *Swanpool* district, follow signs to Swanpool and Gyllyngvase beaches along a right fork as you enter Falmouth. (There is only a short gap between Penryn and Falmouth towns along the main road.) Continue along a suburban B-class road for $1\frac{1}{2}$ miles ($2\frac{1}{2}$ km), then take a signposted right turn downhill past the cemetery. Arriving at the top end of the pool, stop to check marginal vegetation and trees behind. (**Note** Do not trample down reeds as some irresponsible birdwatchers have done in the past.) Drive down to the seafront car park, from which gulls are clearly visible flying in to bathe. Spend time here but also try walking east (left) along the tarmac footpath overlooking the shore rocks, round to Gyllyngvase beach ($\frac{1}{2}$ mile/0.8 km), or farther if large groups of gulls are visible ahead. Most scarcer species, however, are seen near Swanpool end of the bay. Also try walking up past the cafe right from Swanpool and along the muddy $\frac{1}{2}$-mile (0.8-km) track to Pennance Point for close views off the sewer.

Maenporth is reached by following Swanpool beach road over the hilltop past the cafe, then forking left, about 2 miles (3 km) by minor road, or by coast footpath beyond Pennance.

Rosemullion and Helford Passage Continue beyond Maenporth for 2 miles (3 km) to Mawnan village, parking near the old church. On the coast path, turn left for ¹₂ mile (0.8 km) out to Rosemullion for passing seabirds, or right for a few hundred metres to view the bay for divers, grebes and seaducks in winter.

Resident: Little, apart from Little Grebe.

Calendar

Dec-Feb: Great Northern and Black-throated Divers, Red-necked and Slavonian Grebes, Tufted Duck, Pochard, seaducks, Water Rail, Turnstone, Purple Sandpiper. Gull flocks peaking Feb, inc. Glaucous, Mediterranean and Little among commoner species. Auks, Blackcap, Chiffchaff, Firecrest, Black Redstart, in small numbers.

Mar-May: Wintering divers, grebes and gulls present to early Apr, with further migrant groups arriving, but total numbers drop from mid Mar. Possibly a rare gull Mar-Apr, Sandwich Tern, early hirundines and singing warblers end Mar, summer migrants and maybe an overshooting rarity from mid Apr. Manx Shearwater, Arctic, Pomarine and maybe Great Skuas, Sandwich and Commic Terns all possible off Rosemullion, especially May.

Jun-Jul: Breeding Reed and Sedge Warblers. Off Rosemullion possibly seabirds, inc. Manx Shearwater, Storm Petrel, skuas, auks. Fulmars breed.

Aug-Nov: Quiet period. Maybe skuas or terns off Rosemullion Aug-Sep, Grey Phalarope or Little Auk at Swanpool in Nov.

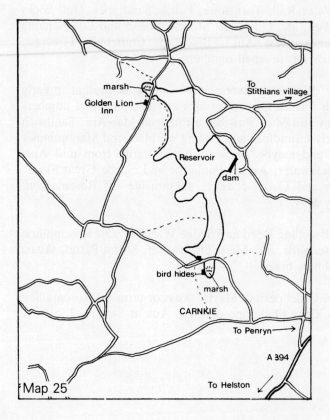

marsh

Golden Lion
Inn

Reservoir

dam

bird hides

marsh

CARNKIE

To
Stithians village →

To Penryn →

A 394

To Helston →

Map 25

25 Stithians Reservoir (Map 25 and OS Map 203)

Habitat

At 274 acres (111 ha), this reservoir, south of the large town of Redruth, is Cornwall's largest lake. It lies within a large area of high, rough ground, much of it semi-moorland covered by Bracken and heather, reaching 250 m altitude. This setting produces weather conditions far removed from those on the sheltered south coast. Even on otherwise warm days, a chill wind often blows across this exposed water.

The reservoir is quite shallow over large areas, having steeper sides only towards the dam, and a margin of mud is quickly exposed at its further perimeters when water levels drop. No islands break up the lake's expanse. There is only minimal human habitation immediately surrounding the reservoir.

Species

This is the region's most important reservoir for birds; Devon, unfortunately, has nothing which even remotely compares. As ducks and waders are the main species, most interest centres on autumn and winter. The surrounding rough open terrain is attractive to small numbers of birds of prey, which also hunt near and over the reservoir, providing added value for birdwatchers. Winter is particularly bleak here, so few of the waders which typically winter on the region's sheltered estuaries remain at Stithians throughout. Conversely, autumn wader counts for some species are the highest for either county, and many rarities have been found.

There are more dabbling ducks than diving species, possibly owing to the shallow grassy margins which they favour. Numbers, however, are not that large, and variety of species is limited. Teals and Wigeons are approximately equal in number, averaging 100 each and sometimes reaching double that, while Mallards total only about 50. Up to five Gadwalls are usually present, but can reach 20 in some years. Few other species occur regularly, and then only in ones and twos. The most numerous diving duck is Tufted, with about 50 usually present; Pochards are less common, reaching only about 20. Counts of four or five Goldeneyes, mostly females, can rise to more than 20 for short periods some years. Scaups are almost annual, visiting from late autumn on, often in twos and threes, and may include grey-backed males. Goosanders do not arrive annually, but two or three might be present, usually brown-heads. Probably because of the reservoir's expanse and relative solitude, various wandering grey geese sometimes visit. The region as a whole is poorly served for grey geese, so any occurrences are noteworthy. White-fronted Geese pre-dominate, and once a group of the Greenland form, which winters in large numbers in Ireland, was identified; Pink-footed and Greylag Geese have also been seen. Occasionally Bewick's Swans have also visited, in very low numbers.

Two or three pairs of Little Grebes breed. In winter up to 15 are seen, but other grebe species are almost non-existent, with just a couple of sightings of Great Crested on record. Divers, although only ever accidental on our inland waters, also shun this locality, but a few single Black-throated have been reported. Cormorants fly far inland to feed, and four or five are not unusual. Coots can muster over 100 from late autumn onwards, and five or six pairs breed. Moorhens, which visit in small numbers, are not known to breed. Few uncommon species of gull are seen, and gull numbers here are fairly low, but the odd Mediterranean Gull has been identified among Black-headed Gulls.

As spring approaches, wintering ducks and other species are quick to depart. A combination of high water levels and poor spring wader passage generally in Cornwall means that very few pass through here at this season. If Stithians does not stand out as a 'hot spot' for spring waders, the same certainly cannot be said in autumn; indeed, waders pass in high numbers from late summer. Most of those early high numbers are created by Green, Wood and Common Sandpipers. This reservoir is certainly the best venue in both counties for these three birds. Green Sandpipers tend to disappear into narrow gullies, and hug grassy margins; over 20 may be seen at once. Wood Sandpipers are much less common, but here ten or more have been seen together, four or five being more normal. More elegant in stature, they feed more in the open. Soon a wide range of other waders appears, the plover family being well represented. Ringed Plovers, reaching over 30, are found more on this reservoir than any other in Cornwall. Another plover which passes through with reasonable regularity is

Little Ringed, and one or two may be watched among their similarly-marked, chubbier cousins. Lapwings congregate early, over 1,000 spending winter in the general area. Golden Plovers, too, return early, one of the few places where they do so, numbering perhaps less than 100 at first, although they may reach several thousand later. This small early flock is enough to lure one of Stithian's specialities: often one of the autumn's first major rarities is the American Lesser Golden Plover, here almost annual, and two or three are identified in some autumns; in flight their underwings are dusky grey, as opposed to the commoner bird's white. Dotterels have also been recorded.

Greenshanks reach over 20 at a time, but few Redshanks occur. Dunlins average 30, and Ruffs can be equally common in some years, although ten is more usual. Each year at least two or three Ruffs overwinter. As the autumn advances more species arrive, including Little Stints and Curlew Sandpipers from Russia. In years when numbers are generally good, 15 or more of each may be seen together; such large numbers do not usually stay more than a week, and about five of each is more usual.

By now rarities, either extreme or semi-rare, will have shown up. One of the more regular comes into the latter category: Pectoral Sandpiper is almost an annual visitor, and seven together have been recorded, but one or two are seen most often. Long-billed Dowitcher is another fairly regular American species, visiting singly, and has been known to stay the winter. Lesser Yellowlegs, which resembles Redshank but has long, slender, yellow legs and lacks white on the wings, has turned up more than once. Solitary Sandpiper and Semipalmated Sandpiper, both Americans which have been found here, are extremely rare anywhere in Britain. Snipe, on the other hand, reach over 200 in late autumn and winter, possibly accompanied by a Jack Snipe or two.

Teals arrive back early, and attract other closely related species. Garganeys have visited here in spring, but this is one of the very few places in southwest England where they are seen more often in autumn, a careful search revealing one or two in most years. Two American teals have also been found among their European relatives; Cornwall's first record of Blue-winged Teal came from here, and the European Teal's New World subspecies, the Green-winged Teal, has stayed.

One or two Little Gulls, often immatures with black-marked wings, and similar numbers of Black Terns pass through, both typical of reservoir habitats. The much-hoped-for White-winged Black Tern has also been seen.

As with any good birdwatching spot, the variety of different species seen, sometimes quite accidentally, heightens interest. Birds of prey other than the residents are seen quite often. Probably most regular are Peregrines, mostly single immatures, clumsily chasing whatever comes their way. The moorland attracts numbers of Skylarks and Meadow Pipits, and contains many small rodents. Merlins have specialised their feeding techniques for chasing small passerines over open ground; these tiny dark falcons have on several occasions been watched hurtling and twisting among panic-stricken flocks. There have also been sightings of the opportunist Hen Harrier, dropping into bracken after prey. Rodents are probably of most interest to the one or two Short-eared Owls which are seen most winters and often stay through to spring. Dead sheep are more to the liking of the few Red Kites which have drifted over. Lucky, and brief, sightings of Osprey and Hobby have been made of birds moving through.

Timing

Factors are few. If winds are high elsewhere, they will be worse here, from whatever direction. This makes observation difficult for the watcher, and encourages birds to huddle together or seek whatever shelter is available. Windsurfers use this water and disturbance is probably worse on weekend afternoons; this sport does not normally disturb waders but can disrupt waterfowl.

Access

The nearest A road is A394, from Helston to Penryn, from which you take Stithians sign north (left). The reservoir is reached by a minor road signposted to Carnkie. Roads run beside the lake at several points. Most people watch from these, which happen to be the most important wader spots, providing good views.

A road cuts off a small marshy part of the reservoir's southern tip, and here two hides have been erected, one either side of the road. From here, views are also gained of a large stretch of open water, often used by ducks. At the northern boundary of the reservoir, near the roadside Golden Lion Inn, a road again divides a small marshy area from the main lake. Here access around the western perimeter of the reservoir, generally the best side for waders, can be gained; open water is also seen from here. A road runs from this area to the dam.

Keys for both hides, and access permits, are available if required, from SWWA.

Resident: Little Grebe, Coot.   **Calendar**

Dec-Feb: Possible Bewick's Swan or grey geese, e.g. White-fronted; Teal, Gadwall, Wigeon, Pochard, Tufted Duck, possible Scaup and Goosander, Goldeneye, possible Hen Harrier, Merlin or Short-eared Owl. Golden Plover, Lapwing, Ruff, Snipe, possible Jack Snipe and Mediterranean Gull.

Mar-May: Most waterfowl leave by end Mar. Light wader passage possible, inc. Ruff. Possible Short-eared Owl Mar-early Apr.

Jun-Jul: Breeding species. By beginning of Jul first returning waders, especially Green, Wood and Common Sandpipers.

Aug-Nov: From early Aug, first Golden Plover and Lapwing. Ringed Plover, Dunlin, possible Lesser Golden Plover and Pectoral Sandpiper. From late Aug through Sep, Teal, maybe Garganey, Peregrine. Sep-Oct, probable Little Ringed Plover, Little Stint, Curlew Sandpiper, Ruff, Greenshank, possible Long-billed Dowitcher and other American rarities, Little Gull, Black Tern. Most waders left by end Oct. Lapwing, Golden Plover and Snipe increase. Most waterfowl begin returning Nov.

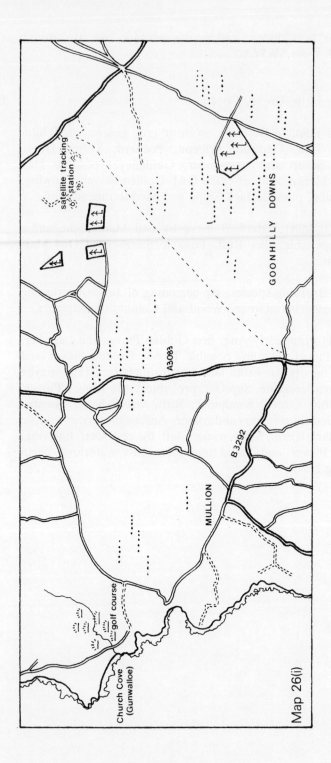

Map 26(i)

26 The Lizard

On Cornwall's south coast, this is the most southerly peninsula in England. It is flat-topped, with few trees, and large areas inland are not particularly scenic, but with high cliffs (of serpentine rock in places) the coastline is spectacular, wave-lashed and rugged. Coves such as Kynance have superb scenery; their valleys often contain little dense cover, as soil is sparse, with a few wind-blown bushes, bramble and Bracken. Church Cove offers more shelter than Kynance, with Cornish Elms towards the valley head. Cottage gardens scattered through the valley provide further shelter. Towards the mouth, the bushes peter out to Bracken and bramble. A brook runs through the valley. Another smaller bushy valley runs parallel about 100 m to the north. Gunwalloe valley has trees towards its head, but the valley bottom consists of reed-bed and marsh, lacking open water; a golf course flanks the south bank.

Habitat

Towards the tip of the Lizard are very large tracts of wet maritime heathland, a habitat of European conservation importance. Most is owned by the NT; a large, especially interesting stretch lies above Kynance Cove. Predannack Downs Nature Reserve is renowned for its specialised habitat. Here, lilac-coloured flowers of normally rare Cornish Heath are abundant. A wide variety of heathers mingles with bright yellow flowers of Western Gorse. Open heathland also predominates on the west side of the Point, the nearest sheltered area from the tip being small Caerthillian Cove

Among other interesting plants on the Lizard are Lesser Quaking Grass, both Dwarf and Pygmy Rushes, and several unusual clovers, including Upright and Twin-flowered Clover. High populations of Adders and Common Lizards are found on the heaths. Among a variety of butterflies, such as skippers, are Dark Green Fritillary and Grayling, as well as migrants such as Painted Ladies.

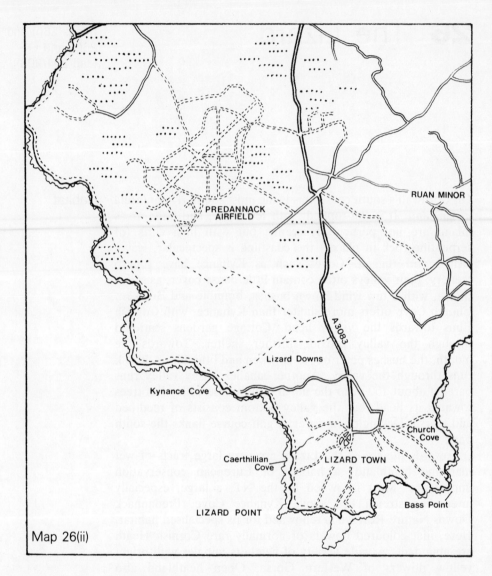

Map 26(ii)

RUAN MINOR

PREDANNACK
AIRFIELD

A 3083

Lizard Downs

Kynance Cove

Church
Cove

Caerthillian
Cove

LIZARD TOWN

Bass Point

LIZARD POINT

Species   The peninsula, a huge area, deserves more watching for birds and doubtless many more occur than are reported, especially migrants. Some parts, however, have difficult access, requiring long walks over rough or steep terrain, and land-ownership denies access to other places good for birds. We have therefore concentrated on southerly coastal sites, relatively accessible.

During winter, apart from Gannets fishing or passing in hundreds, especially off Bass Point on the southeast corner, or an infrequent Black-throated or Great Northern Diver, only a few Razorbills or Guillemots, commoner gulls and abundant Shags are expected at sea. Purple Sandpipers and Turnstones feed in small groups among seaweed-covered rocks. On land, too, interesting birds are few, with little suitable shelter from winter storms. The Lizard is home to small numbers of the locally distributed Corn Bunting; it forms small flocks in winter, often harder to see than in summer when the male, perched on posts or telegraph wires, endlessly repeats its jingling song. Jackdaws, breeding in clefts and holes in rock faces, flock in thousands from late autumn onwards. Most common woodland species, however, are very scarce in this relatively treeless area. Birds of prey hunt over open expanses, with Peregrines, Merlins and Hen Harriers all present annually outside the breeding season. The fast, agile Merlin hunts largely over heaths, as does the larger Hen Harrier, also unexpectedly agile at times when pursuing a small bird desperate to escape its snatching talons. Peregrines range more catholically, often choosing for their prey a white-plumaged feral pigeon from a flock of more darkly marked birds. Two or more of each raptor usually winter. There is a light spring passage of Merlins, and a small autumn passage of all three species. Much rarer is the Red Kite, but several have passed through, and one or two have wintered. During spring further species of migrant raptors occur, including annually a few Hobbies. Increasingly rare in Cornwall, slim Montagu's Harriers are still noted some springs, now only singly. At least two or three Short-eared Owls arrive in spring, often staying a week or so before moving on; few, if any, regularly overwinter. There are two recent spring records of the lovely little insectivorous Red-footed Falcon, a true rarity.

Early spring brings the first passerine migrants, a group of chestnut-tailed Black Redstarts, a Wheatear or two, and less often but equally early a white-gorgeted Ring Ouzel, nervously perching atop a high boulder. A few Firecrests are also early arrivals. In general, high numbers of migrant passerines are not the order of the day. Throughout spring a scattering of short-staying migrants passes through in small groups; Chiffchaffs, and rather more of the later Willow Warblers, arrive in parties of ten or more. Later still, Whitethroats come, and Wheatear numbers increase; some Wheatears breed, with up to ten pairs around Kynance area alone. Whinchats pass in groups of two or three throughout later spring. Far more Hoopoes are usually reported by the public than found by birdwatchers, but a few are annually seen in this area, including one or two in autumn when they are less expected. Other exotic overshooting migrants in spring have included Golden Oriole and the white-bellied Alpine Swift. Other commoner migrants are regular in spring, but in tiny numbers (only two or three Redstarts or Spotted Flycatchers at a time). A few Turtle Doves pass in late spring and in autumn.

Seawatching in spring may provide a few coasting skuas, including perhaps a Pomarine or two. Passage of all seabird species, including Sandwich Terns, appears very light, although auks and Gannets are often in hundreds. Fulmars and Kittiwakes breed nearby, including a colony of about 80 pairs of Kittiwakes near Kynance. Occasionally in spring, Manx Shearwaters pass by in hundreds. Oddly, in spring as well as autumn, the majority of movement is westward for all species. Common Scoter and Puffin occurrences peak here in summer, with up to 15 Puffins and 50 or so Scoters passing in a day. Rather more skuas are seen in autumn than in spring. Sooty Shearwaters are annual in very small numbers, while both the rare Great and Cory's Shearwaters have occurred. Gannets can pass at 1,000 per hour, and Kittiwakes peak in late autumn, when hundreds include many black-marked first-winter birds.

Some passerine migrants are far more numerous in autumn than in spring, and probably more unusual species also occur then. Up to 50 Wheatears per day may be seen, and more than ten Whinchats at a time. Spotted Flycatchers, the less common Pied Flycatcher, and Tree Pipits all occur more than in spring. Small groups of both Yellow and White Wagtails pass through, and coasting Grey Wagtails head westward, sometimes a steady trickle of ones and twos through the day, for several weeks. A long-tailed Tawny or Richard's Pipit may be found among wagtail and pipit flocks.

Less common migrants which appear almost annually, often in early autumn, are Wryneck, and Icterine and Melodious Warblers. Although the first is a woodpecker, it often creeps along low stone walls in search of food. The two stout warblers, both possessing a long dagger-like bill, require experience to tell apart. Swifts, late arriving and early departing, pass through in hundreds per day in both seasons. During this earlier autumn period, Red-backed and Woodchat Shrikes sometimes arrive. All shrikes are uncommon, and colourful adult males are a lucky find, but grey-brown immatures are also likely. Among major autumn rarities in recent years was an Upland Sandpiper, an American wader of grassland, seen on extensive heathland around Kynance.

Melodious Warbler

HARRISON 83

From late autumn a few Ring Ouzels, Black Redstarts and Firecrests replace the early migrants. One or two Lapland or Snow Buntings may appear on open ground towards the close of autumn. Finches and buntings are always among the last large-scale passerine arrivals. Chaffinches form the bulk, with many hundreds moving through; among them the similar but distinctively white-rumped Brambling occurs, picked out by nasal 'tchaek' calls overhead.

Timing

Correct weather conditions are always important for migration-watchers. Spring passerine migration in Cornwall is generally small, and conditions need to be very favourable. Fall conditions are ideal, but any winds off the Continent, particularly south or southeast, will bring birds across; even in clear weather, a small proportion of the birds passing over will land. Before travelling on, these less-fit birds will need to seek food and possibly rest; they often take only a couple of hours after dawn if they have arrived overnight, especially in later spring, and, by mid morning, an area which held a scatter of interesting migrants at dawn can be almost empty. Exceptions are day-flying migrants such as Swifts and Swallows, which leave the French coast at first light, arriving here four or five hours later; in mid spring they begin to arrive about mid morning.

During autumn, movements are much more protracted and, although quiet mornings are still often best, many birds remain throughout the day, perhaps several days. For new arrivals the same conditions as for spring apply.

Although the Lizard appears a very good seawatch point, it is useless unless winds are in the southern half of the compass; even if winds are only light from southerly quarters, passage may occur. In spring a seawatch between dawn and mid morning is essential; after this time migration usually ceases. The same applies in autumn unless winds are gale force, when migration can last all day. Sea mist and poor visibility, causing birds to hug the coastline, can also bring results.

For winter landbirds, choose a fine day without high winds, when birds will not shelter and raptors can hunt over moors.

Access

By A3083 down the peninsula from Helston. The first cove off this road is Gunwalloe, also called Church Cove; we have used the former name to avoid confusion with Church Cove near Lizard Point, which is described above. For Gunwalloe, follow a good road, taken opposite the far end of Culdrose Airfield, through Gunwalloe village, following signs to Church Cove where there is a large car park. Try tamarisk bushes along car park hedges, and around adjacent farm buildings, for migrants. Among reeds and marsh are high breeding populations of Sedge Warblers and Reed Buntings. Cetti's Warblers almost certainly breed, but are far more often heard than seen. Public footpaths follow the coastline left and right of the cove. Among the cove's sandy-topped cliffs Sand Martins breed. Public access to the lower part of the reed-bed is by walking along the golf-course edge.

Kynance Cove is reached via a private toll road; at the bottom is a car park. Walk right a few hundred metres to the steep, quite small valley. For Predannack Downs, continue up the steep valley slope. Another, more direct, access to Predannack Downs is by parking in a pull-in opposite Kynance road. Walk towards Helston for about ¹2 mile (0.8 km), where there is a wide track through a gap in the hedge, level with the road, on the left. Small grassy fields along its perimeter are favoured by pipits; open areas are used by raptors.

For Church Cove near the tip, take the road forking left just before Lizard town, immediately past the private Kynance road. Follow signs until the church, where there are limited parking spaces. Walk down through the village after searching through the elms and churchyard area. The tarmac road becomes a rough track near the cove. A NT footpath is taken on the left, and another small bushy valley leads back to the church.

To reach Bass Point, best for passing seabirds, walk from the head of Church Cove along a concrete path to the lifeboat station, then continue to the Point along a narrow clifftop path about 1 mile (1.6 km) to the Coastguard station.

Caerthillian Cove is not signposted anywhere. Park in Lizard town square, following the public footpath beside it, signposted to Kynance Cove and Pentreath Beach. Walk for about ¾ mile (1.2 km) along a wide track, alongside a row of houses; the last house overlooks the small shallow valley. It contains no trees. Cover for small migrant birds is Blackthorn bushes, Bramble, and gorse especially towards its head; although sparse, this is the only cover within 2 miles (3 km) this side of the exposed Point, and surrounded by equally exposed land.

Flat Goonhilly Downs are reached through the middle of Culdrose Airfield, on B3293. Scan moorland around the satellite-tracking dishes. Minor roads left and right, which dissect the open ground, can be taken. Raptors use this area and a few pairs of Curlews breed; use your car as a hide. The B road continues to Coverack Cove.

Calendar

Resident: Shag, Sparrowhawk, Buzzard, Cetti's Warbler, Curlew, Corn Bunting, Raven; Gannets offshore all year.

Dec-Feb: Seabirds inc. Black-throated or Great Northern Diver, Guillemot and Razorbill. Hen Harrier, Peregrine, Merlin, Purple Sandpiper, Turnstone, possible Short-eared Owl, winter thrushes.

Mar-May: A few Firecrests and Black Redstarts by early Mar; mid-end Mar, Chiffchaff and Wheatear, possible Ring Ouzel. Early Apr, Willow Warbler, possible Hoopoe; mid Apr, Merlin, Short-eared Owl, Whitethroat, hirundines. End Apr-early May, Swift, higher numbers of above warblers, other commoner warblers, Whinchat, Redstart, Spotted Flycatcher, possibly Hobby, Turtle Dove; perhaps southern overshoots from mid Apr. Manx Shearwater, possible Arctic or Pomarine Skua.

Jun-Jul: Breeding species, inc. Wheatear, Whitethroat, Sedge Warbler, Sand Martin. Common Scoter and Puffin passage peaks mid Jun-end Jul.

Aug-Nov: Seabirds, inc. a few Arctic, Great or Pomarine Skuas, possible Great or Cory's Shearwater, probably Sooty Shearwater especially early in season. Later in season (Oct-Nov) Kittiwakes peak. Commoner passerine migrants through Sep, especially Wheatear, Whinchat, Tree Pipit, Yellow Wagtail, coasting Grey Wagtail. Possible Woodchat or Red-backed Shrike. Mid Oct through Nov, Firecrest, Black Redstart, Ring Ouzel, possible Snow or Lapland Bunting. Chaffinch flocks contain Bramblings; winter thrushes arrive.

27 Marazion Marsh, Mounts Bay and Waterfront to Newlyn

(Map 27 and OS Map 203)

Habitat

Penzance is probably the best-known locality here, and the last large town on the south coast of Cornwall. The harbour entrance leads out into Mounts Bay, at the east side of which lies St Michael's Mount, a steep, rocky, privately owned island. Marazion Marsh is opposite the island, just inland from the sandy beach.

Penzance harbour and adjoining Newlyn contain most of west Cornwall's fishing fleet, mainly small inshore trawlers, although large trawlers from farther afield have operated offshore in recent winters. The bay's seabed is largely sandy, with the greatest area of rocks around St Michael's Mount; several freshwater streams drain across the broad beaches. As the bay faces south, it is sheltered from all winds from northerly quarters.

Marazion Marsh is not large, covering only some 85 acres (35 ha), but is the largest reed-bed in Cornwall. A main road runs along the seaward side, a major railway line crosses the marsh, and houses are adjacent on one side. The marsh comprises an expanse of dense *Phragmites* reed, relatively small areas of open water, and a larger area of low sedges and Flag Iris, in which clumps of willow grow. There is a small stand of pines at the rear.

Species

Geographical position makes the marsh and bay one of Cornwall's most important sites for birds. Winter is very interesting in each habitat within this area. The bay regularly attracts divers, grebes and a few seaducks, while unusual gulls and several wader species are found along the shoreline. Great Northern Divers appear from early winter and decrease from early spring. In good years up to ten might be present at a time, but four or five is more usual; often they cruise close to shore in search of small crabs, finding them on almost every dive. One or two Black-throated Divers may occur through

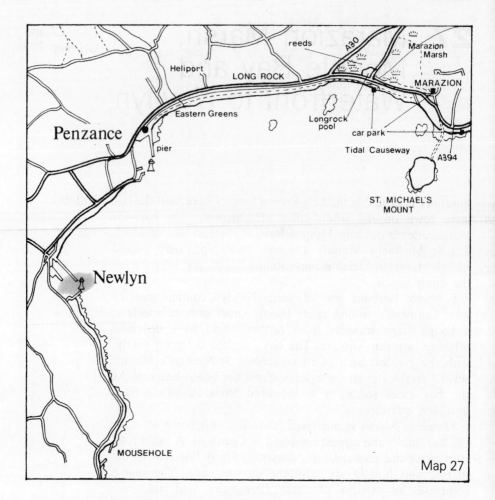

Map 27

the same period, generally increasing from late winter as passage migrants gather; numbers vary, usually fewer than 15. Slavonian Grebes may be present in twos and threes, later birds perhaps attaining summer plumage. Black-necked and Red-necked Grebes are only rare visitors, but one or two a year are expected. Seaducks are irregular in occurrence, and only commoner species are generally seen — two or three Eiders perhaps, or a small flock of Common Scoters, which may contain a large-billed Velvet Scoter with wedge-shaped head profile more reminiscent of an Eider. Dowdy immature or female Long-tailed Ducks have visited, usually singly.

Large numbers of gulls are found throughout the district. Freshwater outlets running across the beaches towards the sea at low tides are used by gull flocks to bathe, preen and drink.

From semi-concealed positions behind rocks nearby, extremely good views may be had of assembled birds. Unusual gulls occur here regularly. The standard uncommon gulls are the same four that occur reasonably regularly throughout coastal Devon and Cornwall: Little, Mediterranean, Iceland and Glaucous. In recent years the American Ring-billed Gull, once considered an extremely rare vagrant, has been proved to occur at least as frequently as Iceland Gull, with individuals staying long periods. Mediterranean Gulls of all ages appear in ones and twos, with a late winter or early spring peak as different birds moving through stop here briefly. A similar pattern of occurrence exists for Iceland Gulls, but most frequently seen are pale-fawn-speckled immatures. Glaucous, also often similarly marked and coloured immatures, arrive less predictably, but Little Gulls tend to be more numerous towards spring. Common Gulls are found in quite high numbers, which rise as more than 300 late-winter immigrants arrive. Gull flocks are further increased by passages of Lesser Black-backed Gulls in similar numbers to Common, while a few Kittiwakes are also present. Other gull species reported in recent years have included further American vagrants, stopping off at this, the first resting and feeding area they reach on the British mainland: Bonaparte's Gull has been seen about four times, and a Laughing Gull stayed to winter.

Other irregular visitors to the bay might include a storm-driven Little Auk or Grey Phalarope, possibly a Red-throated Diver or a passing skua. There is no skua passage as such, although that traditional harbinger of spring, the Sandwich Tern, is normally a particularly early arrival and a small but steady passage ensues. Later, small numbers of Common and a handful of Arctic Terns pass by, with one or two Roseate and Little Terns. In autumn, especially earlier, terns are the only seabirds of interest regularly seen, although, as in spring, numbers are small.

Waders are generally low in number, the sandy beach habitat being responsible for several omissions. One wader specialising in sandy conditions is the pale grey and white Sanderling, uncommon in many parts of Cornwall. Over 100 may gather here, its stronghold on the Cornish mainland. Sprinting along the tideline, they follow receding waves down the beach. Never fewer than 40 winter, but counts at migration seasons are erratic, peaks occurring in spring in some years and autumn in others; some stay to early summer at least, moulting into bright-brown-spangled summer plumage. Ringed Plovers also like this habitat and are scattered throughout. In spring the rare Kentish Plover might be seen; indeed, it is almost annual, two or three having been recorded in a season. Bar-tailed Godwits and Grey Plovers share the beaches, usually small numbers although up to 50 of the latter have been counted. Turnstones will turn seaweed and even tin cans when searching for food, and so are found all along the shore, over 50 being usual. At high tide they often sleep on moored trawlers. Purple Sandpiper flocks, on the other hand, remain loyal to rocky outcrops, especially around Penzance and Newlyn; 20 or more is not unusual and over 50 occur at times.

Marazion Marsh has an interesting and regular wintering population, annually supplemented with unusual visitors. No species of bird is present in very large numbers, although gulls visit in higher numbers for short periods to bathe and preen and may include individuals of scarcer gull species. Ducks are probably most common, Mallards and Teals often totalling well over 50 apiece. More interesting are Shovelers, the gatherings of 30 or more being unusually large for Cornwall. Other dabbling ducks turn up occasionally, mostly in ones and twos, and regularly include Gadwalls. A small number of diving ducks consists mainly of Pochards, with ten or so usual, about the same counts of Tufted, and occasional Scaups. Several Little Grebes and both Coots and Moorhens are present, but only the latter breed. Water Rails are also present at this season, too secretive for their numbers to be estimated realistically but probably under ten. In some winters, particularly in hard weather, a Bittern may briefly take up territory, although such quick sightings as might be gained will be provided reluctantly by this reticent species. Snipe may be 50 strong, remaining largely unseen until they fly. Completing a group of species less likely to be seen than most is a fairly recent immigrant to this country — newer still to Cornwall — Cetti's Warbler: this vocal species has now become a breeding resident, though probably no more than two or three pairs nest.

Grey Herons are far more obliging residents, ten or more of which may be seen at once. Five or six pairs breed, some in traditional habitat high among topmost branches of nearby pines; each year, however, two or three pairs nest on the ground among reeds, a much less usual situation in Britain. During irruption years, when breeding of Bearded Tits has been exceptionally good in East Anglia (or even Holland) with as many as three broods raised in the season by each pair, and five or six young per brood, the species visits reed-beds far outside its normal range in search of food; Marazion is no exception. Every autumn and winter, up to 20,000 babbling Starlings use the reeds as a night roost.

On average over the years, the marsh probably produces some of the earliest returning hirundines in Britain. Sand Martins are by tradition early, but at Marazion a few Swallows and sometimes a House Martin may equal them; later their numbers increase substantially. Other migrants well known for making early landfalls also visit, such as Wheatears, shy Garganeys swimming close to reeds fringing the pools, and perhaps a Hoopoe. Further exciting visitors usually occur later in spring — a white-plumaged Spoonbill or Little Egret perhaps. Common waders passing through early, such as Dunlins, are supplemented by a few Ruffs, sometimes only two or three at a time. Among them may be rarer visitors such as Little Ringed Plovers. Whimbrels are annual migrants, often counted in hundreds through a season. Sparrowhawks and Buzzards regularly hunt the marsh, joined rarely by a Marsh Harrier quartering the reeds. Also hawking over the reeds one recent spring was a White-winged Black Tern in full summer plumage. Yellow Wagtails pass through in small numbers in spring and autumn, and a pair or two have bred in past seasons. Among their numbers birds of differing geographical races sometimes appear, 'blue-headed' most frequently. Migrant parties are joined by a few White Wagtails, and at the same period, or perhaps earlier, the uncommon pale Water Pipit may be seen by freshwater margins. Sedge and Reed Warblers arrive to breed in the marsh; in autumn juveniles of the former can be mistaken for the more brightly marked Aquatic Warbler, one of the earliest autumn rarities that appears almost annually.

During autumn it may be possible to see many species which were noted in spring. Others are restricted to autumn and include the highly elusive Bluethroat; on the rare occasions when this species is reported, it is often by a ringer who has extracted one from a mistnet. Difficult, but not impossible, to see is the intricately marked Spotted Crake; patience and silence pay off when from out of deep cover the buffish crake steps nervously, warily picking insects from a muddy pool. Some years three or four may be present together. Interesting waders may include a few Little Stints, Curlew Sandpipers or Spotted Redshanks. American rarities are expected, though not necessarily annually; the most regular among them is the Dunlin-like Pectoral Sandpiper, but Long-billed Dowitchers have also been seen several times.

Hirundines once again begin to mass, joining large groups of Swifts feeding before departure. Swallows roost at night in the reeds, where over 1,000 may assemble. This late activity attracts another migrant, the Hobby, preying on the Swallow tribe at this time of year. Among the Swallows and martins feeding on the myriad insects, especially flying ants over the marsh, there may be one or two Little Gulls or Black Terns, and always something very special may appear.

Timing

Gulls gather at the beach freshwater outflows when the tide is out. They also throng the tidelines, joined by waders. During rough weather, especially from late autumn through to spring, a wide variety of species may seek the bay's comparative shelter, particularly if winds are from northerly quarters. The beaches are popular with local inhabitants as well as tourists, but may be less disturbed in winter. If possible, early morning or midweek visits are advised, on ebbing tides in good weather. When trawlers unload in the harbour, gulls are drawn from widely scattered areas and this greater concentration may contain unusual species.

Even in very early spring, a spell of settled weather with winds from southerly quarters off the Continent may produce early migrants of a wide range of species, including land- and waterbirds and waders. The marsh is far less disturbed, and most species adapt to interruption from trains and cars. Lower water levels encourage waders to visit and stay, while hard weather may increase numbers of more common birds and produce the odd rarity. Westerly winds from the Atlantic are mostly responsible for the arrivals of American waders. Calm winter days are best for views of Bearded Tits if present.

There is much interchange of birds between here and Hayle estuary complex; conditions, if rough at one site, are often sheltered at the other. Although the two localities are quite close, they are on opposite coasts and there is a slight difference in tide times of which many birds, particularly gulls, take advantage.

Access

A30 runs alongside Mounts Bay, and through Penzance, beside the waterfront. From the marsh to Newlyn is about 3 miles (5 km). There are car parking facilities throughout the area. Public roads fringe harbours and fish quays, where public access on foot is allowed. The beaches can be walked full length, from Marazion to Penzance. Alternatively, the beach named Eastern Green, immediately east of Penzance, may be reached on foot via a level crossing over the railway line (almost opposite the Heliport entrance). This area is a favourite with gulls, as also is the sewer beside the outer wall at Newlyn fish quay.

Marazion can be viewed easily from the roadside pavement. Arriving on A30 from Hayle side, turn left at Long Rock before Penzance and drive east along the front to the marsh. If access onto the marsh is necessary, there is a path opposite the small grassed car park at its east end. Please do not enter the marsh carelessly and disturb birds. Careful approach and concealment is made easier by low clumps of bushes.

Calendar

Resident: Cormorant, Shag, Grey Heron, Cetti's Warbler, Reed Bunting.

Dec-Feb: Divers, especially Great Northern, and grebes, mostly Slavonian. Unusual gulls, Glaucous in earlier part, Little, Mediterranean and Iceland mostly towards end of period, when Common and Lesser Black-backed Gulls and Kittiwakes arrive. Possible Eider, Common Scoter or Long-tailed Duck. Sanderling, Purple Sandpiper, Turnstone, Grey Plover, Ringed Plover, Snipe. Teal, Shoveler, probable Gadwall; Pochard and Tufted Duck. Water Rail. Possible Bittern and Bearded Tit. Black-throated Diver mostly towards end of period.

Mar-May: Unusual gulls may occur throughout, mostly Mar, when Ring-billed possible. Black-throated Divers often peak early Apr. From mid Mar, first Sandwich Terns, Garganey, Ruff, Sand Martin, Wheatear, maybe Water Pipit, possible Swallow or Hoopoe. From mid Apr, Whimbrel, Common Tern, Arctic, possible Roseate or Little Terns. Possible Little Ringed Plover, Kentish Plover, Spoonbill, Little Egret or other southern overshoots.

Jun-Jul: Breeding species, inc. Reed and Sedge Warblers.

Aug-Nov: From mid Aug to end Sep, possible Aquatic Warbler, return tern passage. Light passage of common waders inc. high Sanderling numbers. Unusual waders: Little Stint, Curlew Sandpiper, possible Green and Wood Sandpipers, maybe American waders. From Sep through Oct, probable Spotted Crake, Black Tern, Little Gull, Swallow roost to end Sep, possible Hobby. Starling roost from early Sep. Divers, grebes and seaducks begin to return Nov.

28 Porthgwarra-Land's End Area

Porthgwarra valley, and adjacent south-projecting Gwennap Head, lie only about 3 miles (5 km) from Land's End. Birdwatchers include the whole vicinity south of a line from Carn-Lês-Boel cliffs to, and including, St Levan church to the east. This coastal site is exposed to winds from most directions, except for the lower valley and areas around St Levan church, and in higher winds even gardens and more sheltered areas become affected. At the head of the valley is a small bush-fringed pond, shallow and usually dry from late spring to late autumn. There are small fields of rough pasture and arable land on the landward side of the valley. Above the more luxuriant growth in the valley lies an expanse of very exposed heathland. Gorse and heather, including Western Gorse and Cross-leaved Heath, grow in profusion. The 'moors' in late summer are a mixture of blazing purple and gold. In the stream valley, groups of trees, mostly Sallow and Cornish Elm, are kept low by salt-laden winds. Royal Fern grows in boggy patches near the stream. Dense areas of Bracken, bramble and Blackthorn are also found. The magnificent cliffs contain huge, rounded granite boulders, the heath extending to cliff-edge sea turf. Among this fine, short grass grow blue carpets of Autumn and Spring Squill, Rock Sea Lavender and Golden Samphire. Around St Levan church are sheltered groups of trees, gardens and hedgerows. A brook runs through the centre. Looking seaward on a fine clear day, the outline of the Isles of Scilly can be seen 28 miles (45 km) off. One mile (1.6 km) offshore, from Gwennap Coastguard lookout, lies Runnel Stone reef, marked by a bell-buoy. A powerful tiderace flows past the headland.

Interesting butterflies are seen on land. Graylings are common, some still flying to early October. This is a good spot for migrant butterflies; among Clouded Yellows, a few Pale Clouded Yellows are noted. Some years in early autumn,

Habitat

211

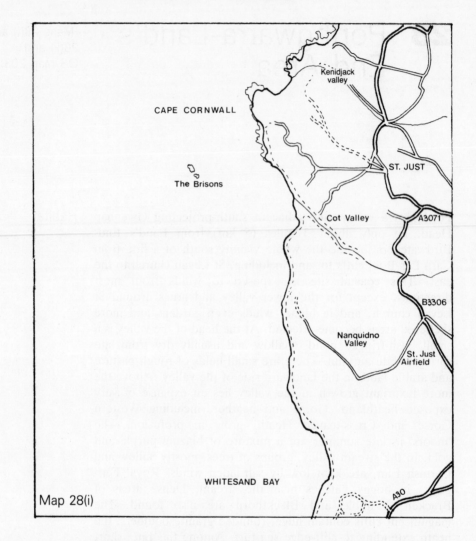

Map 28(i)

thousands of migrant day-flying Silver-Y Moths drink from heather flowers. Adders and Grey Seals are common; Killer Whales and dolphins have been watched offshore.

North of Porthgwarra are other, less-known sheltered coastal valleys adjacent to Land's End. Nanquidno valley, near St Just, has a stream flowing through, lined by bushes and hedges. The small Cot Valley, little visited by birdwatchers, deserves to be better known; many interesting or uncommon migrants are seen in spring and autumn. This picturesque valley, steep-sided and gorse-covered, with rubble from disused mine workings spread over valley sides, has most

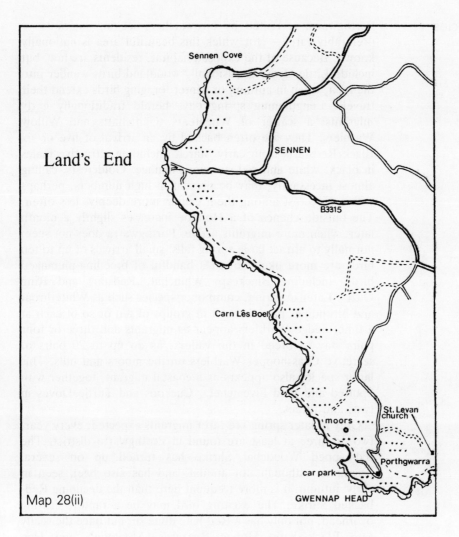

Map 28(ii)

cover including trees and cottage gardens towards its head.
Some Sallow and Elderberry bushes grow beside its stream.
Seaviews are panoramic, facing Brisons Rocks 1 mile (1.6 km)
distant, most notably used by about 100 pairs of breeding
Razorbills. Kenidjack, just north of Cape Cornwall, may also
shelter interesting migrants (recently an American Redstart).
On flat land overlooking the bend of the valley is St Just
Airfield, an open area of short turf. Further inland east and
north along Land's End peninsula, an exposed band of
moorland and hills with heather, brambles and rough pasture
rises to 200-300 m, overlooking the cultivated coastal plain and
extending some 12 miles (19 km) to St Ives.

Species

Porthgwarra is visited by birdwatchers seeking migrants — preferably rare! — for which this beautiful area is nationally known. Because of the exposed habitat, residents are few, but include Little Owls. Occasionally woodland birds wander into the area, when in autumn or winter foraging birds extend their travels. Lengthening spring days herald traditionally early migrants: a scatter of Wheatears, Chiffchaffs and Willow Warblers. They are often backed by an arrival of five or six Black Redstarts from early March, including attractive males in black, white and red summer plumage. Goldcrests, calling almost incessantly, may be present in high numbers, perhaps with a Firecrest among them calling more deeply, less often. The outside chance of a Hoopoe increases slightly a month later, when more migrants arrive. Porthgwarra does not seem normally to attract large spring falls; small arrivals of up to ten birds are more likely, often a handful of breeding-plumaged birds, including Blackcap, Whinchat, Redstart and Ring Ouzel. Later in spring, commoner species such as Whitethroat and hirundines pass through in groups of ten or so of each at a time. Sedge Warblers appear as migrants and three or four pairs stay to breed in the valleys, as do up to 20 pairs of secretive Grasshopper Warblers on the moors and hills. This latter species also appears as a coastal migrant, together with Spotted and Pied Flycatchers, Cuckoos and Turtle Doves in twos and threes.

Only in later spring are rarer migrants expected; every year, two or three at least are found in Porthgwarra district. The red-capped Woodchat Shrike has turned up on several occasions, although not annual, and has also been seen in early autumn; it is more frequent here than the declining Red-backed Shrike. The exciting bird may be a raptor, drifting overhead; not only has a Red Kite done so, but once the really rare Black Kite. Honey Buzzards, Montagu's and Hen Harriers and Hobbies have all been seen on several occasions. Among commoner *Sylvia* Warblers, naturally skulking, was once an even more skulking Subalpine Warbler.

Off the headland, small groups of Whimbrels pass eastward close to shore. The casual watcher will almost certainly see Gannets, and Fulmars just a few metres offshore, but a more sustained watch is required to see more interesting seabirds. The best months to see divers passing are April and May, but probably only two or three in a morning. Most commonly seen is the large Great Northern, with slow wingbeats; next most numerous is the slightly smaller Black-throated with faster wingbeats, showing strongly contrasting black upperparts and white underparts; least numerous, as always in Cornwall, is the smaller, browner, fast-beating Red-throated. A few Common Scoters flying past close to the sea in single file are the only regular ducks. There is very light skua passage; Arctics travel singly, perhaps two or three a day, but rarely a pack is seen, signalling Pomarine. Tern passage is also light, mostly Sandwich, often in small groups of up to ten; a few Common pass, but Arctic or Roseate are less likely. Skua and tern passage is eastward, usually within a mile (1.6 km) range. Seawatching in summer can still be rewarding, with ocean-going Kittiwakes breeding towards Land's End. Feeding parties of Manx Shearwaters, probably from the Isles of Scilly or Welsh islands such as Skomer, pass by quite frequently, sometimes thousands in small groups in a few hours. Strings of auks, constantly passing to and fro, often include a few Puffins. Hard to observe, Storm Petrels are often seen singly, but a group of three or four may 'dance' over the water; only very rarely do higher numbers of 50 or more occur. Rare Cory's Shearwaters, straying from breeding grounds farther south, can be looked for; unlike Manx, which they dwarf, they do not continually bank from side to side, but glide, often on bowed wings, giving a few languid flaps before another extended glide.

Towards late summer, commoner seabird migrants such as terns begin to pass westward and the chance of a Cory's, along with two large shearwaters from the south Atlantic, Sooty Shearwater and the rarer Great, increases slightly. Extra care must be taken when claiming Sooty, as sightings of the browner Mediterranean form of Manx, the Balearic Shear-water, also increase. Through early autumn, seabird numbers and variety improve. Skua numbers are higher, although often only three or four Arctic or Great per day may pass by; Pomarines, now travelling singly, are the least frequent of the three commoner species. Lesser Black-backed Gulls, including many first-year birds, pass westward in hundreds. At sea off here one expects to see unusual or rare birds; apart from those already mentioned, Long-tailed Skua, Leach's Petrel and Black Guillemot have occurred.

Passerine migrants return from early autumn; average numbers are higher than in spring, and birds stay longer. Expected early birds are Spotted and Pied Flycatchers, *Phylloscopus* warblers and Whinchats, which stand out from resident Stonechats by their off-white eyebrow-stripe. Among the first unusual warblers may be a Melodious; although virtually annual, only one may be identified in a season.

Icterine Warblers are less regular. Open-ground species favour the heath and pasture; 20-30 Wheatears, White and Yellow Wagtails, and 100 or so Meadow Pipits gather; among them a few Tree Pipits are often heard calling. The larger, long-tailed Tawny Pipit may visit from the Continent. Looking like a very pale juvenile Yellow Wagtail but larger, it has a similar call, plus a sparrow-like 'chirrup'; one or two are seen each autumn. The Asiatic Richard's Pipit, with rich brown coloration, is similar, but its 'shreep' flight call is distinctive; formerly at least five or six occurred in some years, but recently only the same number as its European relative. Sharing the moorland habitat with pipits and wagtails may be a Dotterel, occasionally two or three, although not every autumn. Whimbrels also stop to feed among the heather, where the 'quip' call of Ortolan Bunting has been heard. Single Corncrakes, now rare migrants, are occasionally flushed from the same habitat. Grassland-feeding species are also attracted to St Just Airfield, where Dotterels and the rare larger pipits have been recorded on a number of occasions; other plovers, and waders such as American Buff-breasted Sandpipers, have visited here in autumn. On the short grass those birds present may be easier to see than at Porthgwarra, although slight undulations in the ground can conceal even Dotterels when sitting. Sometimes, however, particularly if flights have taken place, the airfield is deserted by birds.

Raptors are regular autumn visitors to the area, one or two Peregrines, Merlins and Hobbies passing over the coastal valleys; other less frequent birds of prey include Osprey, Red Kite, Honey Buzzard and Montagu's Harrier.

As the season progresses, numbers and species of birds begin to dwindle. Replacements are likely to be more unusual or rare species. Regular, though only ones and twos per autumn, are exquisite and intricately marked Wrynecks. Barred Warblers, large, grey and white with few markings, are also found most years. Migrants which traditionally arrive late and in larger numbers include Robins, of which 50 or more may be present, and Goldcrests in similar numbers. Firecrests peak at about ten in Porthgwarra, but three or four is more likely. Up to ten Black Redstarts are normally seen at a time, but perhaps over 20 towards late autumn. Other later migrants, visiting in ones and twos, are the harrier-like Short-eared Owl, Hen Harrier and Ring Ouzel. Lapland and Snow Buntings, feeding on heather seeds on the heath above the valley, are difficult to see on the ground; they may also turn up on the airfield. Rare, usually seen only once per autumn, are

Great Shearwater

Cory's Shearwater

HARRISON 83

Red-breasted Flycatchers and the tiny hyperactive Yellow-browed Warbler, both preferring valley trees; such species may also turn up, along with small numbers of Firecrests, Goldcrests and other passerine migrants, in the other valleys.

If conditions are right, large movements of finches pass over the valleys. Thousands of Chaffinches, hundreds of Bramblings, and dozens of Siskins are involved. When such movements take place, with hundreds of Skylarks and flocks of Stock Doves passing, a Twite or Serin may be recorded.

By the end of the season most migrants have departed, but a few individuals linger into early winter. Some may even stay, such as Water Rail, Firecrest, Black Redstart, Snipe or perhaps Jack Snipe, and Woodcock. Short-eared Owls and other predators may also be encountered; two or three of these day-flying owls, plus one or two Merlins and often four or five Hen Harriers, west Cornwall's largest concentration, arrive to winter on the peninsula's higher moorland slopes. By now Porthgwarra will have produced another major rarity for Cornwall, perhaps Pallas's Warbler or a Tree Sparrow! Like the Scillies, this area has an enviable record for producing American vagrant landbirds: three seen here, and nowhere else in Britain before, were American Redstart, Veery and two Chimney Swifts together. Other neighbouring valleys have shared in these surprise arrivals: recently, Europe's first Varied Thrush, a Pacific coast woodland bird, was found at Nanquidno.

Timing

For seawatching off Porthgwarra, a southeasterly or south-westerly wind, light to moderate, is best. Mist at sea could be an advantage, as long as you can see 1 mile (1.6 km) or so out. Strong or gale-force southwesterlies, or offshore strong winds, are least productive, but birds may appear soon after these have abated, or travel before a front passes. Mornings, late afternoons and evenings through spring and summer, and very early autumn, have been good. During autumn migration, seawatching at any time of the day will probably be rewarding in the right conditions. Strong sunlight causes problems, as everything is in silhouette for much of its travel; eyestrain can be a problem. When the sun has moved around later in the day, conditions improve a little. Best is when there is no direct sunlight on the water.

For landbirds in spring, any wind from a southerly quarter, light to moderate, can produce a few migrants; the valleys are adversely affected by high winds. If conditions are clear, most soon depart. Mist or drizzle, of the type associated with wet southeasterlies, may delay them, and produce more birds. The same conditions in autumn are responsible for some of the best bird days. In autumn light easterlies are also excellent, especially if cloud or rain causes birds to land. As a rule birds move off less quickly in autumn, but not always. Strong winds from any direction, funnelling through valley bushes, make the area inhospitable; on such days few migrants are seen. St Levan may be more sheltered, and could be worth checking. Strong northerly winds make visiting largely a waste of time.

Watch St Just Airfield when it is not in use (best early mornings, evenings or weekdays). Fine days are best for moorland raptors in winter; late afternoon, when Short-eared

Owls start hunting and harriers or Merlins strive to make a last kill before nightfall, can be interesting. Two or three hours' watch is needed, ideally over an open stretch, to see raptors coming and going, as they range widely.

Access

For Porthgwarra, from A30, after leaving Penzance towards Land's End, take B3283 through St Buryan. Follow this road to B3315 and continue towards Sennen; at a sharp bend to the right, turn off left on a minor road signposted to Porthgwarra village and car park.

Check for passerines at the base of Porthgwarra valley, among trees and sheltered gardens, especially tamarisk bushes. You can follow a steep path from the cove cliffs, or walk up the road to the Coastguard cottages and heathland. there are good footpaths from here to the cliffs or across the heath. From these paths, search carefully through bushes and trees in the valley.

For seawatching, sit left of the Coastguard lookout, more or less opposite the reef marked by Runnel Stone buoy. Seabirds often feed around the reef and over the tiderace. You can walk to St Levan Church via a highly scenic coast path. Check among the trees and bushes for small birds, and the fields for pipits, etc. A coastal public footpath extends from Mousehole around the entire Land's End peninsula to Hayle.

From B3315 past Porthgwarra, to reach Nanquidno and St Just, continue west towards Land's End, turning north on A30 then B3306 towards St Just. Before reaching the village you pass the airfield to the left. Immediately afterwards, turn left down a minor road along the airfield boundary towards Nanquidno. Good views of the airfield are possible from this roadside. There are several vergeside pull-offs for cars down the valley, but it is better to park and cover the whole valley on foot.

To reach Cot Valley take road signposted to Cape Cornwall, situated in the middle of St Just village, near clock tower; within about 200m take a minor road on the left, signposted to Cot Valley. There is limited car parking beside a narrow road at the head of the valley (this road runs valley length, with further limited parking). On sunny weekend afternoons you may have to park in St Just, as this is a popular tourist spot; but few birds will be seen at these times anyway. Follow public footpaths around gardens at the valley head (good for flycatchers and warblers). An elevated path on the left (facing sea) runs valley length. Check lower rocky areas for such species as Wheatear and Black Redstarts. **Note** There is a Youth Hostel in the valley.

Several good minor roads intersect the high moorlands, and all could probably produce interesting raptors. A particularly high vantage point with the widest possible vista is required to enable sightings of more distant raptors. One of the better places is near Trewey Hill. Turn right off B3306 when heading from St Just to St Ives, along the minor road signposted to Newmill and Penzance; this rather steep road begins to level out, with views over a wide area of moor. Pull off on to the verge and scan the area. Other minor roads near Trewey should also be tried.

Calendar

Resident: Gannet, Cormorant (both non-breeders); Shags breed. Sparrowhawks and Buzzards breed inland. Razorbills and Guillemots constantly passing. Little Owl, Green Woodpecker, Rock Pipit, Stonechat, Reed Bunting, Raven.

Dec-Feb: Few interesting birds winter regularly on coast. Possible wintering passerines. Hen Harrier, possibly Peregrine, Merlin, Short-eared Owl inland on hills, occasional on coast.

Mar-May: Early part of period, Fulmars and Kittiwakes return. First passerine migrants may be Black Redstarts early-mid Mar; end Mar, first Chiffchaffs and Wheatears; by Apr, Willow Warblers and Goldcrests. Mid Apr onwards, Blackcap, Whinchat, Redstart, Ring Ouzel, possible Hoopoe; hirundines pass through. End Apr-May, Whitethroat, Grasshopper Warbler, flycatchers, Cuckoo, Turtle Dove, Whimbrel. At sea in Apr-May, all three divers pass, Manx Shearwaters, Sandwich and Common Terns. Mid May, Arctic and possible Pomarine Skuas. Rarer landbirds expected through May.

Jun-Jul: Breeding species, possible late arriving migrants, and spring overshoots. Seabirds throughout period, inc. Manx Shearwater, possible Cory's, Storm Petrel, Common Scoter, Puffin.

Aug-Nov: Seabirds may now include Great, Sooty and Balearic Shearwaters; Pomarine and Arctic Skuas, Great Skua, Lesser Black-backed Gull, Sandwich and Common Terns. Early Aug on, common *Phylloscopus* and *Sylvia* warblers, especially Whitethroat. Wheatear, Whinchat and

Redstart, Spotted Flycatcher, possible Melodious Warbler or Woodchat. From Sep, the above plus Whimbrel, Turtle Dove, Tree and Meadow Pipits, possible Osprey, probable Dotterel, Wryneck, Barred Warbler, or Tawny Pipit; White, Grey and Yellow Wagtails; other less regular or rare species. From Oct, Goldcrest, Firecrest, Ring Ouzel, Hen Harrier, Peregrine, Merlin, Short-eared Owl; towards end Oct to Nov, Black Redstart, Robins, flocks of finches, Skylarks and Stock Doves, Water Rail, Woodcock, Snipe, possible Jack Snipe, Lapland and Snow Buntings, possible Yellow-browed Warbler and Red-breasted Flycatcher. Moorland raptors arrive to winter from end Oct.

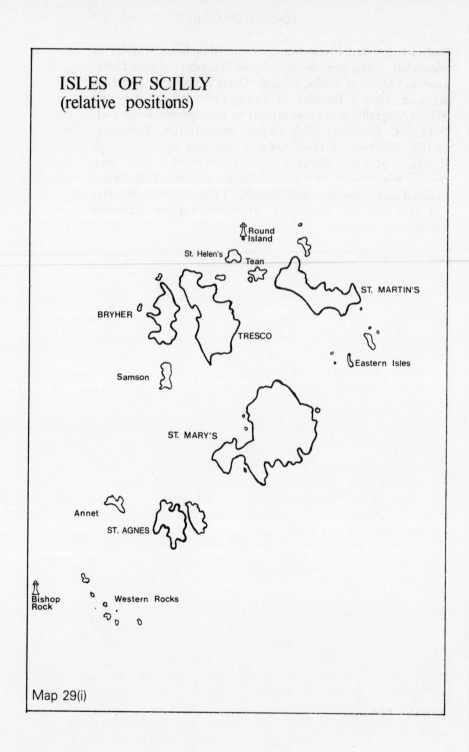

ISLES OF SCILLY
(relative positions)

Round Island

St. Helen's   Tean

BRYHER

ST. MARTIN'S

TRESCO

Eastern Isles

Samson

ST. MARY'S

Annet

ST. AGNES

Bishop Rock

Western Rocks

Map 29(i)

29 The Isles of Scilly

(Maps 29(i) and 29(ii) and OS Map 203)

Twenty-eight miles (45 km) beyond Land's End, and visible from Cornish mainland cliffs on a clear day, the Scillies are a world apart from the rest of the region. Of 100 or so rocks forming the archipelago, only five are regularly inhabited, the largest St Mary's, with a length of $2^{1}2$ miles (4 km) and the major portion of the inhabitants. Within this highly scenic island group, no more than 10 miles (16 km) from corner to corner, the variety of habitats includes rocky and sandy shores, cliffs, farmland, heaths, open downs, sea turf, marshes, lakes and woods. The land is characterised by lush vegetation in sheltered areas, which responds to the mild oceanic climate and lack of frost. Light snowfall is seen every 20 years or so on average. The main limiting factors for vegetation are high winds and blown sea spray. High windbreaking hedges of salt-resistant *Pittisporum* around small flower-growing fields are a characteristic landscape feature on inhabited islands. Other introduced subtropical plants such as tamarisks and palms form a substantial addition to the native flora of the main islands. Island wildlife includes the Scilly Shrew, while Porpoises are often seen in channels between islands; Grey Seals are resident, often seen basking on rocks in fine weather, and breeding on quieter outer isles. Many rare wild flowers or rare local forms of commoner plants are found. Autumn winds have brought large orange Monarch butterflies from America, and Clouded Yellows in groups from southern Europe. Although Rabbits are common, most other animals found on the mainland are unknown here; snakes, Foxes, Badgers, Stoats and Weasels are entirely absent.

The main islands and rock clusters are:

St Mary's Contains Hugh Town, port and main town for the islands, with over 2,000 inhabitants. Although chiefly agricultural, the island has two major boggy south-facing valleys, Lower Moors and Holy Vale-Porth Hellick, with water and sheltered bushes. Areas of open downland with heather and

Habitat

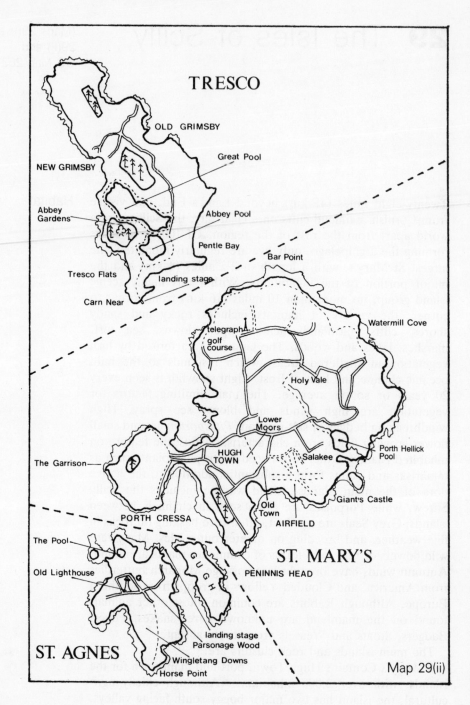

TRESCO

OLD GRIMSBY

Great Pool

NEW GRIMSBY

Abbey
Gardens

Abbey Pool

Pentle Bay

Tresco Flats

landing stage

Bar Point

Carn Near

Watermill Cove

telegraph
golf
course

Holy Vale

Lower
Moors

Porth Hellick
Pool

The Garrison

HUGH
TOWN

Salakee

Giant's Castle

PORTH CRESSA

Old
Town

AIRFIELD

ST. MARY'S

The Pool

Old Lighthouse

GUGH

PENINNIS HEAD

landing stage
Parsonage Wood

ST. AGNES

Wingletang Downs

Horse Point

Map 29(ii)

granite boulders face the coast. The turf expanses of the airfield and golf course occupy prominent positions on the higher slopes of the island. West of Hugh Town is The Garrison headland, with coniferous trees and Bracken, from which wide scenic views can be gained across the sounds to all other main islands.

St Agnes Separated from the others by deep and sometimes rough water, this island, little over 1 mile (1.6 km) long, is the last inhabited outpost of Britain, excluding Bishop Rock lighthouse 4 miles (6¹₂ km) to the west. The island is dominated by the disused lighthouse in the centre, surrounded by a few cottages. Bracken-covered Gugh islet is connected to the east flank of the island at low tide by a sand bar. The windswept south (Wingletang Down) and west of St Agnes are open downland, rocks and Bracken, but the centre and east contain tiny hedged bulb fields. The little Parsonage wood near the old lighthouse is a very sheltered area of elm trees. Beyond this lies a small marshy pool near the north end of the island, which looks out towards *Annet*. This low uninhabited ¹₂-mile (0.8-km) island of rocks and turf, a seabird sanctuary in summer, faces onto open ocean westward.

Tresco Across the relatively shallow, sandy sound north of St Mary's lies privately owned Tresco, with its abbey, subtropical ornamental gardens, lakes and sand dunes. The north end of the 2-mile (3-km) island, relatively little visited, is mostly open downland, but pine clumps and dense Rhododendrons grow on the sheltered east side of the ridge. Lush subtropical gardens surrounding the abbey are bordered by tall mixed woodland. This overlooks the ¹₂-mile (0.8-km) long shallow Great Pool, fringed by reeds and willows, which runs across the southern half of the island. In front of the abbey, separated from the Great Pool by a narrow twisting isthmus of Bracken, is round, sandy Abbey Pool. West of Tresco lie open Bracken-clad *Samson* (uninhabited), with twin hills, and *Bryher* (a little agriculture), which has a small pool on the west side.

St Martin's East of Tresco, the 2-mile (3-km) long ridge of St Martin's overlooks extensive white shell-sand beaches facing back across the sound towards St Mary's. Although mainly agricultural, the top of the island is relatively open fields, lacking deep cover; the east end near Daymark beacon is open downland. Most of the sheltered hedged fields are along the south side of the island above the beach. To the northwest lie rocky *Round Island* with a lighthouse, *St Helen's* and *Tean*.

There are two other main groups of uninhabited rocks and islets: *Western Rocks*, a series of jagged reefs and stacks in deep water 3 miles (5 km) west of St Agnes; and *Eastern Isles*, between St Martin's and St Mary's. These more sheltered isles are covered with grass, Giant Mallow and gorse, with sandy bays between them.

The islands, visited by thousands of tourists in summer, play host to hundreds of birdwatchers, especially in autumn.

Species

The Scillies have built up a reputation as probably THE place in Britain to see stray autumn migrants from all over Europe, Asia and North America. This is probably due to their position on the outer fringe of the European landmass, acting both as a last resort for birds blown across from the east, and as a first landfall for birds which have made accidental ocean crossings from America. Some of these intercontinental wanderers, although very rare on the British mainland, have become regarded as 'regulars' on the Scillies at certain seasons.

Resident species on the islands are few (Song Thrushes seem to replace most other passerines), and many familiar mainland birds, especially woodland types such as woodpeckers, Jay, Nuthatch and Treecreeper, are absent; even Carrion Crows and their close relatives are scarce. The bird population is augmented by important seabird colonies on several islands in summer.

Few birdwatchers visit Scilly in winter, when silver Sanderlings scurry along windy beaches, Turnstones and Purple Sandpipers pick among the rocks, and occasional Merlins wander between islands in search of small passerines. Sometimes a Great Northern Diver is seen in the sounds between islands, where Gannets and Kittiwakes shelter from gales. Parties of Tufted Ducks and Pochards gather on Tresco pools, Pochards usually most noticeable with peaks of 30 or more, while Tufted may not reach double figures. At the same locality the American Black Duck, a vagrant which settled here, and its assorted, puzzling, Mallard-hybrid offspring may be found. Water Rails are confiding, often entering gardens, where Chiffchaffs winter. Black Redstarts are present most winters in sheltered coves, where dead seaweed encourages insect life. There is always a chance of a rarity 'left over' from the previous autumn, particularly a wader. The orange-rumped Killdeer plover from America has turned up several times in late autumn and winter, staying for several weeks on open damp grassland.

Spring is the less-known of the migration seasons on the islands, with room for further discovery, although many rarer birds, such as overshooting Mediterranean herons and warblers, which have been found, have often moved on within a few days. Few watchers are present at this season, although this is starting to change. As with most coastal points in the region, characteristic early spring arrivals are Chiffchaff, Firecrest, Wheatear and Black Redstart. Hoopoes are expected annually, usually several and sometimes two or three together, on coastal downland. Later in the spring large falls of warblers, especially Willow Warblers, can occur, as well as smaller numbers of all common migrants. Exotic overshoots, which increase later in spring, may well include a Woodchat Shrike. No spring passes without the liquid warbling of Golden Orioles in sheltered trees on one or more of the main islands, especially St Martin's, although even brilliant yellow and black males can be hard to spot in thick cover. Sometimes loose parties of several birds arrive in warm weather and stay for weeks.

Among the seabirds, Fulmars and auks (apart from Puffin) tend to arrive early in spring, while the screaming terns do not arrive until up to two months later. Although the seabird colonies are small in comparison with some on the Scottish and Irish coasts, numbers such as 500 pairs of Kittiwakes, 200 or so pairs of Razorbills and over 100 of Puffins (the latter mostly on Annet) are greater than those remaining on the mainland coast of our region. More important regionally is southwest Britain's only regular tern colony, with over 100 pairs of Common Tern in sandy areas of Tresco and Eastern Isles. This species is vulnerable to disturbance, and visitors are asked to keep away from roped-off areas to give them a chance of success. Good views can be obtained of these graceful birds flying over to feed on sand-eels in the shallow sounds and bays. With luck one of Scilly's specialities, the delicate Roseate Tern, may be seen flying past: five to ten pairs of this rare and decreasing seabird still breed among Common Terns. A few Sandwich Terns may also be seen. Out in the sounds there are usually dozens of Shags fishing, and at times 200-300 gather to attack fish shoals.

In contrast to the eastern isles, which shelter terns suited to feeding in shallow seas, the more rocky northern and western sides of the archipelago support deepwater feeders, with most Fulmars and auks in Men-a-vaur, St Helen's and Round Island area, north of Tresco and St Martin's. The most dramatic seabirds are on the reserve island of Annet, on the outer western edge of the main island group, which supports breeding populations of Manx Shearwaters and Storm Petrels. These elusive breeders are hard to census, as they avoid gull attacks by approaching their colonies from the ocean only after nightfall, spending the day either well out at sea feeding or under the ground in burrows and crevices. Recent estimates have given 500 pairs of shearwaters, small by national standards, and perhaps 2,000 pairs of Storm Petrels, an important colony. Both species, particularly shearwaters, tend to flock near the isle towards dusk, but in daytime there is no sign except for corpses of unwary birds killed by the abundant Great Black-backed Gulls, which exceed 1,000 pairs in the island group. The concentration of Lesser Black-backed Gulls, with 500 pairs on Annet and 2,500 total, is the largest in our region.

Breeding landbirds are limited. The best chance is in damp areas of cover, such as near Tresco pools, where a few Reed and Sedge Warblers nest. Gadwalls are regular nesters on Tresco, where Shovelers and Teals may also raise broods in the reed-beds. One or two pairs of Whitethroats or Chiffchaffs might be found in well-vegetated areas of St Mary's. Absence of almost any breeding summer migrant passerines on the Scillies means that new arrivals are easily noticed when migration starts. One influential factor in the number of unusual birds found here is probably the intense scrutiny given to any migrant in autumn, because watchers are always on the lookout for the unusual. Perhaps similar detective work would pay off in mainland areas where many rarities seen on Scilly have never been found. One strange feature of migration on Scilly is that, while numbers of ordinary migrants are often very small, the counts of rarer arrivals can be equal to or even greater than those of 'common' species!

Early autumn is not a peak period for migrants on Scilly, but is probably best for wader variety. Low water levels on Tresco pool margins leave mud, which attracts European migrant waders such as Curlew Sandpiper, Dunlin, Little Stint and Greenshank in small numbers. Likely American species include the stout Pectoral Sandpiper, virtually annual and sometimes in twos and threes, and other rarer visitors such as a pale, slender Wilson's Phalarope. The pool on St Agnes and Porth Hellick Pool on St Mary's may also come up trumps. Along rocky bays, birds resembling Common Sandpipers are checked carefully for that species' very similar transatlantic cousin, the Spotted Sandpiper. The very rare dark-winged Solitary Sandpiper has also been seen on several occasions. At the same time, watchers on open ground may find the autumn's first Dotterel from the mountain tops of northern Europe. Early passerine migrants tend to include several larger Melodious and Icterine Warblers among commoner species, perhaps an Ortolan Bunting, and very often a Red-backed Shrike hawking bees from a gorse or bramble perch, a rare bird now on the mainland.

The pace quickens rapidly from mid autumn as tourists are replaced by birdwatchers from all over Britain. Those crossing by ferry from the mainland often report Sooty Shearwaters and skuas passing close by the boat, or occasionally a raft of dark-capped Great Shearwaters on the sea. St Mary's becomes one of the nation's ornithological centres of communication, with scores of birdwatchers meeting to exchange news. From now on rare birds are the order of the day, with groups of observers hurrying from island to island to catch up with the latest arrivals. Birds become more varied and numerous through mid and late autumn, even common summer visitors continuing to pass through here when nearly all have left the mainland. Next on the list are waders and pipits, turning up on open turf and down such as St Mary's golf course and airfield; the Scillies flock of Buff-breasted Sandpipers, with up to half a dozen sprinting around the seaward side of the airfield, is an annual event. Almost certainly there will still be one or two Dotterels, standing unconcerned while being watched from point-blank range, and a Lesser Golden Plover might drop in with a group of Golden. The same areas may hold a long-legged Richard's or Tawny Pipit, or perhaps a sandy little Short-toed Lark. The inconspicuous Lapland Bunting may also feed in this habitat, although this regular visitor is perhaps more likely on coastal heath such as Peninnis Head on St Mary's or Wingletang on St Agnes. The extra birds arriving will generally attract a few Merlins and probably a Peregrine. 'Lost' larger raptors such as Osprey, Red Kite, Honey Buzzard or a harrier may spend two or three weeks wandering from island to island between favoured feeding spots.

On the edge of the ocean, the Scillies are battered most autumns by at least one severe depressional gale. High winds, rain and sea spray usually prevent much effective birding for a day or two: some people try to seawatch, although numbers of birds passing the islands are low. With luck a passing oceanic migrant such as a Great Shearwater, petrel or scarcer skua may be noted. Observations have been made from Tresco north cliffs or, more usually, southern points of St Mary's and St Agnes. Passengers on 'MV Scillonian' may have better luck, if seasickness permits, with a chance of many larger shear-waters or a Sabine's Gull following the boat and sometimes a flock of Grey Phalaropes sitting on the sea in the lee of Eastern Isles. The real excitement on the islands is in searching for American landbirds when the weather abates; Scilly is Europe's best centre for seeing these lost wanderers. Although numbers of individual birds are irregular, depending on strength and timing of gales, a few are swept across every year. A sighting such as that of an American Nighthawk weaving around St Agnes lighthouse at dusk, flashing white wing-patches, or a tiny striped Black-and-white Warbler scrambling head-first down a tree trunk on St Mary's, is one of the year's high points for many keen watchers. Many 'first sightings for Britain' have been made here at this period.

In favourable conditions, a wide variety of interesting European migrants may be encountered. Spotted Crakes are glimpsed regularly in marshy valleys and poolsides. Firecrests are frequently seen, sometimes amounting to dozens across the islands, and there will usually be several Yellow-browed Warblers, often lingering in waterside trees and thickets where insects are plentiful. Icterine Warblers are still seen and the Red-breasted Flycatcher is another regular, often seen flicking white tail-patches in wooded areas. Towards late autumn almost anything from the northern hemisphere might be found, setting identification puzzles, particularly when little-known Asiatic warblers such as Paddyfield and Booted are reported. Weedy fields prove attractive to elusive small buntings such as Rustic, and perhaps rare pipits including Olive-backed from the Far East. Black Redstarts can be astonishingly numerous around coves and buildings at this season, with falls estimated at several hundreds in the whole island group. A Woodcock or Short-eared Owl may be flushed from coastal Bracken, and one or two northern wildfowl such as Barnacle Geese appear most years, usually not staying for long.

Birds can continue to arrive right through to the end of autumn, while mild weather encourages some exhausted vagrants which arrived earlier in autumn to stay on. Every year the Scillies turn up a Pallas's Warbler, or even several, at the last moment. Then the flood of birdwatchers returns to the mainland, leaving us to speculate on what might still arrive.

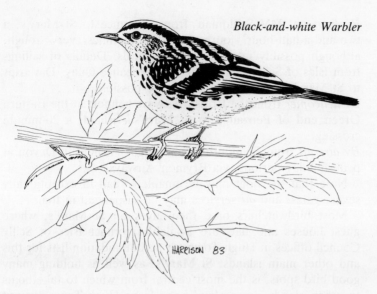

Black-and-white Warbler

HARRISON 83

Most people on pre-arranged visits will be unable to alter timing according to weather conditions. Warm southerly winds are most likely to produce spring exotic overshoots and falls of commoner migrants. Deep depressions which have originated off the American coast in autumn, especially those which start as hurricanes off the Florida and Gulf of Mexico coasts, will tend to move east and affect the Scillies a few days later. Look for American vagrants on the first bright day after the gale, as they come out to feed. In windy weather, sheltered trees such as Holy Vale on St Mary's or the east side of St Agnes are likely to be productive, or perhaps Tresco (if birds can be found in thick cover). In southerly or southwest gales, try seawatching off southerly points such as Porth Hellick or Peninnis on St Mary's and Horse Point on St Agnes. Porth Hellick Point should be the first landfall for birds moving west past the islands. Results are probably best in bad visibility, rather than gales which push birds towards the Cornish mainland. In strong northwesterlies, shearwaters and skuas have been seen from Tresco north cliffs. For breeding shearwaters and petrels coming to Annet, a dusk visit by boat will give a chance of seeing birds gathering nearby. For European and Asiatic migrants, a southeast wind, even if light, usually brings good watching in autumn.

In early morning sun, the trees around the sunken east-facing 'tennis court' area on Garrison hill, or the east side of the battlements path, are good places from which to start on St Mary's. Parsonage Wood on St Agnes can also be very good.

Timing

Access

By boat on 'MV Scillonian' from Penzance to St Mary's, a two-and-a-half-hour journey and sometimes very rough, although possibly interesting for seabirds. Details of sailings from Isles of Scilly Steamship Co., Penzance Quay. Day trips to St Mary's (four hours ashore) are possible.

By helicopter from the British Airways heliport at the Eastern Green end of Penzance to St Mary's Airfield, a 20-minute crossing.

By aircraft from Plymouth (Roborough) Airfield in Devon at peak holiday periods, via Brymon Airways.

Note that the boat may be unable to sail in exceptionally severe gales, and *all* services may be suspended in fog.

Most birdwatchers base themselves on St Mary's, where guest houses and flats are available: contact Isles of Scilly Council offices in Hugh Town for accommodation lists for this and other main islands. St Mary's, as well as holding many good bird spots, is the most central from which to take boats to other islands. *Inter-island boats* leave Hugh Town quay at 10.15 approx. most mornings; details are chalked on the notice board outside the shipping office in the main street. You can usually return in mid or late afternoon. Groups can often arrange by request to charter boats for special outings.

Some visitors may prefer to keep out of the autumn 'ornithological rat-race' and conduct their birdwatching at a quieter, more leisurely pace. Those more attracted by this idea could consider basing themselves on St Martin's or Bryher, which are less visited, probably cheaper, and still provide plenty of scope for seeing birds. For an economical stay on St Mary's (Garrison) and St Agnes, there are basic camp sites.

Note On all the islands, there are lanes, public paths, nature trails or coast walks which enable birdwatchers to search the ground thoroughly. Most fields are small and can be scanned easily from the edge; if a bird fails to appear, wait until it does. There is no reason to enter fields without the farmer's permission. In the past, some irresponsible rarity-hunters have clashed with local residents over access to cultivated land, causing bad relations all round. Muddy boots can bring soil parasites such as nematodes (eelworms) from an infected area into a healthy field, ruining crops and putting the farmer's livelihood at risk. *Please* keep to paths! Note also that stone walls may collapse if leant on.

Migrants, including unusual birds, can turn up anywhere but some of the best-known watching areas are:

St Mary's Garrison trees for warblers; Lower Moors for

raptors, crakes or warblers; Peninnis Point for larks, pipits, Lapland Bunting and possibly passing seabirds; Porth Hellick Pool for herons, ducks, waders; Holy Vale for warblers, flycatchers and other passerines, probably crakes; airfield and golf course for Dotterel and other waders, pipits and Lapland Bunting; fields east of Telegraph Hill for rarer buntings and pipits.

St Agnes Parsonage trees for warblers and flycatchers; the pool and surrounds for waders and crakes; Troytown fields for warblers, pipits and buntings; Barnaby Lane and Covean for warblers; Wingletang Down for Merlin, Short-eared Owl, pipits and Lapland Bunting; Horse Point for seabirds.

Tresco Great and Abbey Pools and surrounding vegetation for ducks, raptors, waders, warblers; north cliffs for passing seabirds.

Bryher Weedy fields across the island centre and near the pool for warblers and buntings.

St Martin's Fields across the top of the island for pipits, buntings and other open-ground birds; also sheltered fields just up from the landing stage.

Access to some parts of *Tresco, Eastern Isles* and the whole of *Annet* in summer is restricted to permit-holders only, by agreement with the Nature Conservancy Council, to protect breeding seabirds. From St Mary's, special boat trips, which do not land, take visitors out past seabird colonies and seals in season, or near dusk to Annet.

Calendar

Resident: Cormorant, Shag, Black Duck (Tresco), Gadwall, Kestrel, Moorhen, Oystercatcher, Ringed Plover, Great Black-backed Gull, Carrion Crow, Rock Pipit, Stonechat. Passing Gannets and Kittiwakes all year.

Dec-Feb: Possible Great Northern Diver, Wigeon, Teal, Shoveler, Tufted Duck, Pochard, possibly Goldeneye, Long-tailed Duck, Merlin, Water Rail, Golden Plover, Grey Plover, Turnstone, Sanderling, Purple Sandpiper, Short-eared Owl, Grey Wagtail, Chiffchaff, Blackcap, Firecrest, Black Redstart. Possible geese and Woodcock.

Mar-May: Fulmar and auks have arrived back. Hoopoe, Chiffchaff, Firecrest, Wheatear, Black Redstart passing through from mid Mar. Manx Shearwater, Storm Petrel, terns arrive Apr; commoner passerine migrants peak late Apr. Overshooting southern species mostly May, best month for Golden Oriole.

Jun-Jul: Breeding seabirds, ducks and Ringed Plover; occasional late migrants and overshoots remain from spring; a few warblers breed.

Aug-Nov: Breeding shearwaters, petrels and auks have departed. Wader movement inc. American species peaks mid Sep. Beginning of passerine movement with chance of Icterine or Melodious Warbler and Ortolan (mid Aug on). Red-backed Shrike (early Sep-mid Oct). Seabirds on 'Scillonian' crossing (mostly early Sep-mid Oct), inc. Manx and Sooty Shearwaters, Great Shearwater (irregular, mainly Sep), possible Cory's Shearwater, Gannet, Grey Phalarope (mostly Oct), skuas, occasional Sabine's Gull. On islands, American waders inc. Buff-breasted Sandpiper (mid-late Sep), European plovers inc. Dotterel (late Aug-mid Oct); raptors from early Sep. Wide range of passerines from mid Sep inc. warblers, flycatchers, chats and pipits, with chance of Richard's and Tawny Pipits; Melodious and Icterine Warblers, Red-breasted Flycatcher, Lapland Bunting all regular. Peaks for rarer species: American landbirds late Sep-end Oct; European and Asiatic birds, e.g. rare pipits, warblers and buntings, early Oct-early Nov. Short-eared Owls arrive mid-late Oct, Black Redstarts often abundant end Oct-early Nov. Late summer visitors and a few vagrants stay into Nov, when Pallas's Warbler may still arrive.

30 St Ives Island and Bay

(Map 30 and OS Map 203)

St Ives is in far west Cornwall, on its north coast. The 'Island' is a 20-m high rocky headland with a Coastguard station on top, from which you can look across the bay to Hayle Sands and Godrevy Point lighthouse, 2^{1}2 miles (4 km) away; directly seawards off Godrevy is a long narrow reef, the 'Stones'. Running in a semi-circle from the edge of St Ives town, Carbis Bay is a particularly sheltered section of the larger St Ives area, the whole of which remains sheltered from most easterly and all southerly winds, including prevailing southwesterlies. Overall it has a sandy bottom, with long stretches of wide sandy beaches, backed towards Hayle Towans by high sand dunes. Some parts have a more rocky shoreline, like that found near the island.

Just below and behind the island, which forms the western corner of the main bay, is a sewage outfall. As the bay and headland face north, strong opposing sunlight is not such a problem as at many coastal points, except perhaps in early mornings. The high light values in the far west produce perfect colour and detail.

Habitat

This area is famous chiefly for large spectacular passages of seabirds off the island, especially in autumn gales when birdwatchers from many parts of Britain come here to see pelagic birds, normally rarely seen from land.

In winter and early spring, St Ives Bay is noted mainly for diving birds, especially when sheltered from rough seas. Most numerous of the interesting species are divers and grebes. Two or three Great Northern Divers are almost always present, sometimes ten or more. Smaller and more snake-necked, Black-throated occur quite often singly, but there can be five or more; numbers tend to rise from late winter and by early spring ten or more may be present. Red-throated Divers are only occasional single winter visitors. Typical of the region,

Species

235

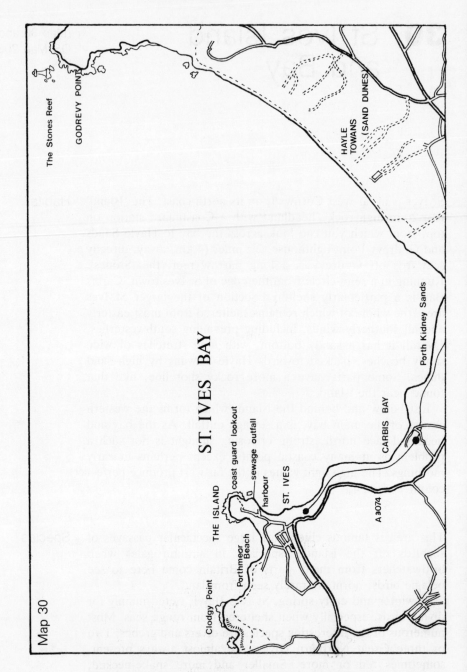

Map 30

ST. IVES BAY

The Stones Reef

GODREVY POINT

HAYLE TOWANS (SAND DUNES)

Porth Kidney Sands

CARBIS BAY

A 3074

ST. IVES

harbour

sewage outfall

coast guard lookout

THE ISLAND

Porthmeor Beach

Clodgy Point

Slavonian is the most common grebe, although fewer than five is normal. Black-necked are uncommon, most years bringing one or two. Red-necked Grebes, as elsewhere, are scarce, and not even seen annually. A very light scattering of seaducks come and go through winter: perhaps a group of three or four female or immature Eiders is present, diving for shellfish off rocky areas, with similar numbers of Common Scoters; the odd Long-tailed Ducks which visit prefer small fish. None of the above diving species competes for food with the 50 or more Shags and dozen or so Cormorants regularly seen in the bay. Small groups of Purple Sandpipers forage with Turnstones along rocky foreshores, often below seafront houses in the town.

When spring arrives, ducks leave quite quickly as a rule, as do most Great Northern Divers and grebes; as is normal in Cornwall, however, Black-throated Divers often increase in spring. Lingering individuals may attain summer plumage. Up to five Glaucous Gulls might appear together, frequenting especially the harbour and fishing boats. They may also be joined by the smaller, slimmer Iceland Gull, but only irregularly. The largest male examples of Glaucous can be larger than the largest Great Black-backed Gull, while smallest males may be little bigger than a Herring Gull. Very early spring is a good time for unusual gulls, especially Little Gulls. These begin appearing in groups of three or four, gradually increasing, sometimes to 15. Mediterranean Gulls, like Little, tend to hover over wave crests and sewer outfalls, picking scraps from the surface; only two or three may visit, sometimes joining together. Rarities such as American Laughing Gull have been found at this season.

Soon the first migrant terns appear in the shape of excited Sandwich Terns, loudly proclaiming their arrival while diving for fish; this is the most common tern in spring. Later small flocks of ten or more, moving through the bay, may be joined by two or three Common or Arctic Terns.

Seawatching from the island is possibly worth a try year-round in any conditions, on the off-chance that an interesting species may fly past. From March prospects become more certain, and, if conditions are favourable, a scattering or even sustained passage may occur. True movement is usually eastward, up the coast, as opposed to seabirds milling around the general sea area, such as a few Gannets. One species present in the general area, as well as passing through, is the Fulmar, but hundreds, even thousands, streaming past the headland indicate real movement. Manx Shearwaters and Kittiwakes are also involved, in similar numbers, heading towards breeding colonies; 2,000 or more of each may pass in just a few hours. Among the Manx may be a few browner Balearic Shearwaters. If divers are passing (usually only in twos and threes), they are most likely Black-throated. A few Bar-tailed Godwits or Whimbrels may fly past later in the season, and there is always the chance of a skua or two, or even a few Storm Petrels. Sightings of the latter are well on the cards throughout late spring and summer, and small feeding parties occasionally wander close to shore. If winds blow strongly from the right direction, even in high summer, especially in early mornings, odd non-breeding birds of several interesting species may be seen: these may include a stray from southern oceans spending its winter here, possibly an albatross!

As late summer approaches and depressional Atlantic gales become likely, the chance arises for the first major seawatch. Really high numbers of seabirds do not occur early on, but some will already have left their natal colonies to begin their westward journey. All true passage will now be westward. **Note** All numbers quoted below are on a per-day basis. Shearwaters, skuas and terns make up the bulk of early passages, if conditions cause them to occur. Fifty or more each of Common and Sandwich Terns pass, perhaps accompanied by two or three Roseate, Little or Black Terns; terns use the bay regardless of winds, small groups fishing or gathering along quieter sandy beaches. Skuas may be present, in ones and twos, skilfully harrying feeding terns; early ones will be predominantly Arctic, maybe 30 or more, with four or five stocky Great Skuas (frequently known by their Scottish name, 'Bonxie'). Groups totalling up to 150 Shags and 50 or so Cormorants move westward. Manx Shearwaters can pass in very high numbers early on; the more usual counts of 10,000 have occasionally risen to well over 20,000, among which may be 20-50 Balearic-race birds. Sooty Shearwaters speed through, attaining peak numbers early; often 30-40 may be seen, rarely over 200; small numbers are also seen outside their main season. Storm Petrels appear off the headland in variable numbers; passing throughout autumn, they may be absent on some days, flit low over the waves in twos or threes, or occur in hundreds.

As the season progresses, tern and skua numbers increase and the two most common terns, Sandwich and Common, can pass in hundreds, though Roseates may not increase from two or three and rarely move through in double figures. Never are there more than a handful of Little Terns. Black Terns usually pass in twos and threes, but more than 30 may be seen. Arctic Terns, later migrants, are usually seen only in numbers up to ten. Both Arctic and Great Skuas can now reach 50 plus.

Bonxies have the longest season, and are not up to peak numbers here until after other skuas have reached their southern destinations. Daily counts of over 100 for either of these commoner skua species are unusual. Pomarine Skuas, more heavily built than Arctic although similarly shaped, fly with slower, more measured wingbeats, resembling their larger Bonxie cousins. Usually only in ones and twos, certain weather conditions can bring this ocean-going migrant closer to shore, producing ten or more per day; odd ones are seen both very early and very late. The rarest skua to pass is the smallest, usually now seen annually — the Long-tailed Skua — which has the most oceanic migration, taking it far from the coast; this lovely skua remains rare at St Ives, in very good years perhaps four or five in a season. Recently Britain's first McCormick's Skuas, a southern hemisphere relative of the Bonxie, were identified here.

From mid autumn, earlier and later migrants merge, numbers gradually increasing. The St Ives speciality is now most likely to be seen. The dainty, fork-tailed, Sabine's Gull has been recorded here more frequently than anywhere else in Britain. Even so, only four or five pass in some years, while in stormy autumns groups of this number may occur, sometimes amid throngs of similarly-marked first-winter-plumaged Kittiwakes. Kittiwakes can number well in excess of 30,000! Such figures are recorded mostly late in the season. Little Gulls, on the other hand, pass in twos and threes, occasionally reaching 20 or more. Few Leach's Petrels are seen early in the season, and in some unfavourable autumns they are absent; rather like Storm Petrel occurrences, some apparently good days produce none, or two or three, while on other days 50 or more move past. Gannets, in hundreds even on quieter days, are easily capable of reaching 25,000, although up to 5,000 is more usual.

As the season moves on, and tern and shearwater numbers decline, other birds come to the fore. Replacing black and white hordes of Manx Shearwaters are auks, in even greater number. They appear to be mainly Razorbills, but distance often precludes accurate identification. The flocks passing on whirring wings act as a backdrop to more exciting species. Counts are made of over 50,000 (average numbers per hour passing, multiplied to give a day figure). Puffins, strangely, are almost non-existent, while Little Auks appear only at the very end of autumn. The latter, too, have good and bad years, in some barely seen, while in others 50 pass a day; up to ten is more usual. Least common, not surprisingly as most populations are non-migratory, are Black Guillemots, one or two being noted some years. Another later species is a sea-going wader, the small greyish-white Grey Phalarope, often stopping to rest on the waves; numbers are similar to Little Auk, but over 50 is exceptional.

Divers come through in higher numbers later on. This is one of the few places in Cornwall where substantial numbers of Red-throated are seen. In fact St Ives probably records most, with daily totals of 20 or 30 attained, as well as at least as many Great Northern although rather fewer Black-throated. No real passage of grebes occurs, but occasionally one passes by. Later in the season, a few other ducks may attach themselves to small parties of Common Scoters, which pass throughout autumn: perhaps a larger Velvet Scoter showing distinctive white wing-patches, a Red-breasted Merganser, or an Eider or two. Geese, uncommon in the far west, have been seen in small flocks, usually 'black geese' (Brent or Barnacle). A thin scattering of northern white-winged gulls, such as Glaucous, occurs. Once an adult Ross's Gull was seen in an exceptionally fierce gale. Herring Gulls can pass in thousands, whereas Lesser Black-backed Gulls, which move in autumn and early winter, reach only 200-300. Keeping birdwatchers company later in autumn may be two or three Snow Buntings on the island slopes, while Black Redstarts confidingly join forces with Rock Pipits feeding among turf and Sea Pinks.

The most notable omissions from the species list are Cory's and Great Shearwaters, which regularly gather in thousands to feed at the entrance to the Western Approaches, off Ushant, Brittany. Fairly frequently following cold-water currents, and associated food, they visit the sea area around Land's End, albeit in quite small numbers; only rarely are they seen from the island, usually singly and a long way out.

St Ives Island has produced some of Britain's highest totals of migrating seabirds, as well as some of its rarest species. Apart from the few already mentioned, recent sightings include Wilson's and Madeiran Petrels, Bridled Tern and Black-browed Albatross. These unexpected, but hoped-for, birds make ten-hour watches in howling gales, squalls and freezing conditions well worthwhile.

Timing

More or less any time could justify checking the headland or bay if you are in the area. Conditions conducive to large passages past the island are highly critical, although birds such as terns pausing to feed in the bay or semi-resident winter divers and grebes may be seen in varying conditions. In incorrect conditions, however, actual passage off the island will be little or nothing.

For substantial seabird movement to be seen, winds should ideally be between WNW and north. An Atlantic depression from the southwest will have just passed through, preferably with its centre not much higher than Northern Ireland. As it passes, the wind veers from southwest towards northerly; at this point seabirds begin to pass. The larger, more vigorous, faster-travelling and more rain-bearing the depression is, the greater seabird passage will result.

There are many variations, but results then become more uncertain. Sometimes a strong front of northerly air alone will produce good results. At other times, days of southwest gales which fail to veer (therefore no birds pass) finally do so, but abate to a breeze; either few birds then pass, although they may include a rarity, or a good passage may take place as tired birds merely track with the wind. On the day of a major gale, those species able to cope pass through. The next day (or morning), provided winds are still from the right direction, smaller species such as terns, small gulls etc. come through when strong winds have decreased. Strong winds from due west usually produce little or no *close* passage; the moment they flick north of west, especially if the weather system contains frequent squalls, the bay can be seething with birds, all of which were passing by, unseen, further out! Sometimes ideal conditions start early in the morning; heavy passage takes place, the wind then dies, or backs to southwest, and passage ceases, perhaps by midday. Conversely, passage may not start until late afternoon, frustrating if you have been watching an empty sea for five hours, knowing what you are missing. Very occasionally correct winds will blow for two or three days, during which passage will be sustained. Until these critical conditions arrive, some years for only three or four days, major passage is non-existent.

Although most passage occurs within a mile (1.6 km) — often very close — it should be remembered that perhaps less than five minutes may elapse between initial sighting and brief views before a moving seabird is lost to view round the headland; the sheer numbers can also cause bewilderment. It is better to learn basic seabird identification elsewhere if possible, or visit on a quieter day.

St Ives is reached by A3074 from Hayle. For the island, head **Access** to the northern tip of the town, following signs to the car park. This car park lies immediately below the steeply rising headland; a tarmac path leads to the top. Watch from areas sheltered from the wind (if possible), around the outer walls of the Coastguard lookout. From the edge of the car park very close views of the sewer and its gulls are gained. The sewer can also be seen well from the island.

The outer part of the bay is also checked from this car park or from the harbour walls, as well as from roads adjacent to the bay. Check the harbour for unusual gulls. Public footpaths lead from the town, remaining close to shore, extending to the mouth of Hayle estuary at Porthkidney beach (part of Carbis Bay), where terns often rest. A branch railway line from London-Penzance main line runs from St Erth to St Ives all year round, daily except Sundays, giving panoramic views en route.

Calendar

Resident: Gannet and Oystercatcher (do not breed but seen all year). Cormorant, Shag, Razorbill and Guillemot breed nearby. Rock Pipit.

Dec-Feb: Black-throated and Great Northern Divers; Red-throated mostly pass the island. Slavonian Grebe. Possible Black-necked and Red-necked Grebes, Eider, Common Scoter. Turnstone, Purple Sandpiper. Possible Grey Phalarope past island, Great Skua, Little, Mediterranean and Glaucous Gulls, possible Iceland Gull and Little Auk.

Mar-May: Apart from Black-throated Diver and uncommon gulls, all above species gradually decline. Fulmar, Manx Shearwater, possible Storm Petrel, especially towards May. Bar-tailed Godwit and Whimbrel pass from mid Apr. Possible odd skuas throughout period. Sandwich Tern from mid Mar, a few Commic from Apr.

Jun-Jul: Breeding species. Chance of seabird movement, particularly Manx Shearwater or Storm Petrel. End of period, terns reappear in bay.

Aug-Nov: Early part of period, Aug-early Sep: Fulmar, Sooty, Manx and Balearic Shearwaters, terns inc. Black, Sandwich, Common and Roseate often peak now. Whimbrel, skuas (mainly Arctic), Little Gull, Lesser Black-backed, possible Sabine's Gull. Middle period, mid Sept-mid Oct: all the above, some peaking now, e.g. Arctic Skua. Leach's Petrel, Common Scoter, Great and Pomarine Skuas, possibly Long-tailed Skua, Mediterranean Gull, Arctic Tern, Grey Phalarope. End period, end Oct-Nov: three species of diver past island. Many species decline past Oct, except: Grey Phalarope, Great Skua may peak now. Possible Glaucous Gull, Kittiwake and auk passage increases, perhaps inc. Little Auk.

Sabine's Gull

Adult

Juvenile

HARRISON 83

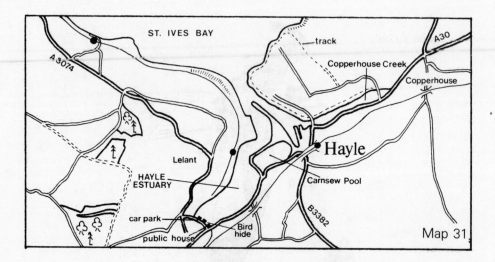

ST. IVES BAY

A3074

track

Copperhouse Creek

A30

Copperhouse

Lelant

Hayle

HAYLE
ESTUARY

Carnsew Pool

B3382

car park

public house

Bird
hide

Map 31

31 Hayle Estuary (including Carnsew Pool and Copperhouse Creek)

(Map 31 and OS Map 203)

Habitat

This estuary and adjoining areas are adjacent to Hayle town in west Cornwall, on the north side of the peninsula. The area is important as the only estuary in the far west, and very sheltered from the sea. The mouth lies at a different angle from the main basin, separated by a long curving channel cutting through a barrier of dunes. The lower estuary is predominantly sandy, becoming muddy higher up. A freshwater channel flows at low tides. At the bottom of the estuary an embankment encloses an artificial tidal area known as Carnsew Pool, where a large sheet of water is retained even at low tides, when soft mud is exposed. Running alongside the town centre is another muddy tidal area, Copperhouse Creek, less than half the size of the main estuary.

Winter temperatures in low, sheltered areas of the far west at times bear little resemblance to those even in eastern Devon. Apart from exceptionally cold years, far fewer days are below freezing, and snowfall is not annual.

Species

Although well known to most birdwatchers for migrant waders and wintering ducks, the first sight as you glance over the estuary in winter is of large flocks of gulls. They congregate mainly towards the middle and upper sections. This estuary does not attract extremely high numbers, perhaps no more than 1,500 Herring Gulls at a time. Black-headed Gulls, which flock in nearby fields, often number less than 1,000 on the mudflats. Normally, about 500 Great Black-backs gather. The two most numerous migrant gulls, Lesser Black-backed and Common, achieve highest numbers in late winter-early spring. Paradoxically, Common Gulls are not at all numerous in Cornwall until fresh migrants (mostly adults) appear, swelling the small winter population; flocks of 500 and more then become commonplace. The build-up of Lesser Black-backed Gulls is even more noticeable, as many fewer remain through early winter: being so far west, concentrations of over 200 soon appear in late winter, reaching 1,000 or more later; autumn passage peaks at around 300.

Uncommon gulls are relatively frequent visitors at any time during non-breeding seasons, but more occur from late winter through spring. Normally present as single birds, some species such as Glaucous, Mediterranean and Little Gulls may total five or more individuals a year. Least frequent are Iceland, normally one or two a year. Apart from odd appearances of truly rare gulls such as Bonaparte's, in recent years Ring-billed Gulls have been identified with increasing regularity, mostly in late winter and early spring. Almost certainly they arrive with migrating Common Gulls, which they closely resemble in all plumage stages.

When conditions are severe elsewhere, weather movements bring higher numbers of ducks and waders to the milder far west. Groups of up to ten Brent Geese may arrive. Average winter populations are not large, nor particularly varied. Wigeons are the most numerous duck, at about 800 (American Wigeons have occurred). Teals peak at little over 300, and sometimes the American subspecies, Green-winged Teal, visits. Mallards and Shelducks reach about 50 and 30 respectively; one or two pairs of each breed. Gadwalls are annual, usually six to ten. Other common dabbling ducks occur annually at irregular intervals. The most common diving ducks are Goldeneyes, usually females (brownheads), perhaps reaching 20 although half this is normal. Goosanders visit most winters, when two or three brownheads may be seen. The closely related Red-breasted Merganser is also seen in groups of three to five, again usually brownheads. Tufted Ducks often occur, in parties of under ten.

Winter flocks of waders are rather low. Dunlins fluctuate, averaging 500. Curlews reach 300 in winter, and up to 700 are often counted in autumn. Lapwings use the estuary as a temporary roost, several thousand sharing local fields with Black-headed Gulls; only a few hundred of these plovers visit the estuary at any one time. Grey Plovers keep to the estuary, totalling about 100 birds. Only about ten Knots stay the winter, although in autumn twice as many are seen. Fifty Bar-tailed Godwits arrive in autumn and stay throughout winter. Black-tailed Godwits visit only irregularly in ones and twos, while Oystercatchers gather in almost static numbers of 100 for much of the year. During autumn a heavy passage of Ringed Plovers peaks at over 300, occasionally as many as 50 overwintering. Whimbrels, often heard before being seen, stop off briefly; small groups of ten or more behave similarly in spring. Redshanks, long called 'sentinel of the marshes' from their loud ringing calls, are present in most months of the year; autumn flocks build to about 300, and 100 normally winter. Turnstones gather in groups of up to 25 in autumn, also staying to winter.

Small numbers of less common waders regularly occur on autumn passage. Both Little Stints and Curlew Sandpipers are annual. Subject to their migration patterns, numbers fluctuate from year to year, though not often over ten; a party of five of either species can be reasonably expected. Higher numbers are more regularly achieved by Curlew Sandpipers, with 12-20 in good years. Flocks of up to ten Ruffs may pass through in autumn, with two or three at a time in spring. Greenshanks and Common Sandpipers appear in similar numbers to Ruffs, but one or two may overwinter. Spotted Redshanks are less numerous, perhaps only three or four visiting at a time in autumn, often only singles. Little Ringed Plovers are now more or less annual, occasionally with two together; in some years they are recorded in both migration seasons.

Rarities turn up annually. Pectoral and White-rumped Sandpipers and Long-billed Dowitcher are American species seen several times over the years. Every year the area is certain to produce a number of such birds. Probably this is due largely to its geographical position, being both the first and the last estuary most migrants will see in Britain. In one recent spring a Broad-billed Sandpiper, a rare European wader, was identified — the first ever recorded in Cornwall. Occasionally a Spoonbill makes a spring visit.

Grey Herons and Buzzards are resident, but, whenever either flies over, gulls and waders take flight in alarm. Peregrines have the same effect, with better reason, and often visit through autumn and winter. One or two Kingfishers are present throughout the same period.

A small passage of terns uses the estuary, either as a temporary roost or to pause a short while to feed. Having followed the main channel up from the sea, they find shelter especially in rough weather. Most common is Sandwich, among the first spring migrants to reach us; later groups of 20 or more may gather and higher numbers are normal in autumn. Arctic, Roseate and Little Terns occur in flocks of fewer than five in spring and autumn. Up to ten Common Terns come through in spring, often many more in autumn. The rare White-winged Black Tern has occurred on several occasions.

In the quiet winter waters of Carnsew Pool, an exhausted diver may be sheltering; single Black-throated and Great Northern Divers are not uncommon. One or two Slavonian Grebes are annual, but apart from up to ten Little Grebes, all other grebes are rarer visitors, though single Great Crested and Black-necked are recorded most years. Red-breasted Mergansers and Tufted Ducks favour the pool rather than the estuary, as do the occasional Long-tailed Ducks which appear. Many birds which use the main estuary, including most smaller waders, also habitually visit Carnsew.

Copperhouse Creek, more open to disturbance, is also quite narrow, and less attractive to wary species. The gull flocks which congregate should be checked for uncommon species, which regularly occur. Mute Swans reach over 30 through autumn and winter. Among the many fewer waders are some which prefer this area: Little Ringed Plovers and Wood and Green Sandpipers in spring and autumn, for example, are less often seen on the main estuary. Pectoral Sandpipers tend to frequent this spot. In an area of grassy wasteland in hard weather, up to 50 Snipe flock; among them a Jack Snipe may be flushed. The same area in autumn may have standing pools which attract interesting waders, once a Temminck's Stint.

Timing

A visit at any time of day, through all seasons, could prove worthwhile with the chance of occasional late passage or non-breeding birds and strays moving through. Low winter sunlight is not much problem here, as you can face away from the sun most of the time. For waders the tide must be out to some degree. A rising tide, or one just starting to fall, forces many waders to alight on relatively small areas of mud at the head of the estuary when close views are obtainable; there is no central high-tide roost. Hard winter weather may increase numbers and species, while rough seas will induce some species such as terns to shelter. Strong westerly airstreams in autumn are responsible for American vagrants.

Access

The main estuary is just west of Hayle town. A30 runs beside the sites, with car parking in the town. At the head of the estuary, beside the main road, a publican has kindly allowed his car park to be used when checking here. The car park is a good vantage point. The RSPB has erected a public hide (again on the publican's land) giving close views of the main channel. A log of watchers' records is kept inside. The estuary is flanked on the north side by a branch railway line, but the main road along the opposite shore allows checking along its length. The hide is near the A30/A3074 junction to St Ives, at the west end, on the right as you turn north off the A30.

Access to Carnsew Pool is by a public footpath located from the road, near the site of some small industrial units beside the lower end of the estuary. From this path, on three sides of the pool, extremely good views are obtained. In addition to the main road, public paths run along the remaining three edges of Copperhouse Creek, including alongside the grassy areas at its head (i.e. on the right as you enter Hayle town from the east on A30).

Resident: Grey Heron, Oystercatcher.   Calendar

Dec-Feb: Probable Black-throated and Great Northern Divers; Slavonian Grebe, Little Grebe, possibly other grebes. Possible Brent Geese; Teal, Gadwall, Wigeon, Tufted Duck, possible Long-tailed Duck, Goldeneye, Red-breasted Merganser, occasional Goosander, possible Peregrine. Ringed and Grey Plovers, Lapwing, Turnstone, Dunlin, Knot, Redshank, possible Spotted Redshank, Greenshank, Common Sandpiper, Bar-tailed Godwit, Curlew, Snipe, possible Jack Snipe; possible Mediterranean, Little, Iceland and Glaucous Gulls, particularly towards end of period. Lesser Black-backed Gull passage from late Dec, may peak at end of period. Common Gulls arrive from mid Feb. Kingfisher.

Mar-May: Most grebes, ducks and waders begin departure from early Mar. Sandwich Terns arrive from second week of Mar. Common Gulls peak first half of Mar. Uncommon gulls continue to pass through. Mid Apr, Whimbrels arrive. Late Apr and May, Common, Arctic, Roseate and Little Terns. Possible Ruff, Little Ringed Plover, Wood Sandpiper and Black Tern late spring.

Jun-Jul: First returning waders end Jul, inc. Green Sandpiper. Possible Roseate Tern. Shelduck and Mallard breed.

Aug-Nov: Most common waders gradually increase throughout period. Exceptions are: Whimbrels pass through early period, Ringed Plovers peak in Sep, Little Stints and Curlew Sandpipers arrive from early Sep (leave by early Nov), Ruffs, Spotted Redshank, Greenshanks and Common Sandpipers peak early Sep. Possible American waders from early Sep. Possible Little and Mediterranean Gulls through period. Lesser Black-backed Gulls peak Sep. Black, Sandwich, Common, Arctic and Little Terns, Aug to Oct. From mid Sep, Wigeons and Teals begin to return, other ducks towards end of period.

32 Camel Estuary and Amble Marshes

(Map 32 and
OS Map 200)

On Cornwall's north coast, near the town of Wadebridge, this **Habitat** very interesting diverse habitat combines marshy meadows, mudflats on the upper Camel estuary, and sandy lower estuary and around Padstow and Rock towards the sea. Near the river mouth are extensive high sand dunes along the north shore. At low tide two very large sandbanks and several smaller ones are exposed.

Along these lower estuary shores few trees grow, unable to survive salt-laden Atlantic winds. Farther up the estuary, sand gives way to mud, trees grow on the more sheltered margins, and the estuary forms a much wider basin towards the head. The Camel river meets the smaller Amble river at the head of the flats; the Amble flows through the marshy ground around Amble Chapel, which is now, in part (about 50 acres/20 ha), Walmsley Sanctuary. There is little human habitation over much of the area, which therefore remains relatively un-disturbed.

Among interesting plants on the sand dunes are Rock Rose, and butterflies of note include Brown Argus.

The varied habitat results in a good selection of species, the **Species** area being particularly important for waders and wildfowl. During winter Amble marshes attract a couple of hundred Snipe, often difficult to see as they crouch among rough grass; one or two smaller Jack Snipe may associate with them. Walmsley Sanctuary was created mostly to protect a regular wintering flock of White-fronted Geese, which formerly attained 100 or so individuals each year. In recent years, either the flocks have not arrived or 20 or less have visited briefly. During very hard weather their numbers increase as the geese home in on this traditional site. Unusual species include other geese, mostly in ones and twos, perhaps a Barnacle Goose, or the odd Greylag or Bean Goose; the orange-billed Greenland

251

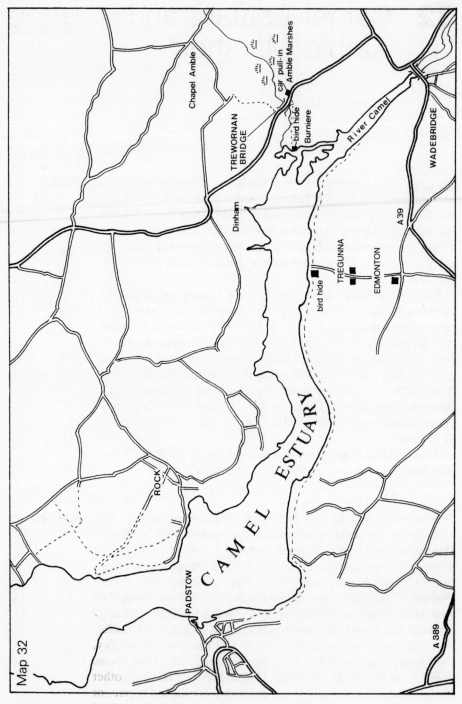

Map 32

White-front has been recorded on several occasions, in addition to the normal Russian form. Bewick's and Whooper Swans, mostly the former, occur in small groups from time to time, but neither is annual. The marshes here support huge concentrations of Lapwings and Golden Plovers; in normal winter periods both species can easily exceed 1,000 apiece, but with prolonged hard weather numbers become quite phenomenal, exceeding 10,000 of both. Dabbling ducks, mostly Wigeons and Teals, use both estuary and marshes, flighting to and fro, when Wigeons can be heard giving their high-pitched whistling 'wheeoo' calls; over 1,000 of each may gather (nowhere else in Cornwall receives this number of Teal). Pintails are seen in small flocks, over 20 at times. Among these regular visitors a few Gadwalls or Shovelers may stop over. On the higher estuary diving ducks are few. Most numerous is Goldeneye, about 15 usually, nearly always brownheads. A few Tufted Ducks can occur, but more interesting are one or two Smews, seen most winters. In harder weather very small numbers of other ducks may visit, including Goosanders. Other unusual birds seen around the estuary's upper reaches and marshy areas have included Bittern. Green Sandpipers often overwinter, and recently a Cattle Egret frequented the area.

Through winter on the lower estuary, and around the mouth to where it meets the sea at low tide, interesting waterfowl are expected. Three or four Great Northern Divers are often seen, and both Black-throated and Red-throated Divers in ones and twos. Up to five Slavonian Grebes at a time is not unexpected, and one or two Red-necked and Black-necked Grebes occur most years, along with a few Great Crested Grebes. Seaducks are not infrequent, but only in small numbers. Most numerous are Common Scoters and Eiders, the latter mostly brown females and patchy black and white immature males; both species reach small groups of about ten. Red-breasted Mergansers rarely attain this figure, three or four being more usual. Only one or two Velvet Scoters or Long-tailed Ducks occur. In the lower estuary Shags are common, but fail to penetrate further upriver, the Cormorant occupying this niche; here the division in habitat between the two is clearly marked. Along this lower sandy stretch, ten or more white and pale grey Sanderlings run along the tidelines.

Farther upriver the waders mass, as usual little grey-brown Dunlins being most common with over 1,000 probing the soft mud. More than 500 Curlews winter here and 1,000 may occur in early autumn. Oystercatchers, however, average only about

400. Ringed Plovers tend not to winter in large numbers in the southwest, but 100 or so have been counted here, often favouring lower sandy reaches. In winter plumage Grey Plovers are well named, having only a jet-black patch at the base of their off-white underwing (a diagnostic field mark) as a noticeable marking; over 200 can sometimes be seen.

Quite high numbers of gulls use the estuary in winter, over 5,000 Black-headed Gulls being most common; Herring Gulls average 2,000, often with 500 Great Black-backed. Some 100 Common Gulls winter, looking rather like miniature Herring Gulls but adults differing in their greenish bill and legs, and darker grey upperparts; by late winter northbound migrants can increase their numbers greatly, and 1,000 have been counted. Lesser Black-backed Gulls arrive at about the same time, and up to 500 may assemble for a week or two before moving on. There are very few sightings of unusual gulls, except a few Little Gulls in autumn; perhaps other species are overlooked.

The Camel is well known for terns, seen from the estuary mouth and flying up to the highest reaches to feed. High numbers are recorded in spring as well as autumn. As always Sandwich Terns are first to arrive and most numerous, with up to 50 in both seasons. In spring only two or three each of most other tern species are seen, although Common may reach ten or more. Arctic are also seen, and the rosy-breasted Roseate, whose long tail-streamers and graceful flight help make this uncommon bird the loveliest of sea terns. The Little Tern is diminutive, and a decreasing species in Britain. Black Terns are seen practically every spring, resplendent in summer plumage; their autumn and spring numbers are roughly similar, as with other tern species (although in autumn over 50 Common Terns may flock). Terns greatly favour sandbanks which become exposed and on which they settle, or where they dive for sand-eels among the shallows; as incoming tides submerge this habitat, they follow the rising tide up the estuary.

Whimbrels constitute by far the strongest spring wader migration, with sometimes over 100 passing in flocks overhead giving their distinctive multiple whistling calls, or resting for short periods; there is also a strong autumn passage. As autumn approaches, waders begin to gather. Among the first to arrive are Greenshanks; very high numbers pass through in some years, in excess of 50 in loose flocks, one or two staying to winter. Common Sandpipers may also be seen, about 20 at a time, again two or three spending winter on sheltered stretches. Each autumn one or two Wood Sandpipers pass through. About ten Spotted Redshanks join over 300 shorter-billed Redshanks, and may stay on with them. Up to 15 Ruffs are seen and a couple stay through winter, while two or three at a time may also pass in spring. Both godwit species use the estuary, perhaps no more than ten of the larger Black-tailed, but Bar-tailed can reach 80, as can Knots; godwit numbers usually decrease by half in winter. Only about four or five Curlew Sandpipers are usual, with about the same number of Little Stints; the latter species has a history of one or two birds passing winter here. When all the other waders which sometimes winter on this estuary are present together, there are more unusual wintering waders here than on any other estuary in southwest England.

In addition to common breeding raptors, two others regularly hunt through the non-breeding seasons, a third less regularly. Peregrines, often inexperienced juveniles, chase the estuary's waders, and spectacular displays of aerial skill are demonstrated as the hunted attempts to outmanoeuvre the hunter. They are seen from late summer, with two or three different birds during autumn and winter. The Merlin is much less regular but favours this area, appearing from late autumn, and one or two prey on small waders and passerines through winter. A single individual of the magnificent fish-catching Osprey may pass through some autumns, possibly staying several weeks. A few Hen Harriers and a couple of Goshawks have also appeared briefly.

One of the largest heronries in Cornwall is situated among the estuary's bankside trees; about a dozen nests are occupied each year. Kingfishers are resident and one or two pairs breed, along with two or three pairs of Mute Swans. A few Mallards also breed, but their numbers here are rather low. Perhaps six or more pairs of Shelducks breed, and in winter their numbers may rise to over 200.

Timing

Low tides are essential to see waders on the estuary mud, and for terns gathering on sandbanks or feeding in shallows near the river mouth. High, or rising, tides encourage terns to fly upriver. A rising tide, or one just ebbing, is best for watching waders from the CBWPS hide at Amble Dam outflow overlooking the estuary head and at Tregunna, also near Wadebridge. From midwinter, particularly if there is a hard spell, geese and wild swans can occur on the marshes.

Numbers of other species also rise, both there and on the estuary.

A239 north out of Wadebridge leads to B3314 left, just after leaving the town. The B road crosses Trewornan Bridge across Amble marshes, and on to St Minver. At the bridge there is roadside parking. From here good views are obtained over the marshes (Walmsley Sanctuary) on the right; access there should be unnecessary and could seriously disturb the birds. On the left just before crossing the bridge is a gate leading into a field. Follow a footpath, keeping close to the hedgerow so as not to damage farm crops. Continue through another field to Burniere Point at Amble Dam, where the CBWPS hide is situated. While walking along the fields there is marshy ground on the right, and looking through gaps in the hedge might produce something of interest such as Green Sandpiper. Views from the hide are very good, covering the head of the mudflats where many ducks and waders assemble. Gaps in the hedge near the hide allow good views if keys to the hide are not obtained. In the summer of 1983 a new hide was erected at Tregunna. From A39 at Wadebridge take a minor road to Edmonton (to the right, on a sharp left-hand bend). Take right-hand turn to Tregunna, down narrow lanes, where there is limited parking near the farm. Follow a lane for about $\frac{1}{4}$ mile (400 m) to estuary and hide. Alternatively follow the public path along a now disused railway track from Wadebridge; the track runs close to the hide. This track continues along the whole length of estuary to Padstow, giving excellent views throughout.

To reach the lower estuary continue from the bridge to St Minver, and take a narrow but good road signposted to Rock. At Rock there is a car park. From the road good views of this part of the estuary are possible. When the tide is out the sandbanks are well seen. A main channel continues to flow and often contains all the same birds, such as divers and grebes, as when the area is flooded by the tide. At low tides you can walk to the mouth, where other waterbirds, especially terns or Sanderling, are seen. Access onto the dunes is from the car park. From Amble marshes to river mouth is about $4\frac{1}{2}$ miles (7 km). For Padstow take A389 for good views of terns, divers, grebes and gulls off the harbour, near the mouth, opposite Rock.

For keys to the bird hides, contact CBWPS.

Resident: Cormorant and Shag present all year and breed   Calendar
nearby. Grey Heron, Mute Swan, Shelduck, Mallard, Oystercatcher, Kingfisher.

Dec-Feb: Great Northern and probably other divers,
Slavonian, Little and probably other grebes, probably White-
fronted Goose, Teal, Wigeon, Pintail, Tufted Duck, Eider,
Common Scoter, possible Velvet Scoter and Long-tailed
Duck. Goldeneye, possible Smew, Red-breasted Merganser,
Peregrine, Merlin, Ringed Plover, Grey and Golden Plovers,
Lapwing, possible Little Stint, Dunlin, Knot, Sanderling,
probable Ruff and Spotted Redshank, Redshank, probable
Greenshank, Green Sandpiper, godwits, Curlew, Snipe, pos-
sible Jack Snipe. Commoner species of gull, with Lesser
Black-backed and Common Gulls migrants arriving from Feb.

Mar-May: Most above waders and waterfowl begin to leave by
early Mar. End of Mar, first Sandwich Terns, Ruff pass
through. Mid Apr on, Whimbrel and other tern species,
probable Roseate and Black Tern.

Jun-Jul: From mid Jul, commoner waders start returning, also
Green Sandpipers.

Aug-Nov: Most wader species and numbers increase throughout early autumn. Late Aug-Oct, Little Stint, Curlew Sandpiper, probably Wood Sandpiper, Whimbrel. All terns reoccur
in same period. Peregrine, maybe Osprey. From end Sep,
probable Merlin. Waterfowl return from end of period.

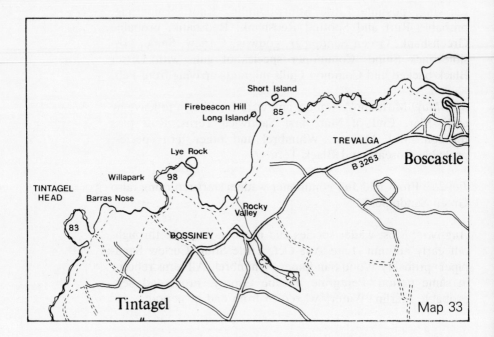

Short Island

Firebeacon Hill
Long Island

85

TREVALGA

Lye Rock

B 3263

Boscastle

Willapark
98

TINTAGEL
HEAD

Barras Nose

Rocky
Valley

83

BOSSINEY

Tintagel

Map 33

33 Tintagel-Boscastle, North Cornwall

(Map 33 and OS Map 200/190)

Habitat

This 5-mile (8-km) stretch of the north coast incorporates some of the most rugged and spectacular cliff scenery in the region. Off the 100-m high mainland cliffs and coves lie a number of rock pinnacles and islets, surrounded by Atlantic surf, a few dozen metres from the mainland. The coast is backed by high open farmland, but much of the coastal strip is covered by heath, Bracken and sea turf. Tintagel Head at the south end of the area projects farther out to sea than the series of promontories which stretch towards Boscastle, with deep water close offshore. Much of the coastline is owned by the NT, and the views attract numerous visitors. Single Grey Seals often appear offshore.

Species

This is the best seabird breeding area on the mainland coast of the two counties. Winter is relatively quiet except for a few passing groups of Gannets, auks and Kittiwakes. On fine days, however, parties of Guillemots may fly in to look over nest sites, while Fulmars are often back on nest ledges after only a few weeks' absence at sea in early winter. Spring proper brings a great deal of activity on the cliffs and islets as birds jostle for nesting space in favoured sectors. Scattered pairs of Shags and Cormorants are found all along the area, while Oystercatchers nest on inaccessible rocks. In recent years Fulmar colonies have expanded to occupy almost all available sites; scores of pairs now breed along this stretch of cliffs. Herring Gulls are here in hundreds, with many nests on offshore islets. Great Black-backed Gulls also breed, a scourge to other species as they search for exposed nests and young. The smaller Kittiwake does not breed here, but large flocks often feed offshore, or move past with Manx Shearwaters and Gannets flying down from Welsh colonies.

This area, in particular Long and Short Islands halfway to Boscastle, now holds the largest Cornish mainland colony of

259

breeding auks. Parties of dozens sit on the sea offshore or whirr past swiftly to land on concealed ledges. In good light the browner backs of Guillemots and black backs of Razorbills can be distinguished. Puffins can also be seen without too much difficulty, sitting in rafts of up to 20 on the sea or standing near their nest burrows on offshore islands; their smaller, more dumpy outline and white cheek-patches usually stand out before the multi-coloured beak can be seen. All auks breeding here are difficult to census, but a watch along the entire area described might reveal up to 70 of each species.

A local oddity is a cliff-nesting colony of House Martins near Tintagel Head, a habit seen in few other parts of Britain.

Although much bird activity is down under the cliffs, with excellent views at times of seabirds passing below, it is worth looking in other directions. Peregrines can be watched frequently, often circling high up over the clifftops to obtain a wide view of approaching prey along the coast. Ravens are a common sight, and the jingling song of Corn Buntings may be heard from posts and hedgerows.

By late summer auks have left, although gulls still have young in the nest.

Timing

The seabird colony can be seen at any time of day during the breeding season. The number of tourists using the area makes little impact. Strong onshore winds with high seas should be avoided if you want parties of off-duty auks sitting on the sea. Such conditions, with west or northwest winds, could, however, force in other seabirds moving down the coast. The clifftop viewpoints lack any cover and watching breeding seabirds is difficult in very wet weather.

One problem caused by the summer tourist influx is that parking can be difficult if you arrive after mid morning, especially on warm weekends.

Access

A39 from Bude to Wadebridge runs past here well inland. Turn off west on one of several B-class roads to Tintagel and Boscastle; B3263 is the main coast road between the two villages, passing through the small settlements of Bossiney and Trevalga en route. There is a coastal footpath all along this stretch of cliffs and the full walk from Tintagel to Boscastle is worthwhile for those with time and energy. If unable to do this:

Tintagel itself is the most visited by tourists. Not the best point for auks, although Fulmars are numerous. The outer headland is a possible seawatching point. Look at the sea caves just west of the head for House Martins breeding.

Bossiney car park is a good central starting point. Walk down the valley footpath which starts at the road bend just east of the village. Near the bottom, turn left onto the steeply sloping coast path. Continue up left to overlook Lye Rock area, which gives good views and often Puffins on the sea (about $\frac{1}{2}$ mile/0.8 km walk). Alternatively, walk right from the cove for 1 mile (1.6 km) to reach Long and Short Islands just offshore, with breeding Puffins and other auks.

Calendar

Resident: Shag, Oystercatcher, Great Black-backed Gull, Stonechat, Raven, Corn Bunting.

Dec-Feb: Occasional passing seabird flocks. Fulmars begin arriving back at sites, Guillemots and Razorbills prospect ledges intermittently.

Mar-May: Fulmar, passing Manx Shearwater and Gannet, Cormorant, Kittiwake, Razorbill, Guillemot, Puffin, House Martin, all best seen late spring although auks may flock offshore in Apr.

Jun-Jul: Main period of breeding activity, but auks depart to sea from mid Jul. Manx Shearwaters, Gannets and Kittiwakes passing may be joined by other migrant seabirds towards end.

Aug-Nov: Most breeding seabirds departed by late Aug. Chance of migrant shearwaters or skuas passing with commoner species at sea.

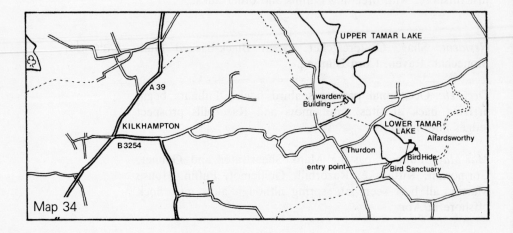

34 Tamar Lakes

(Map 34 and
OS Map 190)

Habitat

Straddling North Cornwall/Devon border, these two neigh-bouring man-made reservoirs with natural banks lie among high rolling farmland in a sparsely populated district. The 40-acre (16-ha) Lower Lake, tree-fringed with shallow marshy areas and rushes at the top end, is now used for recreation only, since completion of the 81-acre (33-ha) replacement Upper Lake, with more open banks. Both lakes, stocked with trout, are used extensively for fishing, and sailing is regular on the Upper Lake. Wildlife includes occasional Otters glimpsed on the banks on quiet mornings.

Species

These two reservoirs have suffered neglect from birdwatchers, partly because of lack of resident watchers nearby. Scarcer migrants, particularly waders, have been reported in the past, and the lakes, although comparatively small, attract a good variety of ducks, waders and waterside species, there being no comparable habitat in this corner of the region.

An attraction at the beginning and end of the year is the fairly regular occurrence of small parties of wild swans and grey geese, both quite scarce and irregular visitors to most of the region. Hardly a winter passes without a visit by a small tightly-knit group, probably a family, of Bewick's Swans, relatively slight in build beside resident Mutes. Sometimes longer-billed Whooper Swans, more on a size par with Mute, are also reported. The swans can be seen on either lake, but the grassy banks of the Upper Lake may be more attractive for a grazing party of half a dozen White-fronted Geese. None of these larger wildfowl stays through winter, although Bewick's Swans have been seen for two- or three-week spells. A smaller winter visitor, found in twos and threes regularly, is the grey-brown Little Grebe. Great Crested, the only other grebe at all likely, is more a passage migrant, odd singles turning up in spring or autumn. Four or five Cormorants usually fish on the

263

lakes. Dabbling ducks, although not found in huge numbers, are attracted by relatively shallow muddy banks, enabling a range of species to find suitable feeding. They often include over 100 Mallards, and varying numbers of up to 200 or more Teals often concealed among marshy vegetation. Flocks of 100-200 Wigeons might be seen at peak periods grazing on grassy banks, the male's yellow crown-stripe conspicuous, while one or two Pintails may join them irregularly. Shovelers are regular, this being one of their most established winter haunts in the region, although numbers are not large; up to 30 have been seen, but often counts are in single figures, chestnut-and-white-sided drakes usually in the majority. Another local speciality is Gadwall, the females often overlooked as slim Mallards but for their white speculum-patch on the wing; up to 15 have often been seen on Lower Lake, and this rather unevenly distributed species is rarely absent in winter. Diving ducks are not present in exceptional numbers, but winter counts of 40-60 Pochards and about half that number of Tufted are normal, with often half a dozen brownhead Goldeneyes feeding in deep stretches. A Goosander may call in, and 'coastal' species such as single Scaups or the dark-winged Long-tailed Duck have spent long periods here through winter, especially on Upper Lake, perhaps staying into spring.

Waders tend not to winter in numbers on reservoirs, where water levels are too high for edge feeding, but Green and Common Sandpipers have been flushed from quiet bays, where several dozen Snipe and occasionally a Jack Snipe can be found. Flocks of several hundred Lapwings, often accompanied by 100 or more Golden Plovers, gather on nearby farmland. These, and reservoir ducks, may attract a passing Peregrine to try its luck, but hundreds of Fieldfares and Redwings feeding in the vicinity may be more to the taste of Merlins, seen dashing overhead at irregular intervals most winters. One or two ringtail Hen Harriers seem to wander large expanses of northwest Devon in winter, and may beat low over the reservoir banks for a day, although they are by no means predictable. Another smaller but no less fierce predator, the Great Grey Shrike, has been seen several times among bushes in open land near the reservoir banks. Gull flocks often bathe and preen, but the totals of 400 or so Black-headed and Herring Gulls are unexceptional and, apart from 20-30 Common Gulls, occurrences of this family are not usually noteworthy.

Warmer weather brings activity among residents. Two or

three hissing cob (male) Mute Swans defend territory vigorously, while a pair or two of Coots and Moorhens nest. A pair of Kingfishers usually breeds in the area and singles may be disturbed from waterside trees, darting off low and straight across the lake. Usually nasal 'buzzing' calls of nesting Willow Tits can be heard in trees by the Lower Lake. Up above, Rooks are busy nesting, and several pairs of Grey Herons build bulky treetop nests nearby. Spring migrants, although less varied than autumn, can be numerous, with hundreds of hirundines and Swifts massing to feed low over the water on their way north. In most springs, probably late on, they are joined briefly by a breeding-dress Black Tern or two, scarce in our region at this season, which benefits similarly from hordes of midges just over the lake surface. At the same time a few pairs of Reed and Sedge Warblers join smart, black-headed Reed Buntings singing in the fringe vegetation of the Lower Lake. Wader migrants usually include Ruff, Green and Common Sandpipers, and one or two noisy Greenshanks. Ringed Plovers are regular inland passage migrants in single figures on both migrations, and the flat 'peeo' calls of a slim-winged Little Ringed Plover have been heard. Curlews, which breed nearby, are also likely to be seen.

In autumn, when water levels have dropped, waders are present for longer periods. The marshy end of Lower Tamar Lake is favoured. Four or five Green Sandpipers are expected, joined by varying numbers of Wood Sandpipers with pale-spangled upperparts, from singles to (more exceptionally) half a dozen birds or more according to early autumn migration conditions. Similar numbers of Little Stints peck at titbits on open mud, and may stay for several weeks with groups of Dunlins, which reach 30 birds at times. Usually one or two Greenshanks, Ruffs and long-legged Spotted Redshanks feed for periods off-passage at this season, along with probably the first few Teals in the shallows. Black Terns are, as in spring, a regular feature, seen through early and mid autumn, with one or two pale winter-plumaged and juvenile birds present almost continuously, although more than four or five is rare. A variety of other migrants has been noted, including a Spotted Crake venturing out from waterside vegetation. American visitors have included single Pectoral Sandpipers, and Long-billed Dowitchers, looking somewhat like very large, greyish Snipe.

This type of habitat repays regular visiting rather than one-off **Timing** visits, as birds filter through over a period. Black Terns and large hirundine flocks are most likely on humid, cloudy days, possibly with drizzle, especially in winds from southerly or easterly quarters. Dry autumn periods with falling water levels leaving mud margins are best for feeding waders. American species are, as usual, most likely after strong west winds. Disturbance from fishing and sailing is normally less on weekdays or early mornings. Wild swans or geese are seen mostly in cold weather, but geese may soon depart because of disturbance.

Access

Although A39 Bude-Bideford road lies only 4 miles (6½ km) to the west, the reservoirs might easily be missed. From Bideford direction, turn left (east) off A39 at Kilkhampton on B3254 towards Launceston, turning left after ½ mile (0.8 km) on minor roads towards Bradworthy and Holsworthy. For the Upper Lake turn first left after 1 mile (1.6 km), then take a left turn signposted to the reservoir car park. For the Lower Lake, continue towards Holsworthy, turning second left after leaving the B road, then pulling into the lower car park. A footpath connects the two. The marshy end of the Lower Lake, overlooked by a bird hide, is maintained as a bird sanctuary from August to April; permits for the hide are available from the SWWA warden's office by the Upper Lake dam. At other times there is open access to the lake banks and the other parts of the lake can be viewed at any time. Visitors to the Upper Lake banks also require a SWWA permit. A bird logbook is kept at the warden's building and information centre.

Calendar

Resident: Grey Heron, Sparrowhawk, Buzzard, Coot, Barn Owl, Kingfisher, Willow Tit, Reed Bunting.

Dec-Feb: Little Grebe, Cormorant, probably wild swans or geese, Teal, Wigeon, Gadwall, Shoveler, Tufted Duck, Pochard, Goldeneye, maybe Scaup or Long-tailed Duck, occasional Goosander, irregular Hen Harrier, Peregrine and Merlin, possible Green or Common Sandpipers, Snipe, maybe Jack Snipe, commoner gulls, possible Great Grey Shrike, winter thrushes.

Mar-May: A few ducks, especially diving ducks, e.g Tufted or a Long-tailed, stay through Apr. Migrants inc. Sand Martin from mid Mar, most species from mid Apr inc. commoner warblers, Reed and Sedge, hirundine flocks, waders, e.g. Ringed Plover, Ruff, Green and Common Sandpipers, Greenshank; probably Black Tern late Apr-May.

Jun-Jul: Breeding species, inc. probably Curlew, a few Sedge Warblers. Migrant waders, inc. Ringed Plover, Dunlin, Ruff, Green Sandpiper, from late Jul.

Aug-Nov: Protracted wader migration peaking end Aug-Sep, with Ringed Plover, Ruff, Spotted Redshank, Greenshank, Dunlin, Little Stint, Common, Green and Wood Sandpipers, maybe scarcer species; most left by late Oct. Probably Black Tern Aug-early Oct, Great Crested Grebe irregular. Winter visitors arrive back during Nov, except some Teals from early autumn.

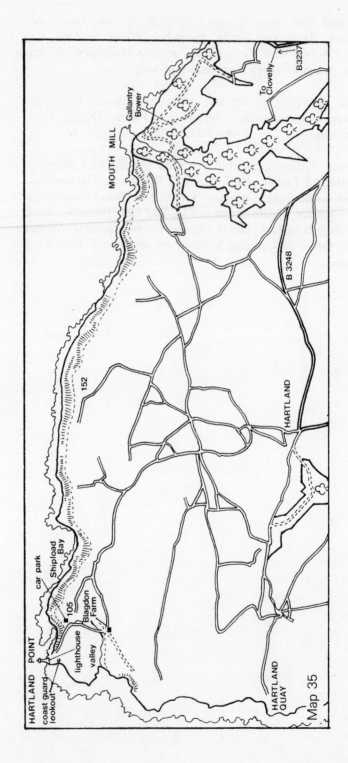

Map 35

35 Hartland Point and District

(Map 35 and OS Map 190)

Habitat

On the corner where the North Devon coastline turns sharply southward towards Cornwall, the high jagged cliffs of Hartland face across deep water towards Lundy island 12 miles (19 km) away. On a ledge below the cliffs stands a lighthouse, overlooking a strong tiderace offshore. The surrounding gorse-clad coastline, backed by high farmland, includes many small coves and rocky promontories. A sheltered, bushy stream valley lies just west of the Point. Eastward towards the tourist village of Clovelly 6 miles (9$\frac{1}{2}$ km) away, the cliffs are heavily wooded. Inland, 4 miles (6$\frac{1}{2}$ km) south of Hartland village, lie the dense conifer plantations of Hartland Forest, and nearby open heaths such as Bursdon Moor.

Species

The Point is well placed for seeing birds moving across from Wales and the Bristol Channel coastline. The powerful lighthouse also acts as a focus for nocturnal migrants. Early in the year the area is very windswept, and the most obvious birds are parties of croaking Ravens foraging along clifftops. Flocks of over 100 divers reported on the sea in recent winters are believed to be mainly Black-throated. There have been a number of sightings of raptors such as single Hen Harriers and Merlins hunting over inland heaths, and once a wintering Goshawk.

Small passerine migrants arrive early in spring if the weather is fine with high barometric pressure, first dates being even earlier in some cases than on the south coast. Possibly the birds have flown through Devon without stopping, coming to rest on the north coast before making another sea crossing towards Wales. Wheatears are often the first arrivals, and passing migrants later in the season include all the commoner warblers. Among these may be a dozen or more Grasshopper Warblers, the males detected by their high 'reeling' song, some staying to breed in coastal scrub. Most other transient

269

species, including a few Lesser Whitethroats (scarce this far west), occur in thick bushes along the stream valley on the west side, where they can be hard to watch. Sedge Warblers stay to nest in the damp undergrowth. Groups of diurnal migrants such as Swallows may often be seen circling up over the Point in early mornings before departing northward, probably via Lundy.

On early mornings in summer, Manx Shearwaters pass westward in long strings, flashing black and white as they bank low over the waves. Numbers may run into thousands (15,000 have been counted in a morning), believed to be breeding adults from Skokholm and Skomer Islands in Pembrokeshire, en route from the colony on a daily journey to oceanic feeding grounds. Some returning birds are confused by the lighthouse beam on dull nights and become injured in collision with buildings. Single Storm Petrels have been recorded fluttering in the beams, but have never been seen in daylight. Other seabirds flying past on summer days include feeding parties of Gannets, Kittiwakes and auks. Bunches of non-breeding Common Scoters are frequently seen passing. Fulmars are abundant breeders, heckling each other noisily on cliff ledges, together with Herring Gulls. Great Black-backed Gulls nest in small numbers on isolated rocks. Several pairs of Oyster-catchers raise young in quiet coves, while coastal passerines include Stonechats and Whitethroats in thickets.

For those wishing to see woodland species, there are breeding season records of a variety of birds in Hobby Drive woods above Clovelly. Singing Pied Flycatchers have started to occur in recent seasons and several Wood Warblers are likely to be heard, while Grey Wagtails flit along the damp woodland tracks. Breeding birds of the inland area are not well known, but Curlews and Grasshopper Warblers are found on open heathland. One or two pairs of Turtle Doves, and some years churring Nightjars, have been reported in Summerwell plantation, the southern half of the forestry area. The dull sooty-capped Willow Tit is a thinly scattered local resident in damp deciduous vegetation, and Barn Owls may still be watched patrolling silently over the damp heaths.

In autumn, westward movement of seabirds off the Point is not fully known, but appears to be sporadic, chiefly in rough weather. There are annual records of Arctic and Great Skuas, usually no more than half a dozen of either in a day, with most years a scarcer species such as a Sooty Shearwater, or a Sabine's Gull beating past in a gale. Morning coasting movement of landbirds may be interesting, with flocks of

Firecrest

HARRISON 83

hundreds of Chaffinches and Meadow Pipits in later autumn, perhaps pursued by a Merlin or Peregrine. As warbler movement slackens after mid autumn, a few Firecrests arrive, often two or three giving hoarse 'zip' calls from sheltered bushes. Large movements involving thousands of Fieldfares, Blackbirds and other thrushes have been seen, with the chance of a scarcer warbler during these falls. Red-breasted Flycatchers and Yellow-browed Warblers have been seen, but so far not the major rarities recorded on nearby Lundy; perhaps there is scope for future discovery. A Black Redstart is often present around rocks and buildings at the start of winter, while flocks of a dozen or more Purple Sandpipers pick over tideline rocks. A flock of up to 200 Common Scoters is often present off Clovelly at the end of the year, and perhaps through to spring.

Timing

To see wintering diver flocks, calm seas are necessary, although a period of high winds beforehand seems to drive birds in. Terns and Arctic Skuas have been seen on early autumn anticyclonic easterlies with haze. The most likely conditions for numbers of other seabirds would be a strong west or northwest gale, after a period of southwest winds has driven birds up into the Bristol Channel (compare with St Ives in Cornwall). Summer feeding movements of Manx Shearwaters take place early each morning, but farther out in calm weather. The largest arrivals of thrushes and warblers take place in typical fall conditions, overcast with east winds, but clear mornings (first three or four hours of daylight) with an opposing breeze are best for diurnal passage, especially finches.

On the heaths and plantations fine weather is needed to see birds of prey. Fine summer evenings are necessary for crepuscular species such as Nightjar and Grasshopper Warbler singing, and in late summer, with hungry broods to feed, Barn Owls might be active before nightfall.

Access

From A39 between Bideford and Bude. For the Point and lighthouse, take signs towards Hartland, bypass the village and follow separate signs down lanes to the Point. The road bends down past a farm entrance and terminates in a clifftop car park. From the car park a lane leads down to the lighthouse compound. Access to the compound is not normally permitted outside daytime visiting hours, but you can seawatch from the lane near the lighthouse entrance. A coastal footpath runs across the clifftops westward above the lighthouse, and eastward past the radar station into the next bay. Westward the path runs across the mouth of the sheltered stream valley, worth a look for migrants. Alternatively, walk down the track into the valley past the farm buildings, on the corner of the road.

For Clovelly woods, take the signposted turn off A39 4 miles ($6\frac{1}{2}$ km) east of the Hartland road. Drive to the main tourist car parks. Walk right along wooded Hobby Drive, which can be followed for 2 miles (3 km) until it rejoins the main road. For the plantation and heaths, continue west towards Bude on A39 past the Hartland turn. From the Forest Office on the left (east) side of main road, signposted woodland walks can be taken. Over the next 2-3 miles (3-5 km) southward, heaths can be seen right of the main road; small roads cross these westward towards the coast.

Calendar

Resident: Shag, Oystercatcher, Great Black-backed and Herring Gulls, Barn Owl, Raven, Willow Tit, Stonechat, Rock Pipit, Grey Wagtail.

Dec-Feb: Divers (Black-throated?), especially end Jan-Feb; raptors, particularly Hen Harrier and Merlin over heaths;

Common Scoter (Clovelly), Purple Sandpiper, auks passing, maybe Black Redstart.

Mar-May: Fulmar, Manx Shearwater (from end Mar), Wheatear and Chiffchaff from mid Mar, other warblers inc. Lesser Whitethroat, Sedge and Grasshopper mostly from late Apr, common summer visitors from Apr, Curlews arriving on heaths, possible Turtle Dove and Nightjar (late May), singing woodland passerines at Clovelly.

Jun-Jul: Offshore Manx Shearwaters, possibly Storm Petrel, Fulmar, Gannet, Kittiwake, auks, Common Scoter. Breeding species inc. Whitethroat, Sedge and Grasshopper Warblers; warblers, flycatchers, common woodland passerines at Clovelly, Curlew on heaths, still maybe Turtle Dove or Nightjar.

Aug-Nov: Fulmar, Arctic and Great Skuas, occasional scarcer seabirds (Sep-Oct mainly), warblers, chats and flycatchers peaking end Aug-Sep, Firecrest (mainly Oct), Black Redstart (late Oct-Nov), winter thrushes (late Oct-Nov), finches, pipits, raptors mainly Oct-Nov.

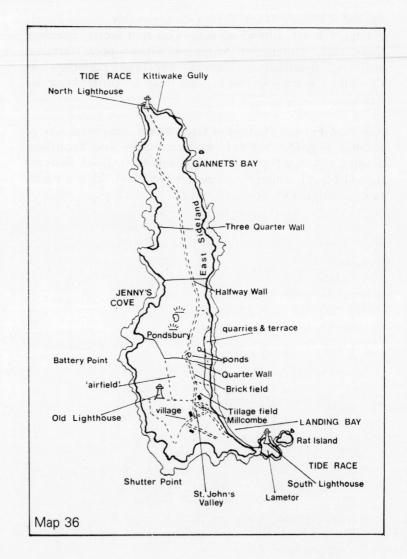

TIDE RACE   Kittiwake Gully
North Lighthouse

GANNETS' BAY

East Sideland

Three Quarter Wall

JENNY'S
COVE

Halfway Wall

quarries & terrace

Pondsbury

Battery Point

ponds

Quarter Wall

'airfield'

Brick field

Old Lighthouse

village

Tillage field
Millcombe

LANDING BAY

Rat Island

TIDE RACE

Shutter Point

South Lighthouse

St. John's
Valley

Lametor

Map 36

36 Lundy

(Map 36 and
OS Map 180)

Twelve miles (19 km) north of Hartland Point, between the northwest corner of Devon and the Welsh coast, lies the rugged granite mass of Lundy. The island, about 3½ miles (5½ km) long from north to south and ½ mile (0.8 km) wide, has a near-level plateau top about 100 m above sea level. Much of the top is boggy and stony moorland, except in the slightly wider southern quarter where there are a few fields, mostly rough pasture. Stone walls cross the island to mark quarter, half and threequarter points northward from the south end. Permanent standing water is found at Pondsbury depression, almost halfway up, and at tiny pools near Quarter Wall and scattered across the southern quarter.

The north and west of the island are flanked by deep gullies, spectacular cliffs and rock buttresses, but the east side is a little more sheltered, with steep slopes clothed in places by Rhododendron thickets and Bracken. At the south end is the partly detached block of Lametor, with a lighthouse. There is also a working lighthouse at the north end, but the old light-tower, a prominent landmark across the top of the island, is no longer used; its accommodation was used for a bird observatory from 1947 to 1973. Nearby, at the southeast corner of the plateau, stands the small collection of inhabited houses, farm buildings and Marisco Tavern. Between village and sea is the steep, sheltered Millcombe valley with walled gardens, a little mixed woodland (chiefly Turkey Oak, Sycamore and Monterey Pine) and thickets; at the foot is the stony Landing Beach. Off the beach the 'Roads' form a calmer, sheltered expanse of sea in prevailing and often strong west winds. Strong tideraces occur off both ends of the island.

Apart from the limited expanse of farmland in the south of Lundy, largely surrounded by stone walls, much of the island is too exposed and barren to support stock. A few sheep, bullocks and ponies graze the turf. Flocks of feral Soay sheep from Scotland, primitive goat-like brown creatures, spend a hardy existence feeding on steep slopes and crags. Offshore, Grey Seals are a frequent sight, and their moaning breeding calls can be heard from sea caves at several points in the northern half of the coastline. Botanical interest includes the unique Lundy Cabbage. No snakes are found, nor larger mammals such as Foxes or Badgers, although Rabbits are quite plentiful. The island is owned by the Landmark Trust charity and preserved as a national heritage.

Species

Lundy has a long tradition of bird observations, encompassing accounts both of its seabird colonies and of many rare and exotic migrants noted over the decades. Since the demise of the full-time Bird Observatory it attracts less systematic ornithological attention, but must be rated as one of the region's top bird migration watching areas.

The barren, windswept nature of much of the island prevents many species from living here all year, although Ravens are often in view as several resident pairs soar over the steep sidelands. Shags, common breeders, can still be seen in small numbers in other months, although the less marine Cormorant is only a passing migrant. In stony coves Oyster-catchers are always present in small numbers, several pairs staying to nest, while Turnstones and Purple Sandpipers are seen occasionally on weedy rocks in winter. Lapwings are commonly met on the rough grassland; winter influxes of a couple of hundred may occur, joining dozens of Golden Plovers feeding with Snipe, Starlings and winter thrushes on the pasture. Even Skylarks and Meadow Pipits, typical summer residents of open terrain, may move away partly in winter. The population of common woodland passerines is very limited; tits, even Blue and Great, are not normally resident here.

Some breeding seabirds return early to the island. Fulmars and Kittiwakes loiter in the area from late winter, coming ashore intermittently, although not fully occupying ledges until late spring. Manx Shearwaters return to burrows on the south and west slopes, although the status of this visitor, which does not fly to land until darkness covers its movements, is hard to determine. Certainly the species is seen at sea in daytime around the island in late spring and summer, often zigzagging low over the tideraces or flying south in lines past the west cliffs; many of these, however, are presumed to be from the scores of thousands breeding on Skokholm and Skomer Islands in Pembrokeshire. Flocks of thousands seen from the

Storm Petrel　　　　　*Leach's Petrel*

HARRISON 83

boat, resting in masses on the sea between Lundy and the Devon mainland on calm summer mornings, are thought to be of similar origin. The wailing cries of incoming birds circling low over the island at night, and occasional remains of an unwary shearwater killed by gulls, prove that some stay to breed, or at least summer, here. Detail is similarly lacking for the dainty Storm Petrel, believed to breed in small numbers along the wildest rocky west cliffs, but rarely seen in daylight except when gales drive small flocks in to patter over Lundy Roads bay or when one is glimpsed from the boat crossing. Gannets are seen frequently feeding offshore, although counts of more than a few dozen are unusual. Most of the seabird breeding population is concentrated on the higher cliff slopes of the west and north. The Lesser Black-backed Gull's summer breeding population fluctuates annually, but reaches several dozen pairs. Herring Gulls are typically abundant, with well over 1,000 pairs. Great Black-backed Gulls also breed, more solitarily, often 20-30 pairs or more on the island. The delicate Kittiwake is particularly conspicuous around the island's north end, the total of pairs perhaps exceeding 1,000.

Many visitors to Lundy's cliffs seek out the island emblem, the rotund Puffin, most commonly seen around Battery Point on the west coast, or near the north end. Numbers of this very localised seabird, after reaching low ebbs as elsewhere in the 1960s, may now be recovering, with perhaps 100 pairs present .

by late spring. Other auks are scattered around the island, Razorbills taking advantage of crevices and fissures between granite rocks to support a population of perhaps 700 pairs (the region's largest). Guillemots nest on sheerer cliffs in similar numbers. All the auks, however, disappear swiftly to sea once chicks have fledged. Formerly Peregrines shared the cliffs with them, but since the 1960s population decline, directly linked with pesticide pollution, have become irregular in occurrence.

Spring migration can be heavy and concentrated, Millcombe valley bushes in particular holding scores of fluttering yellowish-brown *Phylloscopus* warblers in early mornings with 'hooeet' calls from all directions. Many warblers, and other small passerines such as Goldcrests, flycatchers and a few Redstarts as spring progresses, feed in East Sidelands thickets as they work their way northward. Sheltered level areas such as the disused quarries and Terrace with water and bushes, high up on the east slopes, tend to concentrate small migrants. As at the region's other migration points, the main passage is often preceded by a good scattering of Wheatears, which may number scores later, early Chiffchaffs and Goldcrests, with perhaps a couple of Firecrests in the bushes or Black Redstarts on the rocks. The short turf in the south of the island is ideal for a probing Hoopoe, likely to turn up most years. The most noticeable bulk of spring passerine movement consists of commoner warblers, which may be present in mixed aggregations of several hundreds on fall mornings (Willow Warblers being most abundant), and hirundines, which pour northward overhead particularly from mid spring. A very wide range of small birds passes through annually, with always the chance of a really rare sighting, especially towards the end of spring or in early summer. The high, repetitive song of a Greenish Warbler has been heard in Millcombe valley, and one recent year a visiting party of naturalists was entertained by a superb black-hooded Rüppell's Warbler (Britain's second ever) singing in bushes on East Sidelands. Lundy shares with the Scillies the distinction of late spring visits by the beautiful but elusive Golden Oriole, sometimes two or three together, and its fluting 'weela-weeoo' song has been heard a number of times in Millcombe trees.

Up on the plateau there is a steady spring passage of open-ground species, including departing groups of winter thrushes and Starlings, along with Pied/White Wagtails and Meadow Pipits. A Merlin may be attracted in pursuit and a passage Short-eared Owl might be flushed. Small parties of bronze-winged Ring Ouzels often stop to feed in habitat resembling their moorland haunts. Golden Plovers often pass through in small flocks, and resting groups should be inspected for one of Lundy's regular specialities, the Dotterel. Smart breeding-dress birds with white supercilium (eyebrow) stripes and breast-band are virtually annual, sometimes in small groups, en route northward to high mountain haunts. Walls and telegraph wires near the village, or up on the east side, may attract a perching migrant shrike, very occasionally the declining Red-backed, but nowadays perhaps more likely an overshooting south European Woodchat. Occasionally a raptor such as a Montagu's Harrier may also drift over.

In summer an occasional pair of migrant warblers, perhaps Whitethroat or Willow, stays to breed. A surprise southern vagrant could still turn up at any stage. Breeding Curlews (usually two or three pairs present) bubble in song over boggy tracts of moor, joining two or three dozen Lapwings diving in nesting display overhead; a pair of Wheatears may nest on drier ground. In some years late summer has brought an influx of ten or more Continental Crossbills, these stout pine-feeding birds looking strangely out of place here, where they may glean a temporary living from eating seeds at ground level; such arrivals, however, are very irregular and unpredictable.

Waders are among the first migrants to indicate the end of summer: a small party of Dunlins, a shank or Green Sandpiper may drop in beside Pondsbury, or at tiny pools in the south of the island. As autumn progresses, these miniature habitats are worth watching for a variety of waders, although usually no more than a handful of birds. Towards mid autumn, American Pectoral Sandpipers have been recorded often enough to be almost predictable, and any tiny stint-like waders should be carefully inspected for signs of other transatlantic visitors such as Least or Semipalmated Sandpiper, which have both been identified here. Mid autumn usually brings another chance to see the scarce but often tame Dotterel, with small parties most years on open spaces such as the 'Airfield'.

Autumn passage movement is often less concentrated than in spring as far as small night migrants such as warblers and flycatchers are concerned, although a few very large arrivals (over 1,000 birds coming overnight) are on record. The normal daily trickle of migrants may include a heavier-built Melodious Warbler among Willow Warblers and Chiffchaffs. Lundy is one of the region's few localities where skulking East European breeding birds such as the grey Barred Warbler have been found on a number of occasions; ringing has helped to reveal this and other unobtrusive species, such as the rare

Thrush Nightingale recently recorded. Intensive watching of
the East Sidelands bushes and Millcombe is needed to discover
warblers and flycatchers, often busy feeding under cover; the
casual observer may see little without searching, unless there
has been a recent sizeable fall.

Lundy's high open top attracts large numbers of passing
open-ground birds such as pipits, larks and buntings to stop off
in autumn. Numbers of early migrants such as Yellow Wagtail
and Tree Pipit may not exceed a couple of dozen per day, but
Meadow Pipits pass in many hundreds, and occasionally a
rarer pipit such as the heavily streaked Red-throated or larger
Richard's, which often hovers indecisively if disturbed from
the ground, is seen for a few days on the farmland. Seed-
eating species include annual occurrences of Ortolan Bunting
in the fields, a very scarce migrant in our region. Often a few
Lapland Buntings are seen in moorland habitats, recognised
by the hard 'tick-tick-teu' call as they fly up, and Snow
Buntings may also be encountered. Other migrants in open
areas may include a dull immature Red-backed or Woodchat
Shrike, or a passing raptor such as Hobby or Merlin; the latter
often stays for a week or two to take advantage of resting
migrant passerines in the pastures. Late in autumn, flocks of
finches coast high overhead; Chaffinches, sometimes
thousands a day, form the bulk, but Siskins, Redpolls and
Bramblings are also heard calling as they pass over. There may
still be a surprise in store, such as the American Robin which
foraged for worms with Redwing flocks one recent late
autumn.

Timing

As with all islands, most watchers find themselves constrained
by access, which makes timing a visit for special conditions
difficult. Birds may 'filter through' here, between the land-
masses of Wales and Devon, so it cannot always be assumed
that birds will tie in exactly with expected arrival weather.
Nevertheless, larger numbers of warblers, flycatchers, thrushes
and other insect-eating passerines are seen in classic overnight
fall conditions after high pressure, and east or southeast winds
are, as at all migration points, the most interesting, especially
in autumn. Most finch and pipit movements in autumn are
against light headwinds. Fine spells of weather with light
southerlies have brought many scarcer birds, including spring
exotics. Most American rarities have occurred after strong
Atlantic depressions with westerly gales. Such winds have not
proved very good for seawatching, except for common species

and the odd sheltering Storm Petrel. Few seabirds seem to pass here on migration, but poor visibility may bring those that do (e.g. occasional skuas) closer. For Manx Shearwaters or Storm Petrels landing, a night search with flashlights on the west or south cliff slopes would be needed, but great care should be exercised: cliff accidents have claimed lives here.

Note that Landing Beach is not sheltered from east winds; a strong easterly may prevent visitors from landing by boat.

Access

Traditionally by boat from Ilfracombe in North Devon, where the supply ship 'Polar Bear' is based. There is a chance that the service may be moved to Bideford. There is also now a helicopter service from Hartland in holiday seasons. Additionally, steamer excursions may be arranged from Ilfracombe for tourists, although time ashore on Lundy is limited. Steamers cannot unload passengers direct at the shallow landing area, and there may be a delay while small boats ferry passengers ashore. Lundy Field Society also arranges an annual boat trip to the island, with guided tours led by LFS officials; details can be obtained from the Hon. Secretary of the Society at 2 Beaufort Close, Reigate, Surrey, RH2 9DG, telephone Reigate 45031.

For details of regular transport to Lundy, and accommodation in the small Millcombe hotel, cottages, camping field and hostel, contact the Island Administrator, telephone Woolacombe 870870. Most bird news is exchanged in the Marisco Tavern, although on a small island like this, with only a couple of dozen regular inhabitants, 'bird events' are general knowledge.

If time ashore is limited, most visitors usually concentrate on Millcombe valley (and St John's valley, which branches left near the top) for migrants just arrived; the Terrace and East Sidelands for migrants feeding and filtering along; or main seabird colonies such as around North Light or the projecting Battery Point halfway down the west coast, the latter probably best for Puffins. If visiting the north end, try Kittiwake Gully, reached by railed steps right of the lighthouse, for close views. The main track from Landing Beach winds up very steeply through Millcombe, to the village; there is a well-marked track north past the Airfield and other pasture and cultivated areas, through the centre of the island past Pondsbury and to the north end. From the far end to the village is about an hour's walk.

Calendar

Resident: Shag, Oystercatcher, Lapwing, Herring and Great Black-backed Gulls, Rock Pipit, Raven.

Dec-Feb: Reduced winter numbers of residents. A few Water Rails, Golden Plovers, Snipe, Woodcock. Possible weather influxes of open-ground species such as plovers and larks, or winter thrushes. Probably Teal. Fulmar, Kittiwake, Guillemot and Razorbill start to return at end. Occasional Peregrine, probably Purple Sandpiper and Turnstone.

Mar-May: From mid Mar, Wheatear, Black Redstart probable, Chiffchaff, Firecrest probable, Goldcrest; passing winter thrushes, Golden Plover and maybe Jack Snipe, maybe Peregrine, Merlin or Short-eared Owl; most departing winter species have passed by late Apr. Chance of Hoopoe from mid Mar, a few Manx Shearwaters from end Mar. Main passage of small migrants from mid Apr, inc. hirundines, pipits, Yellow Wagtail, all commoner warblers, a few Pied Flycatchers, Redstarts, Whinchats, Ring Ouzels. Probably Dotterel late Apr-May; maybe southern rarities, e.g. Woodchat, Golden Oriole or vagrant warblers, chiefly May. Many Whimbrels pass Apr-May. All seabirds here by May.

Jun-Jul: chance of late commoner migrants, maybe a vagrant. Breeding Lapwing, Curlew and seabirds. Manx Shearwater and maybe Storm Petrel seen on crossing. Chance of wader passage, sometimes Crossbills, and first warblers by end Jul. Auks leave late Jul.

Aug-Nov: Warblers, flycatchers, other small migrants increase through Aug, peak usually early-mid Sep, maybe Melodious Warbler Aug-Sep, possibly a shrike late Aug-Sep. Thin wader passage mostly Aug-Sep, e.g. Dunlin, Whimbrel, shanks, Common and Green Sandpipers, with maybe American species, especially Sep; chance of Dotterel mostly late Aug-early Oct. Probable Ortolan Bunting late Aug-Sep; through Sep-Oct, probably Merlin, Peregrine, Lapland Bunting, maybe Snow Bunting Oct. Scarcer eastern migrants mostly late Sep-Oct. Pipit passage peaking late Sep-Oct. Finches coasting mid Oct on, peak end Oct, winter thrushes arriving, maybe a rarity end Oct-early Nov, when Firecrest and Black Redstart arrive. Probable Short-eared Owl and remaining Merlin into Nov.

37 Taw-Torridge Estuary (Maps 37(i) and 37(ii) and OS Map 180)

Habitat

The exposed, rocky coastline of North Devon is interrupted by only one substantial river system, the combined estuary of Taw and Torridge. This wide, sandy basin is fringed by high sand dunes and low-lying rough grazing marshes. On the north side of the estuary mouth lies the 3-mile (5-km) expanse of Braunton Burrows, with dunes up to 29 m high, part of which is a National Nature Reserve. On the south side of the estuary system is the smaller Northam Burrows area, a Country Park, with a high pebble ridge along its seashore. Between these two peninsulas is the relatively shallow river mouth into Bideford Bay. The estuary's sandy nature creates a less rich intertidal fauna than is found on some of the region's muddy estuaries, but its value is increased by the wide area of scantily populated bordering marshland, especially on the Taw. Main population centres are Bideford on the Torridge and Barnstaple on the Taw, both at the head of the main estuary of rivers concerned.

Wildlife on the marshland still includes an occasional elusive Otter, mainly in winter, and Salmon pass up the rivers in large numbers. Braunton Burrows is of exceptional botanical interest; rarer plants include Sand Toadflax and Water Germander. Other flora of interest include coastal species such as Sea Holly and Sea Stock, or orchids such as Early Marsh, and Marsh Helleborines. In early summer the dunes can be a mass of flowers. Water Germander is also found at Northam, together with Sea Stock and Dune Pansies.

The beaches at Northam Burrows and neighbouring Westward Ho!, as at Saunton Sands fronting Braunton Burrows across the river, are popular with summer holiday-makers and water sports are increasing around the estuary mouth; both create disturbance to wildlife. Parts of the lower estuary, especially around Braunton Burrows, are used for military exercises at times.

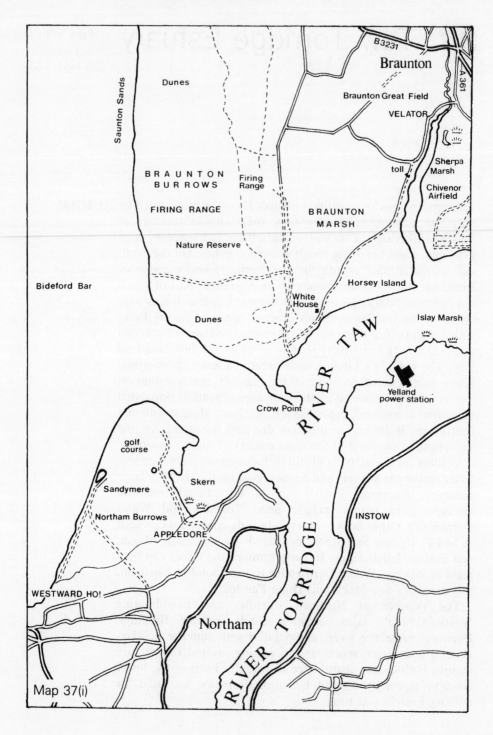

Map 37(i)

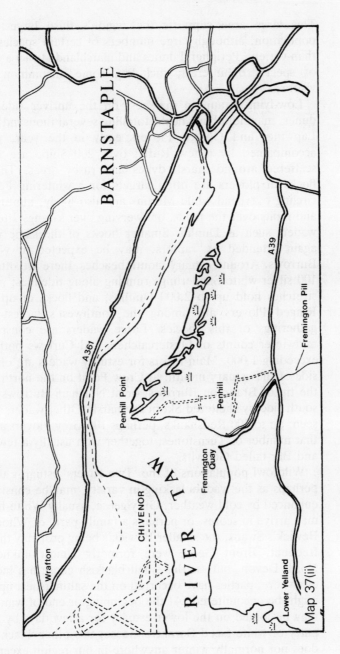

Map 37(ii)

Species

This large area supports the region's third largest wader population, although large numbers of certain species rather than variety. Peripheral dunes and marshland attract a number of species of interest, including some uncommon winter visitors.

Low-lying Braunton marshes, on the upriver side of the dunes, may hold huge flocks totalling several thousand each of Lapwings and Golden Plovers early in the year, perhaps accompanied by a few Ruffs; over 200 Snipe are regular, scattered around marsh dykes and rushy areas. The large flocks of plovers are often targets for a wintering Peregrine circling overhead while Merlins are also likely, hunting larks and pipits over the fields, or swerving over saltings after small waders such as Dunlin. Smaller flocks of the same waders, again attended by raptors, may be expected at Northam Burrows. Around estuary mouth beaches, there are often over 100 silver-white Sanderlings running along tidelines; muddier stretches hold up to 2,000 Dunlins, and flocks of up to 200 Ringed Plovers are among the southwest's largest winter gatherings of this species. Large waders are conspicuous, midwinter counts of Oystercatchers and Curlews both easily exceeding 1,000. Main roosts for estuary waders are on either side of the estuary mouth, at Crow Point on the north side at the tip of Braunton Burrows, or at Northam Burrows on the south side by sheltered Skern saltmarsh. Other waders may be seen: up to 500 Redshanks, perhaps 100 Grey Plovers and half that number of Turnstones, together with usually a few Knots and Bar-tailed Godwits.

Wildfowl populations of the 'Two Rivers' estuary, although perhaps as the waders lacking in variety, may be considerably enhanced by cold weather. Grey geese, usually White-fronted, may arrive in scores, or perhaps a family party of Whooper or Bewick's Swans, the smaller Bewick's being probably the more frequent. Brent Geese were formerly almost unknown in North Devon, but, as this small blackish goose has increased elsewhere, parties have occurred on the saltmarshes; up to 100 might be encountered. At the beginning or end of winter they may be joined on the lower estuary for a few days by a small party of white-faced Barnacle Geese; this other 'black goose' does not normally winter anywhere in our region except for a few tame individuals escaped from wildlife collections (several arriving together probably indicate wild stock). Shelducks are widespread, reaching late winter peaks of well over 100 most years. Regular ducks include up to 1,000 Wigeons, mostly on the lower estuary basin, and often 200 or more Teals, which

Eiders

HARRISON 83

may be scattered in groups over the marshes. Shovelers gather on muddy pools, groups such as 20 together on Northam Burrows being among the largest in Devon; flocks (perhaps the same birds) also occur on outer Braunton marshes, where there is standing water. Other wildfowl such as Pintail and Gadwall turn up sporadically in small groups, generally less than half a dozen. Diving ducks are limited, although two or three Goldeneyes and single-figure counts of Red-breasted Mergansers might be expected. More marine birds such as single Scaups may be driven to shelter in the estuary by winter storms, and Common Scoters are often present in dozens in Bideford Bay, perhaps seen off Westward Ho! front, or Downend rocks beyond Braunton, habitats where a few Purple Sandpipers may be discovered feeding inconspicuously on the shore. One of the outstanding local wildfowl is Eider, of which a non-breeding flock (variable, often 20-30 birds) is habitually present around the lower estuary or mouth; a record recent count of 84 summering shows an encouraging upward trend. Most are brown female or immature birds, some with a confusing pattern of black and white blotches appearing as smart adult male colours show through; full adult males are a small minority.

Rough weather offshore may force a Great Northern Diver to feed in the estuary mouth, where one or two Slavonian Grebes are present most winters. The browner Little Grebe, a marshland breeder here in very small numbers, may also be found diving on the tideway in winter. Colder months can bring increased interest to the marshes and freshwater pools, where a streaky-brown Bittern may lurk camouflaged in reedy margins, joining Water Rails. At sheltered spots, such as Wrafton pond east of Braunton marsh, the 'ping' calls of small parties of Bearded Tits have also been heard.

Farther upriver, in side creeks and bays, Grey Herons fishing may be joined by wintering Greenshanks. This latter species often winters in good numbers of six or more all together in different locations, but Spotted Redshanks found in similar backwaters and creeks are much scarcer, only one or two being normal. Kingfishers are also regular visitors to the estuary head, and the muddiest creeks or the riverside marshes above Barnstaple and Bideford may hold a Green or Common Sandpiper staying through. Gulls also use the marshes, including Black-headed with an estuary total which may approach 10,000. Herring Gulls, usually under 2,000, are not exceptionally plentiful compared with other parts of the region, but coastal gales may drive in several hundred Great Black-backed to the estuary mouth.

Spring wader passage is conspicuous, with dozens of whistling Whimbrels and many scattered Common Sandpipers stopping off. Sometimes migrant parties of up to 30 or more pale grey-backed White Wagtails are seen on marshes near the estuary mouth. Sedge, Reed and occasionally Grasshopper Warblers sing in the marsh dykes, although breeding numbers of these 'waterside' warblers are not large here. Whitethroats singing in thickets on Braunton Burrows are joined by one or two dark-faced Lesser Whitethroats, an increasing species here on the edge of its breeding range; two or three pairs of Turtle Doves are likely in similar habitats. Later, in the ancient Great Field area near Braunton, Quails may be heard calling, probably invisible in the cultivated land; this is a long-established site for the scarce and diminutive gamebird. More common, but perhaps not expected at sea level, are breeding Wheatears in the shingle and dunes around the estuary mouth, utilising Rabbit burrows and man-made pipes or debris for nest holes; good views can be obtained especially along Northam Burrows ridge, where a dozen or more pairs may breed. Several pairs of Oystercatchers and Ringed Plovers lay their well-camouflaged eggs on quieter stretches of the estuary.

Autumn brings varied, although not intensively watched, wader passage. Sheltered bays and creeks where streams flow in, known locally as 'pills', may hold Little Stints or Curlew Sandpipers, generally fewer than six of each; they are seen particularly at muddy feeding areas near the estuary mouth, such as Northam Burrows tip road pool or the River Caen outlet at Braunton Pill behind the Burrows. Occasionally an American vagrant such as Pectoral Sandpiper or Long-billed Dowitcher is reported in these habitats. Passerine migrants move through the dune-slack bushes, where damp conditions encourage rich insect life, and among commoner warblers and flycatchers a scarcer bird such as Wryneck might be seen. Feeding hirundines, often in hundreds over the marshes, may attract a passing Hobby. A few Sandwich, Common and Little Terns feed out around the estuary mouth, but numbers on this coast are small, even Sandwich rarely exceeding a dozen. Common Terns, if seen closely, may be checked for single individuals of the scarcer Arctic Tern, seen most years in autumn. The lower estuary also attracts considerable gatherings of noisy Greenshanks, with frequent counts of over 20, and perhaps a group of passing Bar-tailed Godwits.

Late autumn is often interesting. When Peregrine and Merlin return to harry wintering flocks, there is often a Short-eared Owl in the coastal dunes, and a Hen Harrier, usually a brown ringtail, may quarter the marshes, staying to winter in years when voles are plentiful. Late season also brings specialities such as regular Snow Buntings, seen flashing white wing-patches particularly along Northam pebble ridge, although usually only in twos and threes. Parties of other uncommon northern visitors such as Shorelarks and Lapland Buntings have also arrived on the estuary edges and dunes in some years. A gale at sea may bring in an exhausted Grey Phalarope to spin on one of the pools, a virtually annual visitor in recent seasons. Descending winter sees Ravens circling over Northam rubbish tip, and maybe a Barn Owl floating white across riverside pastures.

Timing

At low tide, the vastness of the estuary system defeats close watching of ducks or waders. An incoming tide, particularly about halfway into creeks and bays, is more likely to bring success, or a visit to the main roosts on either side of the estuary mouth two hours or so up to high tide as birds fly in. Snow and ice in other regions are likely to increase considerably flocks of open-ground species and probably bring White-fronted Geese. Look for American waders after strong, persistent autumn west winds, and Grey Phalaropes after northwest or northerly gales have forced them into Bideford

Bay in late autumn. Quails are more likely if summer is hot and dry.

Water sports may disturb the lower estuary and mouth on sunny weekends; public use of Crow Point beach and Braunton Burrows is increasing at weekends. See Access section for Army restrictions. Some motorcycle scrambling is also carried out on the dunes, mostly at weekends.

Access

Barnstaple, reached by A377 from Exeter, is the usual starting point at the head of Taw estuary. It is linked by A39 west to Bideford on the Torridge. Large areas of estuary are difficult to approach, but are probably not outstanding for birds. We recommend the following areas:

NORTH SIDE —

Braunton Burrows Drive west on A361 from Barnstaple, signposted towards Ilfracombe, then turn left at Braunton town centre towards Saunton and Croyde. After 1 mile (1.6 km) take a minor road left (not conspicuously signposted) to the Burrows. The Great Field area, surrounded by minor roads, is on your left. Drive down the lane behind the dunes; you can stop in signposted Nature Conservancy Council car parks, complete with map boards, or continue down a rough track (driveable with care) towards the estuary mouth. The NCC signs detail National Nature Reserve areas and regulations for those who enter; there is normally access for visitors except when Army exercises take place. Further details from the Warden, Mr J Breeds, telephone Braunton 812552. After 2 miles (3 km) of dirt track, park and walk ahead towards Crow Point at the tip for resting waders and views up the estuary; or right across the dunes by duckboard path to the beach and river mouth. Given time, a walk along the last 2 miles (3 km) of track with stops to check the bushes may be profitable. Eiders may be in sight off either beach or river side of the dunes.

From here you can take a driveable track leading around the perimeter of Braunton grazing marshes behind the Burrows, with the tidal flats and pill across a seawall to the right. Reaching a tarmac road, continue back through Velator tollgate towards the main road. A complete circuit of the dune and marsh peninsula gives chances to see varied ducks, waders and perhaps hunting raptors; do not forget to look in the pill for autumn passage waders.

Sherpa Marsh Across the pill from Braunton lie further

extensive grazing marshes, less disturbed by public access. A path leads along the seawall on the east side of the pill. Geese may use the fields, and the reedy pools can shelter marshbirds such as rails or Bittern.

SOUTH SIDE —

Penhill/Fremington Drive west on A39 from Barnstaple towards Bideford. Between Bickington and Fremington villages, a small lane leads off right towards the old disused rail halt. Park by main road near junction and walk down the creek banks for feeding waders (maybe Greenshank or Spotted Redshank), then turn right along the main estuary bank and walk east for 1 mile (1.6 km) to Penhill Point bend. Look at saltings on the east side of the point, where Shelducks, Wigeons and Teals feed.

Islay Marsh Near the large Yelland power station, a marshy bay and stream outlet where Teals and waders often concentrate to feed. Access via power station property: enquire for permits via Mr T Beer, 'Tawside', 30 Park Avenue, Barnstaple EX31 2ES (s.a.e. please).

Northam Burrows Drive to Bideford and cross the bridge, turning right on A386 for Northam and Westward Ho! For road past Skern saltmarsh and freshwater pools, turn right towards Appledore then second left (Broad Lane) off the main road. Continue across minor road junctions, and on down the mile-long (1.6-km) tip road with close views of marshes on the right (car-window views) and the interesting freshwater pool on left. Golden Plovers flock on nearby turf.

For Northam pebble ridge, follow signs towards Westward Ho! and turn right past holiday camps to Country Park entry points. Drive past golf course and pastures, watching again for plovers, out to Sandymere Pool depression beside the pebble ridge. Wheatears and perhaps Ringed Plovers are here in summer, probably Snow Buntings in winter.

Calendar

Resident: Little Grebe, Cormorant, Grey Heron, Sparrowhawk, Buzzard, Oystercatcher, Ringed Plover, Lapwing, Curlew, Barn Owl, Raven; Eiders stay through some years.

Dec-Feb: Great Northern Diver (sporadic), Slavonian Grebe, maybe Bittern or grey geese, and wild swans (hard weather only), Brent Goose, Shelduck, Teal, Mallard, Wigeon,

Shoveler, occasional other ducks, probably Goldeneye, Red-breasted Merganser, Eider, Common Scoter (offshore), Hen Harrier some winters, Peregrine, Merlin, Water Rail, Grey and Golden Plovers, Snipe, Bar-tailed Godwit, Green and Common Sandpipers, shanks, Sanderling, Dunlin, Turnstone, Purple Sandpiper, Knot, maybe Ruff, Kingfisher, possible Snow Bunting especially early winter.

Mar-May: Wheatears arrive to breed; later wader passage (especially from mid Apr) inc. Whimbrel and shanks, a few terns especially Sandwich, White Wagtail mostly Apr; commoner warblers arriving mostly from mid Apr, inc. Lesser Whitethroat at Braunton. Winter visitors left before then. Turtle Doves arrive May; perhaps a scarcer migrant, e.g. Hoopoe in dunes.

Jun-Jul: Breeding species, inc. Shelduck, Lapwing, Ringed Plover, Oystercatcher, possibly Quail, Turtle Dove, Reed and Sedge Warblers, Wheatear; Black-headed Gulls and first returning waders, inc. Dunlin, Common Sandpiper, shanks and Whimbrel from late Jul.

Aug-Nov: Hirundines feeding Aug-Sep, perhaps Hobby; Yellow and White Wagtails pass. Possibly terns Aug-Sep, inc. Arctic; passage of commoner *Sylvia* and *Phylloscopus* warblers; passage waders peak Sep, with possibly Little Stint and Curlew Sandpiper, perhaps an American e.g. Pectoral Sandpiper. Peregrine and Merlin from late Sep, maybe Grey Phalarope, probably Snow Bunting end Oct-Nov; chance of Hen Harrier or Short-eared Owl.

38 North Devon Coast (Morte Point-Lynton)

(Maps 38(i)-38(iii) and OS Map 180)

Habitat

A highly scenic exposed coastline of cliffs and a few rocky coves, running directly east-west from the Bristol Channel coast until an abrupt southward turn at long, jagged Morte Point on the edge of Bideford Bay. Coastal resort towns such as Ilfracombe, Combe Martin and Lynton are encircled by steep, rocky slopes and backed by high ground, rising especially to the east, on the fringe of Exmoor. Over much of the area, although sheer cliffs are limited and often under 50 m, the land rises very fast, reaching 300 m within ½ mile (0.8 km) inland.

Inland behind the high, open coastal downs, steep sheltered valleys (combes) hold belts of mainly deciduous woodland. Spreacombe Wood in the west of the area is an RSPB reserve. Arlington Court estate (NT), farther east, has a 6-acre (2.4-ha) lake set in mature mixed wood and parkland. On the edge of Exmoor nearby, 43-acre (17.4-ha) Wistlandpound Reservoir is extensively used for sailing and fishing. The whole area is heavily used by summer holidaymakers.

Species

Although much of this area is not regularly looked at by birdwatchers, it offers attractive birdwatching territory with a variety of typical Devon breeding birds, seabird colonies and coastal migration potential.

Through spring and summer, the coastline is occupied by large numbers of breeding seabirds, with countless widespread Herring Gulls, and a number of Great Black-backed Gulls nesting on rocky promontories. Fulmars have spread enormously and are now one of the commonest coastal species, with total counts of hundreds sitting on cliff ledges or veering past on stiff outstretched wings. Breeding Razorbills are scattered along the eastern half of this coastline, particularly around Heddons Mouth-Martinhoe-Woody Bay district, where small groups gather off the towering coastal downs from early

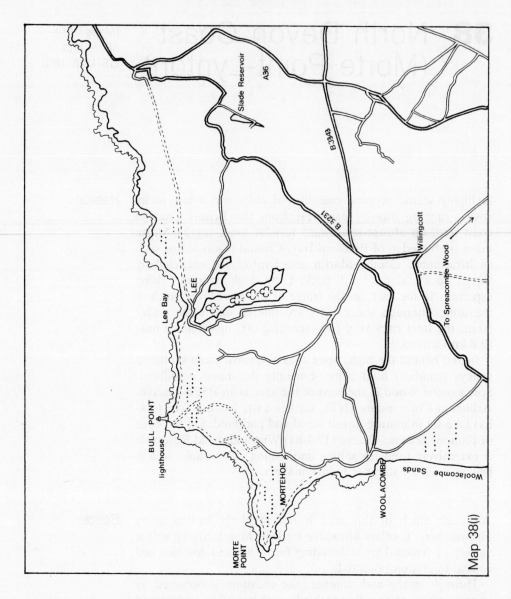

Map 38(i)

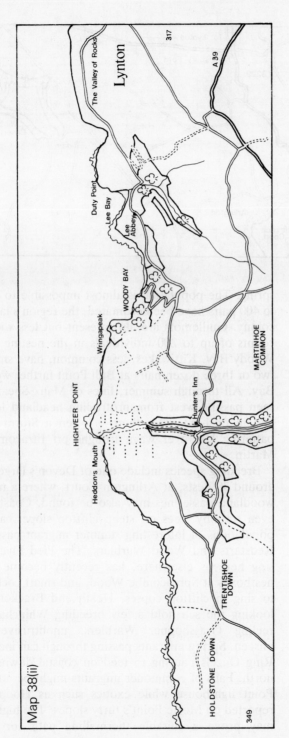

Map 38(ii)

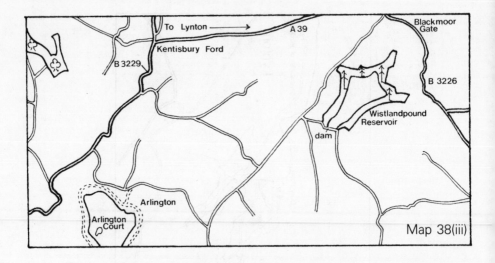

Map 38(iii)

spring. The population is almost impossible to census, but up to 400 pairs have been estimated, the region's largest mainland colony. Guillemots are also present but less widespread, with counts of up to 200 individuals in the nesting period around Woody Bay. Kittiwakes, less common, have small colonies of two or three dozen pairs at Bull Point farther west and Woody Bay. All through summer, lines of Manx Shearwaters can be seen passing west from protruding headland lookout points, and in onshore gales there is often a Storm Petrel or two pattering low over wave troughs off Ilfracombe or Combe Martin.

Breeding species include one of Devon's larger heronries, of around 30 nests, at Arlington Court, where a mix of common woodland passerines may also be found. Coastal valleys, and even scrubby trees on steep clifftop slopes, also hold small populations of interesting summer migrant passerines such as Redstarts and Wood Warblers. The Pied Flycatcher, increasing here as elsewhere, has recently become established in nestboxes at Spreacombe Wood, and smart cock birds turn up to sing in clifftop copses. Heath and Bracken valleys overlooking the sea hold a few breeding Whinchats and regular reeling Grasshopper Warblers, unobtrusive and usually unseen. Spring migrants passing through can include a party of Ring Ouzels pausing to feed on coastal downs on their way north. Falls of commoner migrants might be attracted by Bull Point lighthouse while exotics such as Hoopoe have been reported on Morte Point's turfy slopes. The high line of downs may prove a suitable thermalling path for an occasional migrant raptor; indeed, less common birds such as the intricately marked Honey Buzzard have been watched soaring over. Some of the region's characteristic breeders are particularly common inland. Ravens breed in many woods such as Spreacombe, often choosing large old conifer trees and sometimes competing for territory with mewing Buzzards. Sometimes a dozen or more of the latter can be seen in the air at once. The attractive tail-flirting Grey Wagtail, flashing sulphur-yellow underparts, is a frequent sight by hill streams.

Although migration has not been particularly studied, westward offshore movements of seabirds have been noted, including longer-distance migrants such as skuas and terns, especially in autumn. An occasional Arctic Skua and a trickle of terns, usually Sandwich, might be seen in spring. The Capstone at Ilfracombe has proved a suitable lookout point in summer, autumn and winter, but Morte Point on the corner of the coast might be good, especially in spring. Movements of over half a dozen skuas, mostly Arctic with a few stocky Greats in autumn, and over a couple of dozen terns, mostly Sandwich or Common, normally moving west, are unusual even in autumn; spring up-channel movements probably amount to no more than a quarter of this. Scarcer species such as the oceanic Sooty Shearwater are more likely through late summer and autumn, when a handful of birds probably pass westward each year, although, surprisingly, this wanderer has also been seen off the coast in spring. Brownish Balearic Shearwaters are probably also annual in varying numbers moving west, but are less frequent than off the region's southern and western extremities. Divers of all three species have been noted moving past in winter and especially spring, although (as usual) Black-throated is least often certainly identified and over half a dozen of any species in a day is unusual. Divers appear not to feed regularly along this stretch, although sometimes in winter a Great Northern has arrived unexpectedly on Wistlandpound Reservoir.

Autumn brings large coasting movements of hirundines along the clifftops, followed later in the season by other diurnal migrants concentrated into a stream by the straight coastal escarpment. Passages of finches are a well-known feature, although little watched recently. Sometimes several thousand move west in one day in late autumn, the vast bulk being Chaffinches, perhaps bound for Ireland; at any high point along the coastal downs the flocks can be seen passing over. The 'pinking' calls of Chaffinches are accompanied by a few harsher-calling Bramblings and other finches or buntings.

Cold weather may bring a party of Snow Buntings to rest and feed on open down or moorland, such as Holdstone Down near Trentishoe, and predators such as Merlins often pass down the coast in pursuit of the travelling flocks of passerines.

Winter does not bring major gatherings of birds inland, but, depending on disturbance levels, ducks (mostly diving species) visit Wistlandpound Reservoir, with up to 30-40 Pochards, a dozen Tufted, and four or five Goldeneyes at times; small groups also appear on nearby Arlington Lake. Less common diving ducks such as Scaups are seen singly on either lake in most winters (probably the same individual); and an American Ring-necked Duck, as usual a prominent drake with high crown and grey-shaded flanks, has wintered among the Tufted Ducks. The small wooded areas bordering Wistlandpound are also worth a look if undisturbed; harsh nasal calls draw attention to Willow Tits, and a Woodcock may burst out from ground cover.

Timing

At any time of day, highly scenic wood and coastal walks can bring views of characteristic local birds. Most woodland bird song in spring-summer will be in mornings, which are also best for coastal migrant passerines. Fall conditions might leave resting migrants at dawn around Morte or Bull Point; autumn coasting movement of hirundines and finches, commencing soon after daybreak, is most prominent up to mid morning, especially in westerly winds. Northeasterlies bring the northern birds such as Snow Bunting. Occasional larger raptors circling over the coast are most likely on warm anticyclonic days, later in the morning than other migrants, when thermal currents have had time to develop. At this time of day local Buzzards and Ravens will be seen in strength.

Seawatching is best when seabirds are confused or pushed in against the coast by mist, rain or onshore winds. Strong northwesterlies are often interesting, and likely to produce numbers of passing birds, mostly early in the day. Seabirds breeding locally pass to and fro at any time of day.

Wistlandpound Reservoir, vulnerable to disturbance, is best visited at off-peak periods such as weekday mornings.

Access

A-class roads, such as A39 Barnstaple-Lynton and A399 through Ilfracombe and Combe Martin, serve main holiday resort towns. Minor roads cross the hinterland, running south through wooded valleys towards the Taw valley and

Barnstaple; relatively few minor roads give access to the larger expanses of coastal down and cliff. Public footpaths are the best way to cover these areas; west from Lynton for example, good signposted paths lead from Heddon valley woods near Hunter's Inn, either way along the clifftops, for views of seabirds breeding far below and clifftop passerine migrants. This area can be reached by leaving Lynton southward on A39 and taking narrow right turns to Martinhoe and Hunter's Inn. Park by roadsides near the Inn (can be congested later on summer days), and choose your path beside the Inn: west takes you across high ground towards Holdstone Down; east leads back towards Lynton via Woody Bay. Worth at least two or three hours' walk in either direction.

The Capstone seawatching point is clearly visible as a high, grassed headland beside Ilfracombe seafront. From this town, B3231 and B3343 lead west towards Woolacombe and little-watched Morte Point — worth a try. South of Morte-Woolacombe area, a left turn (eastward) off B3231 ½ mile (0.8 km) before Georgeham village takes you to Spreacombe Wood, a small RSPB reserve. Entry is by permit: contact RSPB regional office or the Warden, Mr C G Manning, Sherracombe, Raleigh Park, Barnstaple (please send s.a.e.).

SWWA permits are needed to visit Wistlandpound Reservoir. The lake can be reached off A39 Barnstaple-Lynton road, turning south at Blackmoor Gate junction on the edge of Exmoor, on B3226 towards South Molton, then right on a minor road after ½ mile (0.8 km).

Calendar

Resident: Sparrowhawk, Buzzard, Oystercatcher, Great Black-backed and Herring Gulls, Grey Wagtail, Rock Pipit, Stonechat, Willow Tit, Raven.

Dec-Feb: A few divers passing. Possible Hen Harrier, Peregrine or Merlin over downs. Diving ducks — Tufted, Pochard, Goldeneye, maybe Scaup — at Wistlandpound, maybe Woodcock. Teal and Wigeon irregular. Fulmar, Grey Heron and Raven start breeding cycle at end.

Mar-May: Passerine migration along coast, Wheatear and probably Ring Ouzel from mid-late Mar. Summer breeding visitors and passerine migrants, inc. warblers, Pied Flycatcher, Redstart from mid-late Apr. Seabirds at colonies from mid Apr (Fulmar earlier), maybe raptors or other overshooting migrants especially from late Apr. Manx Shearwaters pass from Apr, maybe Storm Petrel from May. Divers passing, Sandwich Tern, maybe Arctic Skua.

Jun-Jul: Summer breeding passerines and seabirds, inc. Fulmar, Kittiwake, Razorbill, Guillemot. Passing Manx Shearwaters, occasional Storm Petrel, Gannets offshore, a few Sandwich and Common Terns from Jul. Woodland birdsong decreasing from late Jun. Auks leave mid Jul.

Aug-Nov: Summer breeding passerines depart from Aug. Possibly migration falls on coast (little known). Possible Balearic and Sooty Shearwaters, Arctic and Great Skuas, terns with possibly Black (mainly Aug). Chance of waders at Wistlandpound, e.g. Greenshank or Green Sandpiper, Aug-Sep. Coastal movement of finches and northern migrants, finches peak late Oct-early Nov. Winter visitors returning Nov.

Purple Sandpiper

HARRISON 83

39 Molland Common and Tarr Steps, West Exmoor

(Map 39 and OS Map 181 or National Park Map)

Habitat

Molland Common is a ridge of heather moorland rising to about 400 m on the south edge of Exmoor; we have included neighbouring commons towards Hawkridge and East Anstey, which form a continuation of Molland. Hill farms and sheltered bushy combes at a lower altitude border the ridge. The open common is frequented by moor ponies, and with luck a herd of Red Deer might be spotted; they may lie in long heather or Bracken and sometimes only the spreading antlers of a stag are visible. To the northeast of the ridge, the River Barle, a tributary of the Exe, flows through a steep wooded valley and under the stone clapper bridge at Tarr Steps, a popular tourist feature in summer.

Species

Molland ridge holds a selection of moorland birds, but the speciality is wintering and passing birds of prey. Hen Harriers are always in the district in winter; open views along the ridge mean that hunting birds can soon be located as they beat low across the common. Two or three, often including a smart grey male, may be found in the vicinity, together with a small number of Merlins, which occur in most months outside the breeding season, pursuing small passerines in low, swerving flight. Peregrines occasionally fly over, and common breeding West Country raptors also use the area, giving a variety of species although total numbers of birds are small. Short-eared Owls, hunting diurnally on long buzzard-like wings, also winter some years when voles are plentiful, or after a good breeding season when their numbers are high. Other birds can appear scarce, but a walk through the heather might put up a Red Grouse and there are sometimes large finch flocks, including Bramblings, on adjacent agricultural land. Great Grey Shrikes have been seen several times along the edge of the common and may be regular visitors.

The prominent position of Molland ridge, facing south at

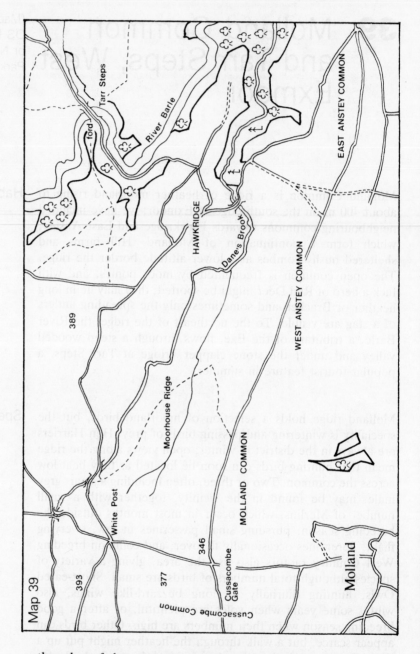

Map 39

the edge of the moor, means that migrant raptors may circle over it on spring passage; a Montagu's Harrier or Hobby, for example, could be seen on a fine day. The summer breeding population of the ridge is not outstanding, but the bubbling song of Curlews may be heard overhead, while Snipe are

Buzzard

believed to breed in the boggy hollows. Wheatears and Whinchats breed in small numbers along this side of the moor, and Meadow Pipits and Skylarks are plentiful. At this season the oakwoods and waterside of Tarr Steps may be rewarding, with a good selection of woodland species including Pied Flycatchers singing close to the bridge, Redstarts and numerous trilling Wood Warblers. There is a good chance of Grey Wagtails and Dippers along the riverbanks.

Timing

Winter raptors are most likely to be active on fine, clear mornings after a frosty night. Hen Harriers, however, will hunt in most weathers. In spring, high pressure with fine weather and winds between south and east is most likely to bring passage birds. Breeding waders are most active in early morning and evening. Avoid peak summer weekends at Tarr Steps when tourist congestion is likely, or visit early in the day.

Access

Turn north off A361 between South Molton and Bampton up minor roads to Molland village. Turn right in village centre, then left uphill onto the common. Explore minor roads across open land; the road east towards Hawkridge gives views over most of the area and raptors might be seen from the roadside. For Tarr Steps, turn north through Hawkridge from the east end of the common and continue on a very narrow road down into the valley. Cars can cross the Barle only by a deep ford beside the clapper bridge.

Calendar

Resident: Sparrowhawk, Buzzard, Kestrel, Grey Wagtail, Dipper, Raven.

Dec-Feb: Hen Harrier, Merlin, maybe a Peregrine or Short-eared Owl, Red Grouse, Great Grey Shrike, finches.

Mar-May: Hen Harriers leave by early Apr, Merlins may occur later. Possibly migrant raptors late Apr-May. Summer woodland visitors from late Apr. Breeding waders arriving.

Jun-Jul: Breeding residents, waders, moorland and woodland summer visitors.

Aug-Nov: Summer visitors depart Aug; migrants and winter visitors appear mostly from mid Oct.

Appendix A:
Additional Sites

While a reasonably sized book such as this includes adequate information about the main birdwatching sites, there are inevitably some omissions from the text. Areas which have less easy access, are less reliable for providing an interesting day's visit, or have no outstanding bird features, have generally not been covered. The following localities, however, are worth bearing in mind (D=DEVON, C=CORNWALL).

Site	Habitat	Birds of Interest	Peak Season	Nearest Town
Axe Estuary (D)	Mudflats, grazing marsh	Wigeon, Teal, Green Sandpiper	Winter, early autumn	Seaton
Chudleigh Knighton Heath (D)	Bushes, open heath	Nightingales	Late spring	Newton Abbot
Hennock Reservoirs (D)	Lakes, pine-woods, meadows	Crossbill, Woodlark	Late winter, spring	Newton Abbot
Rackerhayes Ponds (D)	Flooded pits, bushes	Diving ducks, Siskin	Mid-late winter	Newton Abbot
Teign estuary, Passage House Inn (D)	Mudflats, saltmarsh	Waders, Spoonbill (?), Red-breasted Merganser	Autumn, winter	Newton Abbot
Bolt Head-Soar Mill Cove (D)	Cliff downs, coves	Small migrants, raptors, Cirl Bunting	Spring, autumn	Kingsbridge
Aveton Gifford (D)	Water meadows, estuary	Dabbling ducks, Green Sand-piper, Kingfisher	Winter	Kingsbridge

Site	Habitat	Birds of Interest	Peak Season	Nearest Town
Yealm estuary (D)	Mudflats, woodland	Waders, Kingfisher, woodland birds, heronry	Late autumn-spring	Plymouth
Stoke Point (D)	Rocky coast, clifftop bushes	Small migrants, seabirds, grebes, seaducks	Spring, autumn	Plymouth
Dartmoor: Tavy Cleave (D)	Ravine torrent	Ring Ouzel, Redstart, Whinchat, Wheatear	Summer	Tavistock
Dartmoor: Fernworthy Reservoir (D)	Pinewoods, lake	Siskin, Crossbill, Nightjar, Tree Pipit	Winter, summer	Okehampton
Temple Tor Pools (C)	Moorland, flooded pits	Goosander, wild swans, Merlin, Hen Harrier	Winter	Bodmin
Goss Moor: Tregonotha Down (C)	Moorland pools, bushes	Merlin, Raven, Barn Owl, Short-eared Owl, Hen Harrier, Willow Tit, Woodcock	Winter	Bodmin
Lanhydrock (C)	Woodland, NT estate	Common woodland passerines, Woodlark, Pied Flycatcher, Lesser Spotted Woodpecker	Spring, summer	Bodmin
Par (C)	Bay, small freshwater marsh	Divers, grebes, terns, a few ducks, interesting gulls	Autumn, winter, spring	St Austell
Argal and College Reservoirs (C)	Reservoirs	Diving ducks (sometimes rare), a few waders	Winter	Falmouth
Hayle Kimbro and Loe Pools (C)	Freshwater margin vegetation	A few ducks, (Scaup esp. Loe Pool), waders	Autumn, winter	Helston
Crowan Reservoirs (C)	Open-banked reservoirs	Waders (small number, sometimes rare)	Autumn	Redruth

Site	Habitat	Birds of Interest	Peak Season	Nearest Town
Drift Reservoir (C)	Open-banked reservoir	Waders (small number, sometimes rare), interesting gulls	Autumn, winter	Penzance
Sennen Bay (C)	Rocky coast	Divers, grebes, seabirds, interesting gulls	Spring, autumn, winter	Penzance
Cape Cornwall (C)	Rocky headland, downs	Passing seabirds, small migrants	Spring, autumn	Penzance
Godrevy and Hayle Towans (C)	Rocky headland, sand dunes	Passing seabirds, small migrants	Spring, autumn	Hayle
Reskajeage Cliffs (C)	Sheer cliffs	Fulmar, Shag, auks, Kittiwakes nest	Summer	Camborne
Newquay: Towan Head and River Gannel (C)	Rocky headland, sandy estuary	Passing seabirds, a few waders	Autumn, winter	Newquay
Widemouth Bay and Bude (C)	Rocky bay	A few divers, grebes, seaducks, interesting gulls	Winter, spring	Bude
Winkleigh and Beaford (D)	Grass airfield, damp heaths	Golden Plover, Raven, Barn Owl, Willow Tit	Winter	Torrington
Shobrooke Park (D)	Park lake	Wildfowl, Siskin	Winter	Crediton

Appendix B: Alphabetical List of Species Mentioned with Scientific Names

English Name	*Scientific Name*
Albatross, Black-browed	*Diomedea melanophris*
Auk, Little	*Alle alle*
Avocet	*Recurvirostra avosetta*
Bittern	*Botaurus stellaris*
Little	*Ixobrychus minutus*
Blackbird	*Turdus merula*
Blackcap	*Sylvia atricapilla*
Bluethroat	*Luscinia svecica*
Brambling	*Fringilla montifringilla*
Bunting, Cirl	*Emberiza cirlus*
Corn	*Miliaria calandra*
Lapland	*Calcarius lapponicus*
Ortolan	*Emberiza hortulana*
Reed	*Emberiza schoeniclus*
Rustic	*Emberiza rustica*
Snow	*Plectrophenax nivalis*
Buzzard	*Buteo buteo*
Honey	*Pernis apivorus*
Chaffinch	*Fringilla coelebs*
Chiffchaff	*Phylloscopus collybita*
Coot	*Fulica atra*
Cormorant	*Phalacrocorax carbo*
Corncrake	*Crex crex*
Crake, Spotted	*Porzana porzana*
Crossbill	*Loxia curvirostra*
Crow, Carrion	*Corvus corone*
Cuckoo	*Cuculus canorus*
Curlew	*Numenius arquata*
Dipper	*Cinclus cinclus*
Diver, Black-throated	*Gavia arctica*
Great Northern	*Gavia immer*
Red-throated	*Gavia stellata*
Dotterel	*Charadrius morinellus*

Dove, Stock	*Columba oenas*
Turtle	*Streptopelia turtur*
Dowitcher, Long-billed	*Limnodromus scolopaceus*
Duck, Black	*Anas rubripes*
Ferruginous	*Aythya nyroca*
Long-tailed	*Clangula hyemalis*
Ring-necked	*Aythya collaris*
Ruddy	*Oxyura jamaicensis*
Tufted	*Aythya fuligula*
Dunlin	*Calidris alpina*
Dunnock	*Prunella modularis*
Egret, Cattle	*Bubulcus ibis*
Little	*Egretta garzetta*
Eider	*Somateria mollissima*
Falcon, Red-footed	*Falco vespertinus*
Fieldfare	*Turdus pilaris*
Firecrest	*Regulus ignicapillus*
Flycatcher, Pied	*Ficedula hypoleuca*
Red-breasted	*Ficedula parva*
Spotted	*Muscicapa striata*
Fulmar	*Fulmarus glacialis*
Gadwall	*Anas strepera*
Gannet	*Sula bassana*
Garganey	*Anas querquedula*
Godwit, Bar-tailed	*Limosa lapponica*
Black-tailed	*Limosa limosa*
Goldcrest	*Regulus regulus*
Goldeneye	*Bucephala clangula*
Goldfinch	*Carduelis carduelis*
Goosander	*Mergus merganser*
Goose, Barnacle	*Branta leucopsis*
Bean	*Anser fabalis*
Brent	*Branta bernicla*
Canada	*Branta canadensis*
Greylag	*Anser anser*
White-fronted	*Anser albifrons*
Goshawk	*Accipiter gentilis*
Grebe, Black-necked	*Podiceps nigricollis*
Great Crested	*Podiceps cristatus*
Little	*Tachybaptus ruficollis*
Red-necked	*Podiceps grisegena*
Slavonian	*Podiceps auritus*
Greenfinch	*Carduelis chloris*
Greenshank	*Tringa nebularia*
Grouse, Red	*Lagopus lagopus*

Guillemot (Common)	*Uria aalge*
Black	*Cepphus grylle*
Gull, Black-headed	*Larus ridibundus*
Bonaparte's	*Larus philadelphia*
Common	*Larus canus*
Franklin's	*Larus pipixcan*
Glaucous	*Larus hyperboreus*
Great Black-backed	*Larus marinus*
Herring	*Larus argentatus*
Iceland	*Larus glaucoides*
Kumlien's	*Larus glaucoides kumlieni*
Laughing	*Larus atricilla*
Lesser Black-backed	*Larus fuscus*
Little	*Larus minutus*
Mediterranean	*Larus melanocephalus*
Ring-billed	*Larus delawarensis*
Ross's	*Rhodostethia rosea*
Sabine's	*Larus sabini*
Harrier, Hen	*Circus cyaneus*
Marsh	*Circus aeruginosus*
Montagu's	*Circus pygargus*
Hawfinch	*Coccothraustes coccothraustes*
Heron, Grey	*Ardea cinerea*
Purple	*Ardea purpurea*
Squacco	*Ardea ralloides*
Hobby	*Falco subbuteo*
Hoopoe	*Upupa epops*
Jackdaw	*Corvus monedula*
Jay	*Garrulus glandarius*
Kestrel	*Falco tinnunculus*
Killdeer	*Charadrius vociferus*
Kingfisher	*Alcedo atthis*
Kite, Black	*Milvus migrans*
Red	*Milvus milvus*
Kittiwake	*Rissa tridactyla*
Knot	*Calidris canutus*
Lapwing	*Vanellus vanellus*
Lark, Shore	*Eremophila alpestris*
Short-toed	*Calandrella cinerea*
Linnet	*Carduelis cannabina*
Magpie	*Pica pica*
Mallard	*Anas platyrhynchos*
Martin, House	*Delichon urbica*
Sand	*Riparia riparia*
Merganser, Red-breasted	*Mergus serrator*

Merlin	*Falco columbarius*
Moorhen	*Gallinula chloropus*
Nighthawk, American	*Chordeiles minor*
Nightingale	*Luscinia megarhynchos*
Thrush	*Luscinia luscinia*
Nightjar	*Caprimulgus europaeus*
Nuthatch	*Sitta europaea*
Oriole, Golden	*Oriolus oriolus*
Ortolan, *see* Buntings	
Osprey	*Pandion haliaetus*
Ouzel, Ring	*Turdus torquatus*
Owl, Barn	*Tyto alba*
Little	*Athene noctua*
Short-eared	*Asio flammeus*
Tawny	*Strix aluco*
Oystercatcher	*Haematopus ostralegus*
Partridge (Grey)	*Perdix perdix*
Red-legged	*Alectoris rufa*
Peregrine	*Falco peregrinus*
Petrel, Leach's	*Oceanodroma leucorhoa*
Madeiran	*Oceanodroma castro*
Storm	*Hydrobates pelagicus*
Wilson's	*Oceanites oceanicus*
Phalarope, Grey	*Phalaropus fulicarius*
Red-necked	*Phalaropus lobatus*
Wilson's	*Phalaropus tricolor*
Pheasant	*Phasianus colchicus*
Pintail	*Anas acuta*
Pipit, Meadow	*Anthus pratensis*
Olive-backed	*Anthus hodgsoni*
Red-throated	*Anthus cervinus*
Richard's	*Anthus novaeseelandiae*
Rock	*Anthus spinoletta*
Tawny	*Anthus campestris*
Tree	*Anthus trivialis*
Water	*Anthus spinoletta spinoletta*
Plover, Golden	*Pluvialis apricaria*
Grey	*Pluvialis squatarola*
Kentish	*Charadrius alexandrinus*
Lesser Golden	*Pluvialis dominica*
Little Ringed	*Charadrius dubius*
Ringed	*Charadrius hiaticula*
Pochard	*Aythya ferina*
Puffin	*Fratercula arctica*
Quail	*Coturnix coturnix*

Rail, Water	*Rallus aquaticus*
Raven	*Corvus corax*
Razorbill	*Alca torda*
Redpoll	*Carduelis flammea*
Redshank	*Tringa totanus*
Spotted	*Tringa erythropus*
Redstart (Common)	*Phoenicurus phoenicurus*
American	*Setophaga ruticilla*
Black	*Phoenicurus ochruros*
Redwing	*Turdus iliacus*
Robin	*Erithacus rubecula*
American	*Turdus migratorius*
Rook	*Corvus frugilegus*
Ruff	*Philomachus pugnax*
Sanderling	*Calidris alba*
Sandpiper, Baird's	*Calidris bairdii*
Broad-billed	*Limicola falcinellus*
Buff-breasted	*Tryngites subruficollis*
Common	*Actitis hypoleucos*
Curlew	*Calidris ferruginea*
Green	*Tringa ochropus*
Least	*Calidris minutilla*
Pectoral	*Calidris melanotos*
Purple	*Calidris maritima*
Semipalmated	*Calidris semipalmatus*
Solitary	*Tringa solitaria*
Spotted	*Actitis macularia*
Upland	*Bartramia longicauda*
White-rumped	*Calidris fuscicollis*
Wood	*Tringa glareola*
Scaup	*Aythya marila*
Scoter, Common	*Melanitta nigra*
Surf	*Melanitta perspicillata*
Velvet	*Melanitta fusca*
Serin	*Serinus serinus*
Shag	*Phalacrocorax aristotelis*
Shearwater, Balearic	*Puffinus puffinus mauretanicus*
Cory's	*Calonectris diomedea*
Great	*Puffinus gravis*
Manx	*Puffinus puffinus*
Sooty	*Puffinus griseus*
Shelduck	*Tadorna tadorna*
Shoveler	*Anas clypeata*
Shrike, Great Grey	*Lanius excubitor*
Red-backed	*Lanius collurio*
Woodchat	*Lanius senator*

Siskin	*Carduelis spinus*
Skua, Arctic	*Stercorarius parasiticus*
Great	*Stercorarius skua*
Long-tailed	*Stercorarius longicaudus*
McCormick's	*Stercorarius maccormickii*
Pomarine	*Stercorarius pomarinus*
Skylark	*Alauda arvensis*
Smew	*Mergus albellus*
Snipe	*Gallinago gallinago*
Jack	*Lymnocryptes minimus*
Sparrow, Tree	*Passer montanus*
Sparrowhawk	*Accipiter nisus*
Spoonbill	*Platalea leucorodia*
Starling	*Sturnus vulgaris*
Stint, Little	*Calidris minuta*
Temminck's	*Calidris temminckii*
Stonechat	*Saxicola torquata*
Swallow	*Hirundo rustica*
Swan, Bewick's	*Cygnus columbianus bewickii*
Mute	*Cygnus olor*
Whooper	*Cygnus cygnus*
Swift	*Apus apus*
Alpine	*Apus melba*
Chimney	*Chaetura pelagica*
Teal	*Anas crecca*
Green-winged	*Anas crecca carolinensis*
Blue-winged	*Anas discors*
Tern, Arctic	*Sterna paradisaea*
Black	*Chlidonias niger*
Bridled	*Sterna anaethetus*
Common	*Sterna hirundo*
Forster's	*Sterna forsteri*
Little	*Sterna albifrons*
Roseate	*Sterna dougallii*
Sandwich	*Sterna sandvicensis*
White-winged Black	*Chlidonias leucopterus*
Thrush, Mistle	*Turdus viscivorus*
Song	*Turdus philomelos*
Varied	*Zoothera naevia*
Tit, Bearded	*Panurus biarmicus*
Blue	*Parus caeruleus*
Coal	*Parus ater*
Great	*Parus major*
Long-tailed	*Aegithalos caudatus*
Marsh	*Parus palustris*
Willow	*Parus montanus*

Treecreeper	*Certhia familiaris*
Turnstone	*Arenaria interpres*
Twite	*Carduelis flavirostris*
Veery	*Hylocichla fuscescens*
Vireo, Red-eyed	*Vireo olivaceus*
Wagtail, Grey	*Motacilla cinerea*
Pied	*Motacilla alba yarrellii*
White	*Motacilla alba alba*
Yellow	*Motacilla flava*
Warbler, Aquatic	*Acrocephalus paludicola*
Barred	*Sylvia nisoria*
Black-and-white	*Mniotilta varia*
Blackpoll	*Dendroica striata*
Booted	*Hippolais caligata*
Cetti's	*Cettia cetti*
Dartford	*Sylvia undata*
Garden	*Sylvia borin*
Grasshopper	*Locustella naevia*
Great Reed	*Acrocephalus arundinaceus*
Greenish	*Phylloscopus trochiloides*
Icterine	*Hippolais icterina*
Melodious	*Hippolais polyglotta*
Paddyfield	*Acrocephalus agricola*
Pallas's	*Phylloscopus proregulus*
Reed	*Acrocephalus scirpaceus*
Rüppell's	*Sylvia rueppelli*
Savi's	*Locustella luscinioides*
Sedge	*Acrocephalus schoenobaenus*
Subalpine	*Sylvia cantillans*
Willow	*Phylloscopus trochilus*
Wood	*Phylloscopus sibilatrix*
Yellow-browed	*Phylloscopus inornatus*
Wheatear	*Oenanthe oenanthe*
Whimbrel	*Numenius phaeopus*
Whinchat	*Saxicola rubetra*
Whitethroat	*Sylvia communis*
Lesser	*Sylvia curruca*
Wigeon	*Anas penelope*
American	*Anas americana*
Woodcock	*Scolopax rusticola*
Woodlark	*Lullula arborea*
Woodpecker, Great Spotted	*Dendrocopos major*
Green	*Picus viridis*
Lesser Spotted	*Dendrocopos minor*
Woodpigeon	*Columba palumbus*

Wren	*Troglodytes troglodytes*
Wryneck	*Jynx torquilla*
Yellowhammer	*Emberiza citrinella*
Yellowlegs, Lesser	*Tringa flavipes*

Index to Species by Chapter

Latest Information

Addresses

Cornwall Bird Watching and Preservation Society;
  c/o S M Christophers (Recorder), 5 Newquay Road, St Columb Major, Cornwall.
Cornwall Trust for Nature Conservation Ltd;
  Conservation Officer, Dairy Cottage, Trelissick, Feock nr Truro.
Devon Trust for Nature Conservation Ltd,
  now at 35 New Bridge Street, Exeter. Tel. Exeter 79244.
Both County Trusts have reserves of general natural history interest. Devon Trust (characteristic Dipper badge) have recently established reserves in some good bird areas, including (Chapter 1) leasing Otter marshes – access by public paths unaffected (Chapter 2), part of Venn Ottery area – public paths still available elsewhere – and (Chapter 3) Topsham reedbed – canal bank paths still available for public access. They also own part of Dawlish Warren (Chapter 3), although Teignbridge Council manage the reserve, and part of Chudleigh Knighton Heath (D) (Appendix A). Permits are needed for Trust reserves away from public footpaths.
  National Trust; Cornwall area enquiries to Lanhydrock House, Lanhydrock PL30 4DE, Cornwall.

Other Information

Chapter 3: Dawlish Warren – take care not to trespass onto private golf course. Exminster Marshes – now 'no parking' for cars at far end of access lane.
Chapter 14: Yarner Wood enquiries for party visits via D Rogers, Yarner Wood National Nature Reserve, Bovey Tracey TQ13 9LJ, Devon. Tel. Bovey Tracey 832330. Send s.a.e. for written reply.
Chapter 29: Isles of Scilly Autumn Evening Birdwatchers' Meetings are held at Porthcressa Restaurant, on St Mary's.
Chapter 36: Lundy accommodation bookings now via Landmark Trust headquarters at Shottesbrooke, Maidenhead, Berks SL6 3SW. Tel. Littlewick Green 5925.
Appendix A: Rackerhayes Ponds(D) – Please note that Watts Blake Bearne Clay Company of Park House, Courtenay Park, Newton Abbot, issue entry permits.

We have been asked to stress that birdwatchers should not block country lanes, farm access or private ground by parking thoughtlessly.